# Kansas Jayhawks: A Year to Remember

## Inside the Greatest Season in KU Basketball History

BY JASON KING

Printed in the United States of America by Quebecor World, Taunton, MA.

ISBN 0-615-2130351995

Cover photo by Ann Williamson of Topeka Capital-Journal.
Cover design by Laura Nelson.

# KANSAS *Jayhawks:*
## A YEAR TO REMEMBER

## TABLE OF CONTENTS

## SECTION 3: JAYHAWK NATION, CONTINUED

## SECTION 4: THE MEDIA

## SECTION 5: PROFILES

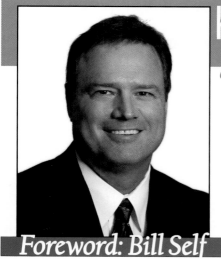

# KANSAS *Jayhawks:*
## A YEAR TO REMEMBER

*Foreword: Bill Self*

A few days after we beat Memphis for the national title, I opened my eyes and it was 12:45 in the afternoon. I had gone to bed around 11 the night before and had literally slept about 14 hours. I guess my body finally gave in.

I hadn't gotten much rest since we'd returned from San Antonio – and, frankly, I didn't care. There was so much excitement in the air after our win and so many opportunities for our staff and our players. Welcome home celebrations ... interviews ... appearances. We were having too much fun to be tired. For awhile, I think we were all operating on adrenaline. We wanted to make sure we enjoyed every minute of it.

As a coach, I don't know that I'll ever experience a greater joy than seeing the smiles on the faces of our players the night they won the title. As proud as I was of their accomplishment, I took an even greater satisfaction in the trophy when I thought about what these guys went through to obtain it.

The stories of the hardships some of our players have endured were well-documented throughout the season. As hard as they fought on the basketball court, some of them have battled even bigger issues off of it – not just this season, but throughout their entire lives.

Through it all, these guys stuck together and kept fighting with one goal in mind. Seeing it all come together at the end and looking at their happy faces as they hugged their parents was one of the more gratifying things I've ever witnessed as a head coach.

These kids are winners, and that would've been the case even if we would have lost to Memphis. But instead we came up big down the stretch. Now – 20 years after Danny and the Miracles - we'll hang another banner in Allen Fieldhouse.

Three things from this season stand out the most.

The 110-year reunion was a reminder of just how special Kansas basketball truly is. Standing in a room and watching generations of Jayhawks mix and mingle made me realize how fortunate I am to be a part of this great program.

Another thing I'll never forget is the emotions on Senior Night. I don't get choked up often, but I definitely had a lump in my throat as I watched Sasha, Darnell, Russell, Jeremy and Rodrick play their last game at Allen Fieldhouse.

You're talking about a group that won four Big 12 regular seasons titles, three Big 12 conference tournament titles and, of course, the big one at the end. There aren't too many classes in the history of college basketball that can make that kind of a claim.

Obviously, the biggest thrill of all was cutting down the nets in San Antonio. The game against Memphis epitomized our entire season. Even though Mario made the biggest shot, every guy that took the court that night played a huge role. Sherron came up with the big steal and the three-pointer, Shady had the two big buckets down the stretch, and then there was Brandon's defense on Chris Douglas-Roberts.

It was a well-rounded effort by a group that spent the entire season sacrificing individual accomplishments for the good of the team. People talked all year about how we didn't have a go-to guy, and they were wrong. We did have a go-to guy, and it was the open man.

Even though we have to move forward as coaches, players and fans, it will always be fun to look back at the greatest season in Kansas history. This book is the perfect vehicle to do just that.

Along with each of our 24 coaches and players, Jason King has collected memories and stories about our championship season from more than 70 people. Whether they come from the cook who caters our meals, the barber that cuts our players' hair or the journalists that cover our games, the tales in these pages are a must-read for any diehard Jayhawk fan.

As a special bonus, Jason has included 10 of his most memorable feature articles and profiles from *The Kansas City Star* and Yahoo! Sports. As much as I liked them the first time, they were even more fun to read again.

I'm hope you will enjoy this book as much I did. More than anything, though, I want to thank you for being such loyal fans during this magnificent season and for supporting our team both on the court and off of it. We couldn't have done it without you.

Rock Chalk!

Bill Self

# KANSAS *Jayhawks:*
## A YEAR TO REMEMBER

The first time I saw Bill Self after Kansas beat Memphis for the 2008 national championship, the Jayhawks coach was riding in a golf cart. That's how it works during the NCAA Tournament. Teams leave the court and spend 10 minutes cooling off in the locker room before designated players and coaches are whisked away in golf carts to fulfill media requests at various locations throughout the arena.

I was hustling toward the interview room in San Antonio's Alamodome when Self rolled up from behind. "Yo, King!" he yelled. I turned and shook Self's hand as his cart came to a stop. Initially, I'd hoped to use my alone time with Self to uncover a behind the scenes angle or anecdote I could use in my story. At that moment, though, the usually-chatty coach appeared too shell-shocked for a lengthy conversation. His mouth hung open, his hair was a mess and his elbows rested on his knees as he leaned forward in his seat. When I offered my congratulations, Self just shook his head. "Unbelievable," he said softly. "Un-freakin'-believable." Then the cart sped away.

Self's emotions certainly weren't difficult to understand. Less than an hour earlier, his team had emerged victorious in one of the most dramatic games in NCAA championship history. You know the story by now: Kansas rallies from a nine-point deficit with 2:12 remaining in regulation ... Mario Chalmers makes a heroic three-pointer to force overtime ... The Jayhawks ride their newfound momentum to a 75-68 victory. Voila! Instant classic.

Still, as Self sat in that golf cart, my guess is that he was reflecting on more than just the championship game. As impressive as Kansas' victory was, it was merely the cherry on top of a season that had been defined by big wins, headline-grabbing story lines and riveting comebacks – both on and off the court.

That's why it was so fun to watch the Jayhawks celebrate on the Alamodome floor. As I looked at them, I didn't just see the players. I saw their stories.

I saw Sherron Collins hugging his mother, Stacey, and thought about how proud she must be that her son used basketball as a way to escape the drugs and gang violence that surrounded his neighborhood in inner-city Chicago.

I pictured Sasha Kaun stepping off a plane in the United States from Russia at age 16 knowing zero English and nothing about basketball.

I remembered all of the pressures and negative stereotypes facing Brandon Rush when he arrived at Kansas. It must have been so gratifying for him to prove everyone wrong.

I thought about the courage Darnell Jackson showed time and time again in the midst of the off-court tragedies involving his family members. And how could anyone not be impressed with the fight and determination of Russell Robinson? Somehow, whenever the odds seem stacked against him, Robinson didn't flounder. He flourished.

Even as an unbiased media member, it was impossible not to like this group of guys – or at the very least, respect them. Apparently Kansas' fans feel the same way.

The championship season has long passed, but the Jayhawks' lovefest continues throughout the Sunflower State. In churches, barbershops, grocery stores, sports bars and living rooms, folks continue to buzz about the team that won more games (37) than any squad in school history.

Everyone, it seems, has a story. Everyone has a favorite moment or memory.

Many of them are captured here.

Thumb through these pages and you'll find the thoughts and reflections of each and every player and coach from KU's championships squad. Still, "Kansas Jayhawks: A Year to Remember" is about more than the men on the court.

In "Section III: Jayhawk Nation," you'll hear tales about the season from opposing coaches such as Roy Williams and Tim Floyd and former players like Drew Gooden. Self's wife, Cindy, chimes in and Rush's brother, JaRon, offers his opinions on the team.

Dick Vitale, Joe Posnanski, Tom Keegan and Fran Fraschilla are among the 20 journalists who contributed excerpts for "Section IV: The Media."

As a special bonus, I've included 10 of my most popular features and profiles from my time at The Kansas City Star and Yahoo! Sports. Some of the articles are a few years old, but judging from the feedback they received, you liked them well enough to read again.

Hopefully, you'll enjoy reading this book as much as I did reporting it. Set it on your coffee table. Keep a copy by your bed or, heck, put one in your bathroom. Even though it's time to move forward, it will always be fun to look back.

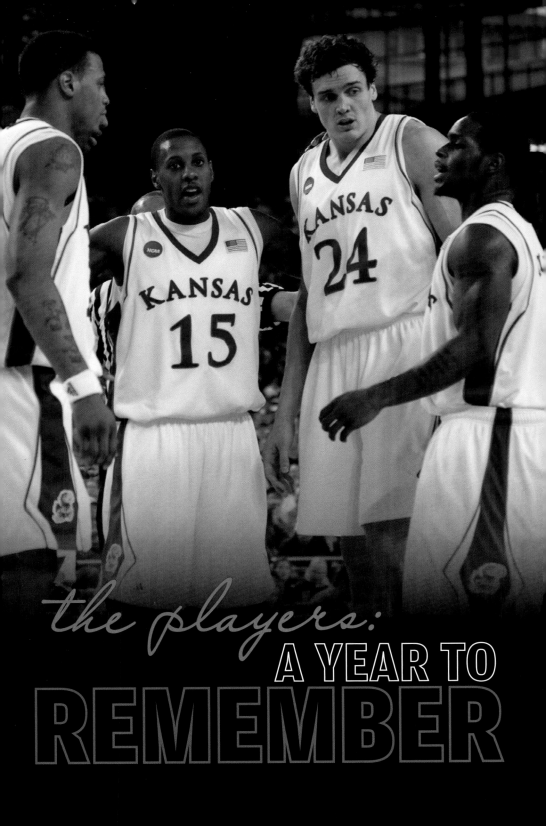

the players:
# A YEAR TO
# REMEMBER

His flight departs in 19 hours, but as he reclines in a chair in apartment 302C at the Jayhawker Towers, Brandon Rush hardly seems ready to admit it's over.

His dresser drawers remain filled with clothes. Magazines are scattered across an end table near his couch and pictures still hang on the wall. It looks like the home of someone who's settling in – not someone who's moving out.

A friend, William Bazzle, motions toward some suitcases and travel bags stacked in a corner. All of them are empty.

"Dang, Brandon," Bazzle says. "When are you going to pack all this stuff up?"

Rush shrugs his shoulders.

"I don't know," he says. "I'll get to it."

*Brandon Rush*

Ironic, isn't it?

Three years ago Brandon Rush didn't want to go to college. Now he doesn't want to leave. If only the NBA had a team in Lawrence.

"I love Kansas," he says. "I love being a Jayhawk."

On April 21 - the day before he left for Chicago to train for the NBA Draft – Rush agreed to an hour-long interview in his living room. As excited as he seemed about the opportunities that stood before him, Rush couldn't help but be sentimental about the life he was leaving behind.

Mario Chalmers hit the shot that propelled Kansas to the 2008 NCAA national title. Darrell Arthur blossomed into the team's top pro prospect and Russell Robinson was the fan favorite who held everything together. Still, make no mistake: Since his arrival in the fall of 2005, Rush has been the face of Kansas basketball.

He led the team in scoring and earned All-Big 12 honors in each of his three seasons. Along with winning a trio of regular season titles, Kansas captured three straight conference tournament championships thanks, in large part, to Rush.

Although he scored just 12 points in Kansas' 75-68 overtime victory against Memphis in the NCAA title game, Rush's menacing defense on Tigers leading scorer Chris Douglas-Roberts was one of the biggest keys to Kansas winning its first national championship in 20 years.

It only seemed fitting that Rush's crowning moment at Kansas came in dramatic fashion during the season's most high-profile game. After all, as the youngest brother of local legends JaRon and Kareem Rush, Brandon has lived his entire life in the spotlight.

**13**

In some ways, KU's victory over Memphis paralleled Rush's journey as both a person and a player. Just as people wrote off the Jayhawks when they were down by nine with 2 minutes remaining, folks have always been quick to give up on Brandon Rush.

Maybe now they'll know better.

"Brandon," coach Bill Self said, "will be better in life because he came to Kansas."

Self was quick to answer when asked if he planned to retire Rush's jersey.

"It's a possibility," Self said. "It's definitely a possibility."

### IN BRANDON'S WORDS

The day I was kicked out of Westport High School, the principal there told my AAU coach that my life would never amount to (squat). The *principal* said that.

I was a sophomore then, and all these years that comment has been in the back of my mind. I actually thought about it the night we won the title. Part of me wanted to drive around Kansas City until I found that lady. I pictured myself holding the trophy in front of her face and saying, "Look at this! Look at what I did!" But I guess that would've been immature, and the last thing I am anymore is childish.

Signing with Kansas was one of the best decisions I'll ever make in my life, and not just because of basketball. I became a man at Kansas. I did a lot of growing up during the three years I spent here. I've definitely come a long way from the days of getting suspended all the time in high school.

I was always in trouble at Westport, but it's not like it was ever anything serious. Usually it was being late for class, goofing off in the halls, talking while the teacher was talking or not turning in assignments. I just messed around a lot and was never very serious about anything.

I kept getting suspended. For awhile, I didn't want to tell my mom. She'd drop me off in front of the school each morning and I'd walk toward the door - even though I knew the security guards weren't going to let me in the building. Usually I'd find somewhere to go or something to get into. One suspension would end, but then another one would come. Eventually, near the end of my sophomore year, it became a permanent deal and I was kicked out of Westport for good.

Looking back on it now, what happened there was probably a good thing because it got me out of Kansas City. I went to Mt. Zion in North Carolina and started to mature a lot, and after that it was Kansas.

I know I had a bad reputation when I got to Kansas. People said I was selfish and uncoachable and that I didn't play defense. On the road fans would taunt me. They'd hold up signs that said, "Rush Can't Read." All of those people that said bad things about me ... none of them knew me or had seen me play. Those people didn't know what type of person I was.

### KNEE INJURY

My first two years at Kansas were great. But obviously nothing compares to winning the title. As upset as I was when I tore my ACL a year ago, I'm almost glad it happened now. I've become a better player and, like my grandmother and Coach Self said, "Everything happens for a reason."

I still remember hearing that pop when I landed funny last spring. I was hoping it was just a sprain. Once they told me it was torn, the main emotion I felt was "scared." I couldn't understand why this was happening to me. I didn't tell anyone at the time but, deep down, there was a part of me that wondered if I'd ever be the same player again. I watched the NBA Draft on television and wondered where I might have gone if I hadn't have hurt myself. I know it would've been in the first round.

The good thing was that I didn't sit around and sulk. For awhile I was going to rehab three times a day, doing all kinds of extensions and other exercises. It got pretty painful at times, but I was determined to get back.

I hated having to miss a few games early on, but overall I was happy with how well the rehab went. By the time I started playing without a knee brace in January, I was pretty much 100 percent. I always wanted to be in the game instead of on the bench, because sometimes, when I was sitting, the knee would tighten up, and then when I went back in, I'd have to get it loosened up all over again. Luckily, I was usually on the floor.

### ENOUGH ALREADY!

One thing I got really sick of during the season was people telling me I needed to be more aggressive. I'd smile and say the right things, but really I wanted to say, "Shut the hell up. You don't have any idea what's it like to play on a team like this – a team full of superstars." Playing for Kansas is different than playing for other schools. We didn't need someone to take the game into his own hands. That would've hurt the team – not helped it.

The whole situation got frustrating. We were 20-0 and I kept hearing about how I wasn't being aggressive enough. Coach Self got on me about it, too. He kept telling me he wanted me to take more shots but, early on, they weren't designing any plays for me or putting me in a position where I could score in places besides the three-point line. I didn't think I had the ball in my hands enough. But I wasn't going to complain. We were winning and everyone – including me – was having fun.

### COACH SELF

Every player has frustrations with their coach at some point in their career. But, overall, I don't have one bad thing to say about Coach Self.

I grew up watching as all these people tried to get at my brothers and take advantage of them. They were young kids and sometimes young kids make wrong decisions. It was tough on them, because they were like pieces of meat, and everyone wanted to take a bite. Before I came to Kansas there were times when I felt like that, too.

That's why I showed up in Lawrence not trusting anyone. Three years later I'm leaving here knowing that I have people in my life that really care about me and want what's best for me. Coach Self is one of those people. I realized that more than ever after I hurt my knee. He was calling or texting every day to check up on me. He told me to call him whenever I needed to talk. He had already treated me well, but I think our relationship got even better at that point. I know it did on my end.

That's not to say that Coach Self couldn't be mean. He could be *very* mean. At halftime of the Nebraska game in the Big 12 Tournament, he called me out like I've never been called out before. I'm pretty sure you can't print the word that he called me in front of the entire team – and I actually didn't think I was playing all that bad. I've always been good about not letting stuff like that get to me. If it affects me at all it's usually in a positive way.

### NORTH CAROLINA

The Final Four was one of the best experiences of my life. Beating up on North Carolina felt good, but it had nothing to do with the fact that we were playing against Roy Williams. I know the media made a big deal out of that situation, but I honestly don't think any of us thought about it. Coach Self didn't mention it one time. There were some things that happened years ago with Coach Williams and my brother, JaRon, that upset my family a little bit. People kept asking me what I thought of him, but I don't have anything to say about the man because I don't know him. To me it's obvious that he's a great coach, and he seems like a great person, too. After we beat them he came up to me in the handshake line and said, "Good luck." Then, after we got through the line, he came and found me again and said, "I mean it. Good luck. I want you to win this thing for you and your family."

### MEMPHIS

The Memphis game was crazy. I thought we may have let it slip away, but Mario hit the shot for the ages. Afterward people were throwing water all over

each other in the locker room and hugging each other. We went back to the hotel and stayed up all night partying. There was a big party on the 22nd floor with everyone: coaches, administrators, players...lots of people. After that the players went to the 11th floor and got after it all night long. Most of us didn't go to sleep before 8 a.m. We were all pretty tired the next day when we got back to Lawrence and went to Memorial Stadium for the Welcome Home rally.

The fans here have always been great, but they've been even better since we got that trophy. I was at IHOP the other day and a couple of people came up to me and thanked me for helping the team accomplish something it hasn't in 20 years.

### FOND FAREWELL

It's all been so much fun that I'm sad to be leaving. There was never a question in my mind about entering the draft. I knew all season that I was going to do it. Still, I'll miss Lawrence and places like The Hawk and Henry T's. I'll miss the fans and I'll miss playing at Allen Fieldhouse. I never have been big on awards, but I can't think of anything better than seeing my jersey hanging from the rafters someday.

I don't know if Coach Self will ever decide to do that, and even if he doesn't, I'll always be glad that I made the decision to come here. I see how great the fans treat Danny Manning, and I realize that I'll always be welcomed here, too – although something tells me I'll probably never be on the coaching staff. I'm just glad I'll always have a home.

For now, though, it's time to move on. I can't wait to get to the NBA. People think it's all about money with me but it's not. More than anything, I'm looking forward to going against players like Kobe to see how I match up with them. You play against a lot of great guys in college, but in the NBA everyone is great. Hopefully I'll be able to hold my own and make a difference like I did at Kansas.

All my life people have compared me to my brothers, and that always bothered me. I wanted to break out of their shadow and be my own person. Finally – after all these years – I think I've accomplished that. People out there now ... they know who Brandon Rush is – and it's for all the right reasons.

*Mario Chalmers*

A few weeks after he made the biggest shot in Kansas history, Mario Chalmers wanted a Whopper. But before he could get his food, Chalmers had to grant a rather odd request from the man working the drive-thru window at Burger King.

"He wanted me to autograph his hand," Chalmers said. "His *hand*! It's times like that when I realize just how much this championship means to people."

Twenty years from now, Chalmers may still be showered with that same kind of love whenever he returns to Lawrence or runs into a Jayhawk fan at an airport. With one flick of the wrist, the junior from Alaska helped Kansas win its first NCAA title since 1988 by swishing a three-pointer that forced overtime against Memphis.

Chalmers' heavily-guarded shot from the top of the key ignited an unlikely comeback that saw the Jayhawks rally from a nine-point deficit with less than two minutes remaining. With the momentum clearly in its favor, Kansas had no problem disposing of the Tigers in the extra period of a 75-68 win.

"The kid has no memory," Kansas coach Bill Self said. "The next thing that happens is the only thing he's ever thinking about. It's remarkable that a guy can have that much poise when the pressure's on like that."

Chalmers' shot capped a brilliant season in which he averaged 12.8 points while collecting a Big 12-best 97 steals. Even more impressive was that Chalmers connected on 46.8 percent of his three-point attempts – a mark that ranks fifth on Kansas' all-time list.

Chalmers, though, has never been concerned with numbers. With him it's always been about big moments and big plays. Goodness knows, there will never be one bigger than the one he made in one of the most breathtaking games in NCAA championship history.

"We just kept saying, 'We gotta believe, we gotta believe,'" Chalmers said. "They'll probably be replaying that game for a long, long time."

### IN MARIO'S WORDS

In Alaska, where I grew up, I hear it's wild. My best friend, Doug Hardy, still lives up there, and he keeps telling me that everyone looks at me as an idol now. Everyone wants to follow in my footsteps. The term "idol" is a little

overwhelming. When I was growing up everyone looked up to Trajan Langdon and Carlos Boozer – two Alaskans that went on to have good basketball careers. I really admired both of those guys. Trajan used to come and play at my high school or I'd go to his. I always wanted to be like him, and now there are kids up there that look at me the same way. It's hard to fathom.

Everywhere I go people want to talk about the three-pointer I made against Memphis. But the way I look at it is this: My shot tied the game, but plenty of other guys hit big shots to win it. Shady had two big baskets near the end of regulation. Sherron had that three-pointer after the steal. Brandon played great defense on Chris Douglas-Roberts. It wasn't just me. A lot of guys came up big when it mattered most.

It's a weird feeling to walk into the grocery store and see your picture

everywhere. You can't get away from it – not that I'm complaining. It feels good. The other day someone asked me what my favorite picture was from the Memphis game. Most people probably think it was the one of me shooting that three, but there are actually a few others that I like better.

One is of me hugging my mom. I like that for obvious reasons. The other is of me and my teammates celebrating after the final horn. It was the last moment we all had together out there, with all of us out on the court. I mean, what a way for our seniors to go out. Not just them, but the guys that are leaving early for the draft and the freshmen and walk-ons that pushed us so hard in practice. That picture showed the bond we all share, the brotherhood.

## HIGH SCHOOL AND RECRUITING

When it came to choosing schools three years ago, I picked Kansas over Arizona. Coach (Joe) Dooley came to a ton of my games in Alaska and we really created a special bond. I knew I'd made the right decision when I came down for Late Night. That's when Darnell and all those guys – who were freshmen at the time – had to dress up and dance on the court. They had the "You Got Served" skit. Everyone treated me like family that night and it's been that way ever since. I played for my dad in high school, and there were times when he was really hard on me. I worked so hard that I got to the point where I didn't make a lot of mistakes. Once I got here things were totally different. I wasn't the best player any more. There were a lot of things I didn't know. Coach Self really stayed on me and pushed me and, eventually, it paid off.

It wasn't always easy, though. In high school I controlled my team. I controlled the ball and I controlled the plays. Once I got here there were a lot of players who were just as good as I was – if not better. Coach Self really stayed on me. It got to me at times. One of the turning points for me was when Jeff Hawkins – who was playing ahead of me – came and picked me up one night so we could talk. He told me Coach Self had been on his case a lot when he was younger and that it frustrated him, too. But Jeff said he stuck it out, listened to what Coach said and that it paid off for him in the end. He told me to do the same thing. From that point forward my attitude got better and so did my play. By the time conference play began I was a lot more comfortable.

### EARLY SIGNS
By the end of my freshman year you could see that we had a chance to be a special team someday. Sure, we lost to Bradley in the first round of the NCAA Tournament. But Bradley was a very good team, and before that, we had won 15 of our last 16 games. One of those wins was against Texas in the Big 12 Tournament championship. Every time we went head-to-head with them we had a lot of fun. There was always a lot of talking going on with me and D.J Augustin and A.J. Abrams.

One of the biggest keys for our team that season – and for the next two seasons after that – was adding Brandon (Rush) to the roster at the last possible minute. I knew we were going to get Brandon from the time he visited. Brandon and I had known each other ever since we met at Adidas Camp. We talked then about playing together in college, but he tried to enter the draft straight out of high school, so it looked like it would never happen. But once he withdrew and decided to visit Kansas I knew we'd get him. Even before he committed, Brandon was coming to Lawrence a lot and just hanging out.

With me and Brandon and Julian (Wright) and Micah (Downs), we felt like we had the best recruiting class in the nation. Micah ended up transferring to Gonzaga that year, but Brandon and I and Julian still won a lot of games together before Julian left for the pros after his sophomore season. Brandon and I had the same goals and the same personality, so that really made us close off the court. Shady (Darrell Arthur) signed with us a year later and he ended up being my roommate. Once Shady got here, Shady and Brandon and I were always together. Not that we were a clique. The best thing about this team was that everyone got along.

### TURNING POINT
Everyone likes to say that our meeting at Henry T's helped turn around our season. But I actually think it happened a few days before that. After we lost to Oklahoma State, the bus pulled into Allen Fieldhouse around 2 in the morning. It had been snowing that night, so we'd already had a long ride home. Still, Coach Self made us get off the bus and head straight to the locker room. The coaches talked and then we talked and aired out a lot of our problems. We were in there for a long time – maybe two hours. I thought it was a really productive meeting. From that point forward, things changed. We won our last 13 games – including the national championship.

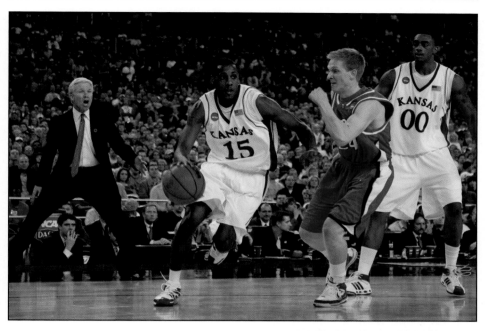

### MEMPHIS

The night before the Memphis game, I actually slept really well. I tried to approach it just like any normal game and not get too excited or worked up just because we were playing for the national title.

Memphis had a great team. Luckily, though, we were able to make some big plays down the stretch to win it. Shady hit his two big shots, Sherron had the big steal and I came through with the three-pointer.

Some people may have been nervous during a time like that, but I love those situations. I'd practiced them with my dad – and even my mom – since I was a little kid. Once that shot went through and we went into overtime, I knew we were going to win because we had the momentum. There was no way we were turning back at that point. It was a great feeling when it was all over and the streamers were coming down from

the rafters. I ran over and found my mom and hugged her. It was a moment I'll never forget.

I thought our whole team handled itself with class that night. We celebrated after it was over – but you didn't see us bragging or mugging for the cameras. One of the main reasons is that we weren't all that surprised. We didn't go to San Antonio hoping we could win the title.

We expected it.

*Russell Robinson*

Throughout his four years at Kansas, Russell Robinson was always admired by the media for his honesty and candor. So no one was surprised that it was Robinson who delivered one of the more moving, heartfelt statements during Kansas' postseason banquet April 13 at Allen Fieldhouse.

"I'm 22 years old," Robinson said. "I still have a lot of living to do, but this will probably be the best moment of my entire life. Enjoy it. Live it up. Rock Chalk, Jayhawk."

Thankful as he is for the opportunities he was given at Kansas, Jayhawk fans are equally appreciative of Robinson. By the end of his career the lovefest for Robinson had escalated so much that the kid from New York, New York may never want to move back to the Big Apple.

Robinson's popularity was easy to understand. He didn't score boatloads of points or contend for first team All-Big 12 honors. But anyone who followed Kansas' team the last three seasons knows that it was Robinson who set the tone. It was Robinson that the Jayhawks looked to for leadership.

"Russell should never be judged on how many points he scored or on what kind of stats he put up," coach Bill Self said. "He should be judged on how many games he won. That's where Russell Robinson's impact can be seen the most – in the win-loss column."

Indeed, in the three years that Robinson started at point guard, Kansas went a combined 95-14. The Jayhawks won the Big 12 regular season and conference tournament title in each of those seasons, which included an appearance in the Elite Eight in 2007 and a national title in 2008.

Think about it: Kansas' championship team featured three probable first round draft picks (Brandon Rush, Darrell Arthur and Mario Chalmers) as well as two more players (Sherron Collins and Cole Aldrich) who could be first-rounders in the next year or two. Yet if you glanced into the stands, Robinson's No. 3 jersey seemed to be the most popular attire among fans young and old.

That says a lot about the respect folks had for Robinson, who in four years went from being a player who refused to enter a game as a freshman to one who was chosen to carry the national championship trophy during Kansas' victory parade through downtown Lawrence. "I wish I could coach him four more years," Self said.

### IN RUSSELL'S WORDS

It didn't take long for me to realize just how special Kansas really was. I came to Lawrence on my official visit in September of 2003 – the same weekend Bill Whittemore and the KU football team beat Missouri at Memorial Stadium. The

**27**

fans rushed the field and tore down the goal posts, and when they went to throw them into Potter Lake, I was right there with them.

I had such a good time on my visit that I called my dad back in New York and said, "Dad, I think this might be the one." He knew I was serious, so he got on a flight that same day and came down here to check it out. He could see why I liked it so much. I ended up committing after that.

When I showed up on campus the following fall, I was full of confidence. The problem was that everything didn't go according to plan. I played a little bit – especially early on – but I felt like I could've been doing a lot more. It was tough to get a lot of minutes, though, because we had some experienced, veteran guards on our team in Aaron Miles, Keith Langford and Michael Lee. They had won a lot of big games in their career. Once I couldn't do what I expected to do – which is play - things started going downhill.

Mentally, I had a tough time dealing with things. I don't want to say that I didn't have any support. In all honesty, I probably just didn't use the support I had. I'm an independent dude and have always figured out a way to handle things on my own. Plus, one of the main reasons I picked Kansas was because of Norm Roberts, the assistant who recruited me. He left to take the St. John's job before I ever got here. It was an awful situation, because I found out from a reporter instead of hearing it from Coach Rob himself. When things went bad for me that year, I didn't feel as comfortable going to talk to Coach Self, because I didn't have the relationship with him like I would've had with Coach Rob.

After my freshman year, everyone assumed I was going to transfer to St. John's. I reached the decision to stay at Kansas on my own, but my parents were certainly a big help. Some parents would've told their kids it was OK to back out since the coach who recruited them backed out too. But my parents told me I shouldn't use that as an excuse. I wasn't going to do it anyways, but it helped that they didn't say, "It's OK with us. Just transfer." They wanted me to honor the scholarship I signed with Kansas, which was fine with me, because I never wanted to be known as a quitter. I came back and played really well. Sherron came in during my junior year, but I never gave up my job. I sacrificed some points and some minutes to him, but nothing is greater than accomplishing something with sacrifice. That's the motto I went by during my junior year.

I've never been afraid to be around the best. I think that makes my job easier. Sherron and I have become really tight. We're both from the inner-city, so we have a lot in common. We're really good friends. Most people in that situation wouldn't have been able to take a back seat, but I did my job.

**MEMORIES, SWEET MEMORIES**

Other than beating Memphis for the national championship, the biggest win of my career came in the Big 12 Championship game against Texas my sophomore year. That was huge. Texas had beaten us by 25 points in Austin a few weeks earlier, which was kind of understandable since we started three freshmen and two sophomores. Still, we had a talented team and we came out and played really well. I thought I played really well in that game. Jeff Hawkins hit some big shots and Julian had his 360 dunk. It was a big moment. I always liked playing Texas. They have a great program and a great coach.

Still, nothing will ever compare to this year's NCAA Tournament. We were lucky to survive against Davidson. But the way I saw it ... I'd been watching UCLA play all year. They'd dodged some bullets and then played well after that. So we dodged ours against Davidson. Everyone has games like that.

Once we got to the Final Four, the pressure was off. At that point, no matter what happened, we had had a great season. I felt good for Coach Self. That was

the hurdle that he needed to clear in his career, so once we got to the Final Four, pretty much all the pressure was off of him, too. We could just go out and play our game.

We didn't talk much about the situation with Roy Williams – but we talked a lot about North Carolina. We were more concerned about them going on a run and about Tyler Hansbrough going off than we were about Coach Williams.

I took a lot of pictures during the tournament, and one of them was actually with Roy and I and some of the guys. I saw him at the Salute dinner we had Thursday night in San Antonio. I'm a college basketball fan, so I couldn't help but be a little nervous and star-struck. But I had the camera ready and we took the picture. He was very nice about it, and I know he said later that it meant a lot to him that we asked him to do that.

As far as the game itself ... we couldn't have played much better. The toughest thing about that game was catching our breath. We were pretty tired after getting up and down the court like that. The clock seemed like it was taking forever. North Carolina was good. We knew they were going to make a run eventually. They did, but we withstood it and won.

I don't think it's any secret that one of the main reasons we won that game was Cole Aldrich and the defense he played on Hansbrough. One of our main concerns was that Hansbrough is a very physical player who loves contact. We weren't scared of him, but we were very cautious. We didn't want that to be a factor in the game.

Luckily, Cole stepped up and played huge for us. We had seen it coming. At

**From left:** Sherron Collins, Darrell Arthur and Russell Robinson with rapper Lil Wayne

practice he had been playing very well. He just had some talented guys in front of him on the team, but he came through when we needed him the most.

### MEMPHIS

We beat Memphis two nights later. By the time I got back to the hotel, I was on Cloud Nine. We had a reception on the 22nd floor and everyone was there, including my mom and my dad and one of my former coaches from back in my AAU days. We all just sat around and talked and took a bunch of pictures.

I couldn't sleep that night so I went to Scot Pollard's room and hung out with a bunch of former players. They were talking about their time at Kansas and about how they wished they could've come through and accomplished what we did. It was interesting listening to those guys. You could hear in their voice how much they loved their university. I kept thinking, "Wow, this is going to be me someday."

It was also good to see Coach Self so happy. I'm always going to have a lot of respect for him no matter what. He's probably going to be at my wedding. I'm definitely going to keep that relationship open. I owe him a lot for sticking with me. A lot of coaches would've been cutthroat. After my freshman year they would've said. "Hey, you've got to go. I've got to get someone in here with a better attitude." But he stuck with me and I respect him for that.

### LOOKING AHEAD

As much fun as I've had celebrating, my focus has shifted to playing in the NBA. I don't want to ride on this championship cloud for too long, because I'm sure everyone I play against from this point forward won't care if I'm a national champion or not. I'll have the rest of my life to enjoy that, but right now I've got to move on. The good thing is that I'll always have a bunch of memories stored away in photo albums or in my head. What happened this year is something that's never going to be lost.

We've had one lottery pick so far (Julian Wright) and there are probably a lot more first-rounders to come. For me to come out here and earn the respect of these guys after what I went through my freshman year is a real accomplishment. It's a compliment to me more as a person than as a player.

Kansas, to me, means more than I can even put into words right now. I never would've imagined Kansas could be like this. Growing up in New York City, all I knew about Kansas was tornadoes and "The Wizard of Oz." I never thought this place could make me a better person. It's going to be tough to leave. I still haven't decided where I'm going to live, but I like Overland Park. The people here are so nice and it's a lot cheaper than New York. Still, whether I have a house here or not, I'll be coming back to Kansas for the rest of my life.

*Darnell Jackson*

Somehow – in the aftermath of one of the most embarrassing upsets in school history – Kansas forward Darnell Jackson found the strength to look toward the future instead of dwelling on the past.

It happened back in March of 2005 at Oklahoma City's Ford Center. As his teammates sat stone-faced in the locker room following a first round NCAA Tournament loss to Bucknell, Jackson turned and whispered to a staff member standing nearby.

"It's our time now," Jackson said. "It's our time now."

Jackson was referring to himself, Russell Robinson and Sasha Kaun. At the time all three were freshmen who had played a limited role on a senior-laden team. But with Aaron Miles, Mike Lee, Wayne Simien and Keith Langford all graduating, a new era of Kansas basketball was about to begin - and Jackson was determined to be a big part of it.

Over the next three years, Jackson became one of the most heart-warming stories in all of college basketball, a guy whose struggles off the court made you appreciate his success on it.

Following his sophomore year, Jackson's grandmother was killed in a Las Vegas car wreck that also caused serious injuries to his mother. His uncle was beaten to death with a hammer and his cousin was shot and killed.

"And that was only half the stuff," Jackson said. "There were other things that I never talked about, things I wanted to keep private."

With each new tragedy, Jackson began having more and more trouble focusing on the court. His fortunes changed, though, midway through his junior year after a meeting with Coach Bill Self outside his home in Oklahoma, where Jackson had fled when the stress became unbearable.

"I broke down out there and just hugged him for a long time," Jackson said. "That was a turning point for me. Everything started going uphill after that."

Jackson made nine of his 13 field goal attempts in the 2007 NCAA Tournament and was one of the few Kansas players who didn't look intimidated in an Elite Eight loss to UCLA. Nothing, though, compared to Jackson's senior season, when he earned a starting spot for the first time in his career and responded with an 11.2 scoring average and a team-high 6.7 rebounds per game.

"You could tell from the start that Darnell was going to be one of Coach Self's favorite players," Langford said after attending KU's regular season game at Texas last season. "He was a challenge for him, a project. He could be stubborn

sometimes and tough to coach. But he's one of those guys that, once you have him, he'll break his back for you out there."

### IN DARNELL'S WORDS

After we beat Memphis, when we got back to the hotel, I didn't hang out and celebrate with the guys. Instead I just went to my room, laid in bed and texted back and forth with my girlfriend all night. I remember telling her, "It's over." I knew that was the end for me. I knew that, starting the next day, it was going to be all business from now on. In some ways that thought excited me, and in some ways it made me sad.

All through the night, I started thinking about my experiences at Kansas, both the good and the bad.

I remember the first day I showed up on the Kansas campus. Me and my mom and Don Davis carried all my stuff from the car up to my room at Jayhawker Towers. I saw Keith and Wayne and Aaron and Mike. Sasha was my roommate, and that night we went and played pick-up. Aaron stopped by later that night and we had a nice visit. We talked about how things were going to be for the next four years.

It was hard not to respect those four seniors, because they had accomplished so much during their careers. It's crazy to think that we actually surpassed that great class when it came to accomplishing all the goals we had set as a team.

### TOUGH TIMES

A lot of things changed for me after my freshman year. I ran into this big

wall. No matter how hard I tried, it seemed like I couldn't climb over it or break through it.

Mentally, some days I was there and some days I wasn't. I kept telling myself that I had to be there every day, every game. I couldn't just be there and go hard in practice one day and half-speed the next. It wasn't helping me at all.

Everyone knows by now that I was dealing with a lot of stuff away from the court. I had lost my grandmother in a car accident the summer before my sophomore year, and that same accident left my mother with a lot of injuries that made things difficult on her. I had an uncle that was killed and later on a friend and a cousin. All of it caused me to have to deal with a lot of emotions – a lot of guilt and a lot of pain. When it came to basketball ... there were times when it was tough to focus.

My lowest low came during the winter of my junior year. Instead of being here playing basketball, I felt like I should be at home in Oklahoma, helping my mom. One night, around 1 a.m., I packed up some of my things and drove home with my brother and my ex-girlfriend. It was a long, quiet ride. I did the driving. There wasn't really any talking, because they slept the whole way there. When I finally got home it was about 6 a.m. I walked through the door, dropped my bags on the floor and crawled into the bed with my mom.

When I didn't show up for practice the next day, Coach Self knew that something was wrong. He found out I was in Oklahoma, so he and Coach Chalmers got on a plane and came to talk to me. We were in my living room with mom and my uncle, Edred, and I asked Coach Self if I could talk to him outside. I broke down out there and just hugged him for a long time. We had a talk, and everything he told me that night ended up proving true. He said we were about to start winning, and winning big. He told me that, during the next year and a half, I was going to start playing basketball at a level that I had never imagined playing. He said anything I had ever wanted or dreamed about was about to happen for me. Looking back now on that conversation ... he was right.

I'll never forget what Coach Self did for me that night – but there were other people that helped, too. I sometimes get asked, "What kept you going, Darnell?" and my answer is, "Everybody." There were so many people that tried to help me. One of the main things that drove me was that I didn't want to let them down. From my mom to Don Davis to Gloria to Scooter in the academic office, all of my coaches ... I thought about those people every day. There were all these people that helped me out and they didn't have to do that. The last people I wanted to let down were the KU fans, the people who supported me the whole four years.

## LAST SHOT

It goes without saying that my senior year was the most fun I had during my time at Kansas. Every day was a new day. It was an adventure. It was a long process and it took me a long time to understand that. Once I understood that the journey was going to be a long one, I settled in for the ride. It helped that I knew that this was the last hurrah for me. This was my last year.

I really enjoyed playing against teams that down-talked us, and I liked playing in games when the guys on television were questioning how we were going to match up with someone or how we were going to stop this player or that player. That really boosted my energy. One person would say we couldn't win a game, and the next thing you know, everyone was on the bandwagon.

That was definitely the case at the Final Four. The whole time we were down there, nobody believed that we were going to win the whole thing. Other than our own fans, no one was giving us a chance. Those are the situations when we play our best.

I thought we really stepped up when we played Tyler Hansbrough and North Carolina. He's a great player, but to me, he also had been given a lot of hype. A lot of players come into college with hype. There's nothing wrong with that. But I like going against a guy who people say you can't stop. It's fun to go out there and stop that person and stop that team. People are like, "Wow – I didn't think he was going to be able to do that." The next thing you know, you've won the game.

## THE ROAD TO KANSAS

Sometimes I wonder how my basketball career would've gone if I hadn't signed with Kansas. I remember calling Coach Self when he was at Illinois. I wanted to see if he'd be interested in me coming up there to play for him. He told me to wait, because he was about to get the job at Kansas. Not long after that, he ended up in Lawrence – and I ended up committing to Kansas. He needed to sign a power forward and he was looking at me and Kalen Grimes, who ended up at

Missouri. Kalen was mad when I got the scholarship, because I think he wanted to come here, too. I still remember seeing a quote from him that said, "I can't wait to play against Darnell Jackson." He didn't get the chance this year, because he was suspended. It's too bad, because I would've given him the opportunity if he wanted it that bad. I loved playing against those kind of forwards – guys like Kalen and Joseph Jones at Texas A&M. I learned something from all those guys.

### ROLE MODEL
Along with winning the title, another thing that happened during my senior year was that I got a lot of publicity for some of the things I'd been through off the court. *Sports Illustrated* wrote a nice story, and after that it seemed like every reporter wanted to ask me about the tragedies that had taken place in my life and how I persevered through them. I did most of the interviews, but what those guys never knew was that I was only telling them half of the stuff. There were so many other things that happened in my life, but I didn't want to put it out there and scare anyone away. Most of those things are things I'll always keep private.

Still, I'm glad the media helped get my story out there. I didn't realize this would happen at the time, but it ended up having an effect on a lot of the people who read it. Even now, everywhere I go, people walk up to me and tell me I'm one of their role models. I'm talking about men that are 48 years old telling me I'm their role model. I'm only 22. It makes me feel good that I helped someone out. When I go out and people walk up to me and ask for an autograph ... it doesn't bother me. I enjoy stuff like that.

Whenever I start feeling bad I just remember that there are always people out there that are having a worse day than me. There are people that are homeless and starving. At least I have a roof over my head and enough money to get by.

Now that it's all over, I've got a lot of new opportunities ahead of me. Whether it's in the NBA or somewhere else, I want to keep playing basketball for a long time. I don't get overwhelmed when I start thinking about what's next. I get excited. I can't wait to get started. I've got a lot of energy right now, a lot of momentum thanks to the way we finished the year – and the way I finished my career.

### FINAL THOUGHT

Every day I was out there on the court, I told myself that I didn't want to be one of those guys that looked back on his career and said, "I could've done this and I could've done that." I wanted to be someone that looked back on things and said, "I *did* that. I *went* to the Final Four. I *won* a national championship. I *walked* down that hill and *got* my degree." I wanted to be that guy who achieved his goals and made everyone proud. Hopefully, I did that.

He praised his players, credited his staff and expressed gratitude toward the fans. Still, during his countless victory speeches following Kansas' victory over Memphis in the 2008 national title game, Bill Self forgot to thank one person.

David Stern.

It was only two years earlier, you may remember, when Stern – the NBA commissioner - implemented a rule that prevented players from entering the draft until they were at least one year removed from high school.

Had Stern not enforced that policy, Darrell Arthur may have jumped into

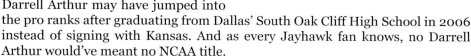

*Darrell Arthur*

the pro ranks after graduating from Dallas' South Oak Cliff High School in 2006 instead of signing with Kansas. And as every Jayhawk fan knows, no Darrell Arthur would've meant no NCAA title.

"He was the best player in the game that night," Self said of Arthur.

Indeed, Mario Chalmers hit the biggest shot. But from start to finish, no Jayhawk performed as well against Memphis as Arthur. The 6-foot-9 sophomore scored a team-high 20 points on nine-of-13 shooting and grabbed 10 rebounds – including five on the offensive end.

Even more impressive was that eight of Arthur's points came after the 3:30 mark of regulation – a sign that he flourishes during the pressure-packed moments when so many others flounder.

Arthur actually entered the Memphis game on a bit of a slide. He had scored in double figures in just two of his previous eight contests – mainly because of the foul problems that plagued him throughout the entire season.

In terms of sheer, God-given talent, though, there was no better player on the Jayhawks' 2008 roster.

### IN DARRELL'S WORDS

One thing I remember about the championship game was looking across the court into the stands. My little brother, Juicy, was crying. He's only six, and later my mom told me he was saying, "We're not going to win it, are we momma? We're not going to win it, are we?" That was with about two minutes left in the game, and I'm sure a lot of people were probably thinking the same thing. Our team, though ... we never lost confidence that we could get it done.

I had 20 points that night. When I look back on it, I can easily say that that was the best game of my career at Kansas – mainly because it happened in the

national championship, the game that every player grows up dreaming about. It was one of those games where I felt like I could score each time I touched the ball. I was in such a good rhythm that night. I hadn't had a ton of nights like that during the season – mainly because I'd had a problem with getting into foul trouble. There were so many games when I picked up two quick fouls and had to sit out for most of the first half. I don't know what the problem was, but it led to a lot of frustration. Luckily, against Memphis, I was able to play smart and stay on the floor.

I made two shots during our comeback against Memphis that I'll never forget: a 17-footer with a hand in my face and a turnaround jumper from the baseline that rattled in. The big one was the baseline shot, because we were down by four with one minute left, and it pulled us within two, 62-60. Memphis made one more free throw after that, and then Mario made his big three-pointer to force overtime. It was one of the most exciting NCAA championships ever. Every day I realize more and more how lucky I was to be a part of it.

The best part about winning the whole thing was that we did it as an underdog.

Everyone kept talking about how we were the worst of the No. 1 seeds and about how we didn't have a chance. I'm not going to lie. That frustrated us. It made us mad. If you look back, we always played our best basketball in games that we weren't supposed to win. Florida in Las Vegas when I was a freshman, Texas in the last two Big 12 Tournaments and then North Carolina and Memphis this year. We knew we were a better team. We knew we were deep and we knew we could do it. No one should be surprised. It lights a fire under us when people say we can't do something.

Going into the tournament, people kept telling me how important it was for me to play well so I could help my NBA draft stock. You can really help yourself by having a good game on that big a stage against the best competition in the country. There were a lot of scouts in the stands, and I'm sure plenty of others were watching on television. I'm just proud of myself for not letting that situation become a distraction. The good thing was that I was already used to playing in front of NBA people like that. We've got so many good players on our team that we had scouts at almost every game to watch guys like Brandon and Mario and Sasha and Darnell and Sherron. Other than the times the media asked me about it, I never really worried about going out there and trying to impress scouts. Coach told us that as long as we were winning, the pie at the end would be big enough for everyone. So that's all I focused on: playing the role I was supposed to play – and winning.

### TURNING POINT

Obviously, you'd like to win every game. But I think the best thing that happened to us all year was losing to Kansas State and Oklahoma State. We started off 20-0 and everyone started feeling really comfortable. People were telling us how good we were and stuff like that. Then K-State came out and took

it to us, and we ended up losing three of our next seven games.

Our confidence was pretty low after we lost to Oklahoma State. We were going through a lot, and there were some issues in our circle, some problems that needed to be addressed. We all got together at Henry T's and talked about what we needed to do to turn this thing around. That talk helped a lot. Our seniors stepped up and talked about how they wanted to go out. They talked about how they wanted to be remembered and about how they wanted this team to be remembered and what we needed to do to turn things around. After that meeting we won our next 13 games and never looked back.

Even though we were having some issues at that time, it's not as if this team wasn't ever close. All

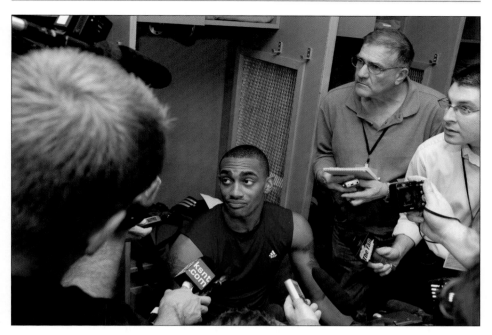

through the year, we never had situations where it was players vs. players or coaches vs. players or anything like that. The best part about us was how much we all got along.

**RECRUITING**

Sometimes I think about what would've happened if I hadn't chosen Kansas and been able to be a part of this national championship. I had so much trouble deciding on a college that I waited until the last possible minute to sign. I visited Indiana, North Carolina and LSU, but in the end it was between Kansas and Baylor. Some of my relatives, including my grandmother, wanted me to go to Baylor because it was close to my home in Dallas. Plus, it was a program on the rise. They had some good players there like Kevin Rogers, who I played with in high school, and their staff did a great job of recruiting me. I scheduled a press conference on May 8 and I pretty much decided that that was where I wanted to go. But in the end I still wasn't sure, so I slept on it and had a dream where I saw myself in a Kansas uniform, playing for the Jayhawks. That's how I came to my decision.

It was tough at first. I was used to being in Dallas around my family. I knew it would be good for me to get away, but I didn't know how much it was going to hurt me. It hit me pretty hard when I realized that I was here on my own. I got pretty homesick, so my mom came up and stayed with me for a few days when I was a freshman. Eventually I got over it and everything was fine after that. I'm glad I made the decision I did. It forced me to grow up and become a man.

No matter what happens in the future with me and basketball, I know this

championship is going to stick with me for the rest of my life. People will be talking about that Memphis game 20 and 30 years from now. We'll come back for reunions and people will talk about how we were the best team that ever came out of Kansas, the team with the best record in school history. It's crazy what happened. Just crazy.

Sherron Collins

Stacey Harris has a message for anyone struggling to raise a young son or daughter.

"Get your kids involved with sports," she said. "Sports can change a kid's life – and maybe even save it."

That's certainly been the case with Sherron Collins, Harris' youngest son. Just a few years ago Collins was a teenager trying to avoid the influences of the drugs and gangs that infested his Chicago neighborhood. But because of his involvement with basketball, Collins was able to escape to a better life at Kansas.

"At Kansas," Collins said, "I've turned into a different person."

And the Jayhawks have become a different team.

No KU player can change the course of a game quite like Collins, a hiccup-quick point guard with the burst of a sprinter and the strength of a fullback. Collins' biggest attribute in 2007-08 was his ability to make game-changing plays during the final moments of postseason contests. Glance at his resume of big shots and it's clear that Kansas would've never won the NCAA title if not for Collins' heroics in the clutch.

• In the championship game of the Big 12 Tournament, Collins dove out of bounds to save an errant pass. His effort kept the possession alive, and Kansas capitalized by scoring a key basket that catapulted the Jayhawks to a victory over Texas – and, eventually, a No. 1 seed in the NCAA Tournament.

• In the Elite Eight against Davidson, Collins hit a three-pointer that turned a 51-49 deficit into a 52-51 lead. Kansas never trailed again.

• Against North Carolina in the Final Four, Collins made a lay-up at the halftime buzzer that gave the Jayhawks a boost at intermission. In the second half, he threw a lob pass that Sasha Kaun turned into a dunk to give KU a 62-53 lead. Moments later, with the Jayhawks clinging to a 64-59 advantage, Collins swished a three-pointer that gave Kansas the momentum for good.

• Two nights later, in the championship victory over Memphis, Collins stole an in bounds pass under Kansas' basket and swished a three-pointer from the corner that shaved Memphis' lead to 60-56 with 1:46 remaining in regulation. Mario Chalmers hit a trey moments later to send the game into overtime, and Kansas emerged with a 75-68 victory. "Sherron has always had that drive," said Walt Harris, Collins' uncle. "In basketball they say you have to have that dog in you, that you can't play passive. That's always Sherron. He's always had that dog in him."

### IN SHERRON'S WORDS

I never thought I'd be a guy who would pass a family on the street and hear a little kid say, "Momma, that's Sherron Collins." But ever since we won the championship, that kind of thing is happening everyday. I realize now that I'm a role model, and I'm going to do everything I can to make the most of it. I want to reach out to others to show that, no matter where you came from, no matter where you live, you can use your God-given abilities to make a name for yourself.

I'm getting messages on Facebook from people asking, "How can I get as good as you?" or "What can I do to get better?" I respond to as many of them as I can. I just tell people to stay positive and to stay focused. I tell them to find people they trust and to stay off the streets.

After we won the title, I went back home and visited the barbershop in my neighborhood. There were all these people there asking for autographs. A television crew came out and filmed the whole thing. I went over and spoke to the kids at the Boys and Girls Club where I grew up, and now I'm supposed to be doing something with Jesse Jackson. They're going to call it "Sherron Collins Day" in Chicago.

The attitude I have now ... I owe it all to Kansas. Coming here from the inner-city, I was worried about how I'd interact with people who had a better lifestyle – people that hadn't gone through the same things that I'd gone through growing up. I thought that would be the hardest thing about making the transition to college, but it turned out to be the easiest thing. The people around here are so nice that you can't help but adjust to this way of life. Your maturity level grows without you even trying.

## FAMILY

As proud as I am of myself, I'm also proud for my mother, my uncle and my grandmother. They made me who I am today. My dad has never been around much, so they all pitched in and looked after me and my brother to make sure we stayed on the right path.

My mother had it rough when we were growing up. Being a single parent, she was always working to make sure we had food on the table. A lot of times we were on our own because she was off trying to earn a living. She hurt her back when I was in high school, so she was never able to come to many games because sitting in those bleachers caused her a lot of pain. Now she's able to see me play a lot more. She jokes that she's traveling the country just like a pro basketball player.

After we beat Memphis, all I remember is her hugging me and crying. She didn't say much. It was just a long, tight hug. That moment really touched me, because I could tell she realized just how far I'd come, and hopefully she knew that she was a big reason for that.

## CHILDHOOD

Growing up, I had every opportunity in the world to get into trouble. A lot of my friends were in gangs and into drugs. I lived in the projects, where there were fights all of the time. I had friends that were dropouts and others that were killed. My high school wasn't a safe place to be. One time, I saw a kid get beaten unconscious in the hallway with a padlock. This year I got a call from my old principal. He told me that a guy I knew had been shot and killed as he walked out of school that day. Gang members shot him right there by the front steps. The same people beat up another guy I knew with a golf club, and he had to be rushed to the hospital. It was all because of an argument over a ball cap. I wasn't surprised. I saw that kind of stuff all the of time back in Chicago. It was the same story, just different people.

## TRAGEDY

The summer before my freshman year, I had a son that died a few days after he was born. It was one of the most painful experiences I've ever been through in my life. Luckily, I got a second chance at fatherhood last spring when my girlfriend and I had a baby boy. We named him Sherr'Mari. I had some tough times with injuries this year, so it was always nice to be able to fly them to Kansas. Whenever I would walk through the door and see them, the pain and the frustration of the season just went away. They kept me positive and lifted me up. Without them things would've been harder on me this year.

One good thing about the season was that I kept my weight down. I was at 200

pounds for most of the year. When we went to the Final Four I was actually at 198. Still, I was always in a lot of pain because of my knees and ankle. Coach Self kept telling me that I could use my brain to do anything. He just said to think positive things and to forget about the pain and just play through it. Before the NCAA Tournament, he said something that I'll never forget. He said, "Sherron, if we win, all the injuries and frustrations you've been through this year will be forgotten about. It will all be irrelevant. All you and anyone else will remember is that in 2008, you were a champion."

### THANKS, COACH

Coach Self and I have always had a special relationship. He likes tough-minded players, so he definitely appreciates and respects kids that grew up playing in the parks of Chicago. I'm stubborn, and I think he likes that. He likes the toughness I bring to the team. In Chicago, you've got to have a swagger on the court or you're not going to survive. Period. You can't make a name for yourself unless you have a swagger. Without that, people will look at you like you're nothing. I'm easy to coach and I want to win, but no one is ever going to take my attitude away from me. No one is ever going to take away my swagger.

I like to compete and I hate rules. When something needs to happen – when we're down or struggling – I get a burst of energy. I love to be the guy that

boosts a team. In those situations you see a different Sherron Collins – a more focused Sherron Collins. That's when I'm at my best, when I'm hitting big shots and doing a little jaw-jackin'. I want to be ultra-aggressive and take it to the next level. That's how I was during the NCAA Tournament.

## POST SEASON

By the time we got to the Final Four, I was starting to feel 100 percent healthy again. It happened at just the right time, because when we played Memphis, I had to guard Derrick Rose. I was really excited for that matchup, because Rose is from Chicago, too, so I took it as a personal challenge. It was Chicago vs. Chicago, so I knew a lot of people back home would be talking about it. At the same time, I didn't want to get into a situation where it was all about me and him. My main goal was beating Memphis – not Derrick Rose.

Rose is a great player. He's athletic and strong. He's a pro, and we knew we had to slow him and Chris Douglas-Roberts down if we wanted to have a chance to win. I didn't want to give Rose anything. You've got to be tough with him, so I tried to put my body on him every time because he's so strong. I'm strong, too, though. Every time he tried to make a move I knocked him off line. I also knew I'd have to attack him and make him guard me on the defensive end. At the end of the first half, he had three points and three turnovers, so I thought I did a

pretty good job.

As the game went on I got more and more confident. Toward the end I made a big steal and then swished a three-pointer from the corner. As soon as I shot it I yelled "Boom!" because I knew it was going in. With about 30 seconds left, with us losing by two, I went in for a fastbreak lay-up against two guys and got my shot blocked. I probably should've pulled up and played for a better shot, but Mario ended up hitting that three to send it overtime, and the rest is history.

Russell and I were the last ones to make it to the locker room. When we got there everyone was just sitting there in disbelief. But then Russell started yelling and throwing water on everyone. That got the whole celebration started. Within a few seconds everyone was throwing water on everyone. We stayed up pretty late that night, enjoying ourselves. It took about a week for everything to hit us. There may be people out there who still can't believe what we did.

Sasha Kaun

Sasha Kaun said basketball has taken a toll on his body – but not in the way that most would think. "I like to dunk a lot," Kaun said, "but sometimes it really hurts. Especially when you do it with one hand. You slam your wrist on that rim and it stings."

You can imagine, then, the bruises that dotted Kaun's arm following the 2007-08 postseason. With each game came a new alley-oop flush or tomahawk jam. Not that he was complaining. Any pain he felt was worth it for Kaun – and for Kansas.

After struggling with consistency issues during his first three seasons in Lawrence, Kaun couldn't have ended his college career on a much higher note. Kaun blocked a career-high 49 shots in 2007-08, when he earned a reputation as one of the top defensive centers in the country despite coming off the bench for the first time since his freshman year.

Kaun's biggest impact came in the Jayhawks' 59-57 victory over Davidson in the Elite Eight. While many of his teammates appeared nervous and stiff, Kaun was clearly the aggressor against the Wildcats. His 13-point effort on six-of-six shooting catapulted Kansas into the Final Four for the first time in Bill Self's career.

When Self fell to his knees at the final horn, you can bet he was thanking God not just for the victory – but for Sasha Kaun, as well.

"Sasha," Self would say later, "clearly saved his best for last."

Indeed, Kaun's emergence couldn't have come at a better time. By midseason NBA scouts were buzzing about the big Russian's pro prospects. One of them had this to say about Kaun:

"Kansas has a lot of players that will get picked ahead of Kaun in the draft but, because of his size and his smarts, he may end up hanging around the league longer than anyone on this team. He's got a chance to make a lot of money."

Even if he has to do it overseas, Kaun knows how fortunate he is to have the opportunity to earn a living playing basketball. Kaun's father, Oleg, died when Kaun was 13. Three years later his mother agreed to let him move to the United States so he could receive a solid high school education at the Florida Air Academy. At the time, Kaun knew zero English – and he'd never played organized basketball. Within two years, though, Kaun had become one of the hottest prospects in the country, with schools such as Duke, Georgetown and Michigan State offering scholarships before Kaun decided on Kansas.

"I'm very fortunate," Kaun said. "Looking back, it's obvious I made a series of good decisions."

## IN SASHA'S WORDS

I knew Kansas was a place I was going to love from the day I first came to campus on my visit. It was definitely a lot different than Florida. Instead of it being all palm trees, there were actually some normal trees, too. It reminded me of home a lot. In Russia we have the same kind of trees. It was a little bit cooler, especially in September, whereas in Florida it still would've been really hot.

As a freshman, I lived in the Towers with Darnell. I was definitely happy to be in the Towers because, in high school, I was living with five other guys in one room. Florida Air Academy was basically like a boarding school. We had bunk beds. They had extra-long ones for some of the taller players. I was still able to sleep OK, but it still wasn't all that comfortable. It was really cramped, so it was a nice change to come to Kansas, where I had my own room. There was a lot more freedom living in a two-bedroom apartment with just one other person.

Once I got to Kansas it was all basketball, all the time. Even in the summer, we played pick-up almost every day, and we were always lifting weights. It was such a big difference than what I was used to. It wore me out. I was tired all the time and didn't have much energy to do anything else.

I tried to make some friends outside of basketball. I met a few people here from Russia, which was nice because we had a lot of things in common and a lot of things we could talk about. When I was in high school it was really expensive to make calls to Russia to talk to my mom. But once I got here I started using the internet to call her. There are certain days when you can make free calls to landlines. Other times it was only like two cents per minute. It's ridiculously cheap. I'd call her at least once a week and make sure everything was OK. I heard her voice and she heard mine. That was more comforting than anything.

### BULKING UP

One of my favorite things to do at Kansas is lift weights. I did a pretty good job of lifting in high school, too. When I moved to Florida I only weighed 180 pounds, but after the first six months I was putting up some pretty good weight. It's fun to see the changes that you can make in your body by lifting weights.

Here at Kansas, lifting is so much more important than it was in high school. We have a separate lifting coach named Andrea Hudy. She did such a fantastic job of developing us and making us stronger. She loves what she does. She takes such pride in her work. She knows so much about every little detail and aspect of weight lifting. She makes us better not just by doing simple basic exercises, but by doing stuff that's related to basketball. She's really strict in the weight room. Even if

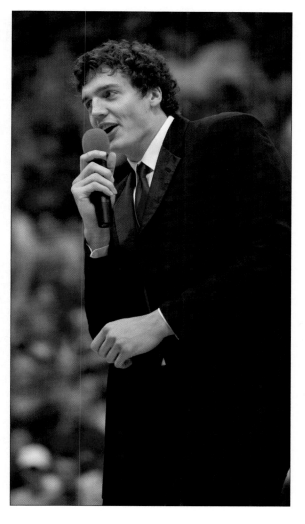

you wanted to slack off there's no way that you could. A lot of weight lifting coaches don't watch your every move like she does. I've heard stories from friends who go to other schools. They say their weight lifting sessions aren't as hardcore and that they're more relaxed.

When you don't do what you're supposed to do – or if she sees you talking and losing focus – Coach Hudy gets on your butt. One of her big things is "No Music in the Weight Room." A lot of people love to listen to music when they lift. But she thinks it's a distraction, because a lot of people start dancing. I think she has a point. When you're on the basketball court, you're not out there listening to music during the games. You've got to focus and get the job done. It should be the same way in the weight room.

53

Obviously my upper body is a lot stronger than my lower body. I do a lot of curls and I love the bench press. The most I've ever benched is about 285 pounds. I usually work out with about 225 or 245. It depends on what part of the week we're in, or what part of the season. The past couple of years they've really tried to get me to focus on improving my lower body.

### SENIOR YEAR

Coming into the season, everyone knew that we were going to be a good team, and a lot of that was because we were so unselfish. Coach Self came to me early in the year and told me that Darnell was going to start and that I would be coming off the bench. Honestly, I didn't mind. When I looked at the stat sheet I saw that my minutes hadn't gone down at all. My role hadn't changed. It was definitely better for the team – and it ended up being a good thing for me, too.

One of the biggest focuses for me during the year was improving my free throw shooting. I was terrible at the beginning of the season. It was frustrating because I'd spent some time during the summer trying to change my shot a little bit. I started bringing the ball back just a little bit more and trying to make it a little more fluid. With me, though, the problem was a mental issue – much more so than form. I could walk into the gym by myself and make 80 out of 100 without any problem. But then I'd get into game situations and it'd be completely different. Before the USC game, I went to see our sports psychologist, Megan Brent. I talked to her for an hour, and it's crazy how much she helped me with just one conversation. We did a couple of exercises. It was nothing too insane or anything. Just some relaxation exercises where I'd close my eyes and talk to her and visualize things and tell her how I was feeling. It was really cool. If computer science weren't going to be my profession, I'd probably go into sports psychology. I could make a lot of money by not doing a whole lot. Just have a little conversation with someone and make X amount of dollars. Sounds pretty good to me.

After we beat Texas in the Big 12 Tournament, I thought we were on a pretty big high. We really came together as a team. Things were going really good for us. Everyone had a lot of confidence. I thought losing a few games earlier in the season helped us come closer together. It's a long season. You can't win every game. That's almost impossible, in my eyes. You can't bring 100 percent energy to every game. Energy is such a big factor. Look at the games we lost: Kansas State, Texas and Oklahoma State. We were completely flat. I watch those tapes and think, "My gosh. We look like we want to crawl in bed and take a nap."

The Kansas State game in Manhattan was the toughest environment we played in all season. They came out ready to go and we were a little bit flat. They definitely did a phenomenal job of having their energy up. Their fans were unbelievable. It was a combination of poor play by us, incredible play by them and a crazy arena that made us lose. That game is a perfect example of what I said earlier: Energy changes everything. It doesn't matter what kind of player you are. When you're playing with passion you can be unbelievable. That's what happened with them that night.

I always liked to play against Aleks Maric at Nebraska. He was a good big guy that I could match up with and test myself against because he was very strong. I liked to play against true big guys – true centers instead of power forwards. There aren't a lot of them. Jiri Hubalek of Iowa State was kind of like that. He played with his back to the basket but he could still step outside and shoot.

### REUNION

One of my favorite parts of the season was the 110-year anniversary, when all of the former players came back. I thought that was pretty cool, pretty amazing. It shows you how much tradition there is at this place and how much people care about basketball. Someone like Matt Kleinmann or Brennan Bechard or Tyrel Reed ... any of the players that grew up around Kansas basketball recognized those guys and knew their names. For me, I looked around and maybe knew two or three people in the crowd – and those were people I'd played with a few years ago, guys like Wayne Simien. I started walking around and introducing myself to different people and they all knew who I was. It was amazing to me how people still follow their

school and care so much about basketball. That was also my first time to really talk to Larry Brown. He was unbelievable. I talked to Clyde Lovellette, too. People tell me he was one of the greatest to ever play the game of basketball and, again, he knew who I was. He was a really, really nice guy. It made me feel good.

### POST SEASON

We had a lot of critics going into the NCAA Tournament. When critics talked about us this year, I know a lot of them said, "They didn't play anyone." But I thought our schedule was all right. We had some tough road games. I wouldn't say USC was a weak team with O.J. Mayo and Taj Gibson and Davon Jefferson. Arizona wasn't bad. Their record suffered a little when they lost Nic Wise and Jerry Bayless for a few games, but whether it happens this year or next, there are three first round draft picks (Bayless, Chase Budinger and Jordan Hill) on that team. College basketball is a crazy sport. Sometimes you'll play a team at a point during the season when they're hot, but then things go downhill for them. Or vice-versa.

As much fun as Senior Night was, the best part of the season was obviously the NCAA Tournament. I was so happy after we beat Villanova, because that meant we'd have another chance in the Elite Eight. We'd come as far as we'd been the previous season, and now we were facing a very underrated opponent – a phenomenal team. Davidson was kind of like Bradley. Just like I had no idea how they got a No. 13 seed, I had no idea how Davidson got a No. 10 seed. They had played well against North Carolina, UCLA, Duke ... a lot of big name programs. And they had just defeated Georgetown, which was in the Final Four last year. I knew they were good. I wanted to win so badly. I couldn't sleep well the night before because I had a big knot in my stomach. I just told myself, "No matter what happens, I'm going to perform as well as I can." There was a different feel for me throughout that whole game.

There was one shot I made against Davidson where, afterward, I let out a big scream. I don't do stuff like that very often. But this game was big. It was the seniors' last chance to go to the Final Four. I knew I had to use my size advantage in that game. They had very good guards but they didn't have very good bigs. Their inside play was kind of poor, so that really helped me which, in turn, helped us.

For the semifinal game, you couldn't have had a better matchup than Kansas and UNC. Just from the hype alone, we were so excited to play. I knew Tyler Hansbrough was going to go 110 percent the entire game. To be able to guard him, I knew I had to match his intensity. He's not advertised as being an incredibly skilled player. You always hear commentators questioning whether he can play at the next level. He doesn't have the skills of someone like Michael Beasley, but he's definitely the hardest-working kid you'll find. That's what makes him so good. He'll outwork you and he'll out-rebound you because he out-hustles people. On his cuts and stuff like that ... I mean, everywhere he goes, he goes full speed.

The thing that helped us – the thing that a lot of other teams didn't have – is that we had a lot of different people to throw at him. A team that has just one really good big, like Louisville and David Padgett ... if that's all Hansbrough has to worry about – just one player – then he'll wear his opponent down with his intensity. You can't match it with one guy. Luckily we had four guys to throw at him. Cole had a phenomenal game that night. That helped guys like me and Darnell and Darrell, because we were able to rest up and be fresh once we got in there. We could go just as hard as Hansbrough was going. I think that wore on him.

In the championship game, with Memphis and Joey Dorsey ... he's a very athletic big. He's a Ben Wallace-type of player that rebounds well and gets a lot of nice dunks. He's such a presence. I just wanted to box him out and keep him off the boards and make him guard me so he'd be in tough positions. I thought we did a good job against him, too.

After we beat Memphis I went over to the stands and hugged my mom before we left the court. It was a pretty special moment. She took a chance by letting me move to The United States when I was 16 because she knew there were better opportunities for me here. She could see then that it was paying off. She gets it now. She understands the game. She knows the magnitude of what we accomplished.

**FUTURE**

It's been a great four years. It's been a fun time. I think the community will remember us for years to come. It's cool to be able to leave your mark on the program.

I'm one of those guys who likes change. I'm really looking forward to what's next – whatever that ends up being. I'm excited and anxious to try new things. I'm looking forward to being able to focus 100 percent of my attention on basketball. For the last four years, I've always been stressed about basketball and school and all these other things. Now I can dedicate all of my attention toward getting better on the court.

No matter where I end up living, I'm sure I'll always make trips back to Lawrence. Ever since we won the championship, I've been amazed at how excited this town is about what we did. We had 80,000 people at the parade – and Lawrence doesn't even have 80,000 people. Where did they all come from? It's been fun to be a part of it all. It's something I know will stick with me forever.

*Rodrick Stewart*

When it was over – when it finally sunk in that he'd played the last game of his college career – Rodrick Stewart was riding back to the Hilton Palacio del Rio in San Antonio. Ninety minutes earlier, in practice, he'd sustained a knee injury that would keep him out of the Final Four, and now it was time to break the news to his dad.

"I called to tell him, and he thought I was lying," Stewart said. "I had to put the trainer on the phone to get him to believe me."

Indeed, so disheartening was the situation that it was almost hard to fathom. A day before Kansas played North Carolina in the national semifinals, Stewart fractured his knee cap while attempting a dunk at the end of the Jayhawks' open shoot-around at the Alamodome.

A fifth year senior, Stewart would never take the court as a Jayhawk again.

"I've got to get it together," a visibly-shaken Bill Self said that afternoon. "I feel terrible for him. For a fifth-year senior to not have a chance to run out of that tunnel at the Final Four – to not be a part of the game-time atmosphere – is incredibly disappointing."

Actually, Stewart *was* able to soak up the atmosphere – albeit from the bench. Instead of having surgery immediately, Stewart insisted on waiting until the Jayhawks returned to Lawrence. That way he could remain in San Antonio to support his teammates during the most exciting weekend of their lives. It was the type of selfless act that defined Stewart's career.

Stewart transferred to KU in January of 2005 after beginning his career at USC, where he started as a freshman. Still, even though he was one of the most highly-touted prospects in the nation coming out of high school, Stewart never found a permanent place in the rotation at Kansas. That wasn't a knock on Stewart, but rather an indication of the talent that dotted the Jayhawks' roster during Stewart's time in Lawrence.

Instead of moping or complaining about his situation, Stewart chose to make the best of it. That was especially the case during his senior season, when he came to relish his role as a defensive stopper.

With Brandon Rush being brought back slowly from offseason knee surgery, Stewart started seven games early in the season and averaged 6.9 points and 3.1 assists. The highlight of his season came in a 13-point, six-rebound performance in Kansas' overtime victory against Arizona at Allen Fieldhouse. He also logged

29 minutes in a win against his former team, USC.

"Rod did a lot to help our team this year," guard Sherron Collins said. "But the thing he did that helped us the most was when he stayed in San Antonio – even through all that pain – to support us. He proved then what he's all about."

### IN RODRICK'S WORDS

Throughout the whole NCAA Tournament, I had never dunked during warm-ups. I always just let the freshmen go. But in San Antonio – the day before we played North Carolina - I heard someone say, "All the reserves ... go ahead and dunk." I thought, "Why not? It's the Final Four."

My plan was to bounce the ball up in the air and do a windmill – a dunk I've done hundreds of times. I could tell the timing was going to be off, so I should've stopped after the bounce. But instead I thought, "Let's go ahead and finish this off for the crowd." I

lost my footing and fractured my knee cap. That was the end of my college basketball career.

At first I thought I'd torn my ACL, but then I looked at my kneecap and saw that everything was out of place. I started pointing at it and everyone ran over. All the guys thought I was playing. So did Coach Self. Then he took a closer look at what I was pointing at and he freaked out. He was like, "Trainer, trainer, get over here!"

The main thing I remember is that it hurt like hell. It was the worst pain I ever felt in my life. You'd have to experience it to know what I'm talking about. The pain lasted until I got surgery five days later.

They had a machine that actually x-rayed me at the arena. They asked me if I wanted to go into surgery immediately, but I said I didn't want to do anything that was going to keep me away from my teammates.

I didn't sleep at all that night because of the pain. I had some strong painkillers, but I've never been very big on taking pills. I wasn't going to have surgery and be away from my team during the most important weekend of our lives. I just decided to deal with the pain as best as I could and be there to support my team.

I got real emotional during the North Carolina game. I was so happy for my teammates and how they came out and played. I was trying to sit there and cheer but, at the same time, I was in a lot of pain. With about five minutes left I just broke down. The crowd was chanting my name and the magnitude of what had happened to me started to set in. I was crying in front of everyone, and I didn't care.

Two nights later, after we beat Memphis for the title, the announcers interviewed me on the court after the game. It meant a lot that they would single me out and recognize me like that. As happy as I was that we won, part of me was like, "I wasn't a part of that." I think anyone in my situation would've gone through those kinds of emotions. Sherron helped a lot. He came over during our last timeout in regulation and said, "Rod, we're going to win this for you tonight." He came right up to me and grabbed my wrist and shook it and said, "We're going to win this for you – seriously."

Knowing that I was part of their motivation made me feel really good.

I had surgery right when I got back to Lawrence. Right before surgery I was sweating and springing up. I'm not a big fan of being put to sleep. My brother, Lodrick, went through the same thing when he got his wisdom teeth pulled. He chose to stay awake during his surgery. He said it was the most painful thing he'd ever experienced, so he definitely said I needed to be put to sleep.

I'm glad I waited until I got back to Lawrence. The Final Four is a once in a lifetime experience. Being in pain for five days to win a national championship ... it was worth it. That was the only chance I'd ever have in my life to experience something like that.

It's unfortunate that it ended the way it did, but I don't regret anything that happened. If I had to do the same thing all over again to win a national championship, I'd do it in a second.

Still, I had worked my whole life for that one moment – just to be a part of a Final Four. Part of me says it was all worth it. But I definitely would've rather been out there with my team trying to help them win.

### A COACH, A FRIEND

One of the main people who came up to console me was Coach (Kurtis) Townsend. He's one of the main reasons I came to Kansas. He recruited me to USC, but he ended up leaving for Miami right before I got there. So I never got to play for him at USC. Kurtis and I have always been close. He recruited Jamal Crawford – who went to my high school in Seattle, Rainier Beach – so he was always around. I've known him since I first started playing ball in seventh grade. I couldn't help but

grow close with him. He was kind of like a father figure to me. After he left Miami for Kansas, I felt like it was only right for me to go where he was.

C.J. Giles was another reason I came to Kansas. He was my high school teammate, so I felt like it would help if I went somewhere where I already knew someone. Even though C.J. had some problems and had to leave, I was fine because I'd hit it off with my other teammates from Day One.

Every day was like one big joke. People didn't really get to see that side of us. This is the closest group of guys I've ever been around as far as joking with one another and having a shoulder to lean on. We all have fun and make the best of every day. In the Towers we're always having water balloon fights. Sometimes we'll go up to someone who's asleep and slap them in the face. We all just get along so well. I think that carried over onto the court.

Darnell Jackson and I have probably been through more than anyone in the country as far as losing family members and friends. People don't even know half of the stuff we've been through because we kept it within the team and the coaching staff. That's why I love my teammates so much. They've been there for me through thick and thin. We're all there for each other, and that goes a long way.

A good example of that happened during my first year at Kansas. I was second-guessing myself when I first got here. I was like, "Man, should I be here?" There were times when I wanted to leave. I felt like I should be playing more – and I'm not trying to sound selfish. Every player who's competitive wants to be on the court. People just told me, "You've got to be patient. Everybody has a different route to take, and you're going to help us when it counts." I think that held true. I think I helped this team in a lot of big games. I'm very satisfied with how my career went at Kansas.

More than anyone, I was probably closest with Sherron Collins. He called me his big brother. He's just really tough. He's a tough dude. From the first day I met him, he reminded me of me so much. We've always clicked. We have the same attitude toward basketball. We play with so much emotion.

About a year ago things got pretty heated between us in practice. We were both playing great defense on each other. It was getting physical. That's the thing. We bring out the best in each other. We started pushing a little bit and Coach Self got a little mad. But at the same time Coach Self knows we're like that. He knows that's how we do it. That's how we play. I think he'd tell you it was a good practice.

**BIG GAME**
One of the highlights of the season for me was our game against Arizona. Sherron was out that game, so I played 27 minutes. I had 13 points, six rebounds – and no turnovers. Before the game Coach Self just told me, "Go out there and play big. Don't even look at the bench if you make a mistake." When he says something like that you can't help but have confidence. I went out there and played just like I did in high school. I played with a free mind and let everything come to me. Great things happened that game – including one of my favorite

63

dunks. I got a rebound at the three point line. I did a little in-and-out move and Jerry Bayless got behind me a little bit. He tried to cut me off as I took off and I just dunked on him. Before the game, I was like, "Man, I'm one of the most athletic dudes in the country." I'm glad it happened. I loved that dunk.

Growing up, I was pretty athletic. A lot of that was because my father, Bull, was world champion power lifter. My brother, Lodrick, and I always tagged along to see him compete. It always made us want to be faster, quicker and stronger than everyone else. We always had weights around the house, but we didn't really lift that much in high school. We mainly did a lot of conditioning: sit-ups and push-ups and stuff like that.

I've always liked working out, so hopefully that will help me while I'm rehabbing this knee. I'll only be good again if I take this rehab more seriously than I've ever taken something in my entire life. Slacking off isn't an option.

### MORE TO COME

My basketball career isn't over. I'm sure I could go play overseas, but first I want to pursue my dream to get to the next level. Playing in the NBA has always been my goal, and I don't want this injury to be the thing that stops me from getting there.

I've given it a lot of thought, and I can honestly walk away from Kansas with my head held high. I came here to be a part of history and to be on one of the best teams ever. I feel I've accomplished that with this team. I played a role in us winning a national championship and I made friends that I'll have for my entire life. I couldn't ask for anything more.

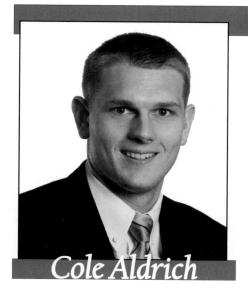

*Cole Aldrich*

Cole Aldrich entered Kansas' national semifinal showdown against North Carolina intent on stopping Psycho T. Funny, by the time the final horn sounded in the Jayhawks' 84-66 victory, Aldrich's performance against All-American Tyler Hansbrough had earned him a nickname of his own. Tenacious C.

"Yeah, I like that," Aldrich said a few weeks later. "You think it'll stick?"

Probably so – especially if Aldrich continues to show the flashes of dominance he displayed during the 2008 postseason.

A freshman, Aldrich played a season-high 17 minutes against the Tar Heels and finished with eight points, seven rebounds and four blocks. The effort hardly surprised Bill Self and the Jayhawks, who said after the game that they had "seen it coming."

A month earlier, Aldrich had turned in an 11-point, 11-rebound performance against Texas Tech. His play in practice was elevating right along with his aggression level. After being overwhelmed by the speed of the game throughout most of the season, things were finally beginning to slow down for the 6-foot-11 center from Minnesota. Still, with a front court that featured three NBA-caliber players in Darrell Arthur, Sasha Kaun and Darnell Jackson, most of the talk about Aldrich centered on next season. His number was rarely called.

Until, of course, the Jayhawks took on North Carolina and Hansbrough, who days earlier had been named National Player of the Year by the Associated Press. "For three or four minutes he was the best player on the floor," Self said.

### IN COLE'S WORDS

Some basketball players spend years worrying about where they're going to go to college. But I pretty much knew I was coming to Kansas in the ninth grade. That's when Coach Self and his staff started recruiting me, and I fell in love with the school on my very first visit.

The summer before my freshman year was a blast. I was going to classes and meeting a lot of new people and, basketball-wise, no one was coming down too hard on us because the NCAA limits the amount of time a coach can spend with a player during the offseason. I thought everything was great. I was like, "This is going to be a lot of fun."

But then fall rolled around and things changed. I was a freshman, and as everyone knows, freshmen can't do anything right. I remember one practice

65

we were running an offense that I had never run before. The whole time I was running up and down the court, the coaches were yelling at me. I was like, "What the hell am I doing out here?" It was stressful for me, because I wasn't used to someone yelling at me constantly like that. Plus, there was a lot of pressure to perform, because everyone knew how good of a team we could be, and I didn't want to be the one to mess that up.

When the season started, things were even more mind-boggling. Guys out there were just flying by me. The pace of the game was way too fast for me at first. Darnell Jackson really helped me out.

A couple of times he stopped by and said, "Cole, let's go grab something to eat." We'd sit there and talk and he'd say, "Don't let things bother you so much." I really listened to what he had to say, because he'd been in the same position a few years earlier. He worked through it and became an outstanding player. I hoped I would, too.

66

## FRESHMAN SHENANIGANS

Off the court, I couldn't have been having any more fun with my teammates. Tyrel Reed was my roommate and we always goofed around like the stupid little kids that we are. We played video games once in awhile. I have "Virtua Tennis 3," and for some reason, Tyrel would never play me. It's probably because he knows I'd kick his butt. One weekend I went home to Minnesota and, when I came back, he had left the game on the screen. Apparently he'd been practicing, although he wouldn't admit it. He still won't play me. I guess my Roger Federer is too good for him.

Another fun thing I did during the fall was go trick-or-treating. I know I may be a little old for it but, hey, it's a tradition. I never miss trick-or-treating on Halloween. I'll probably still be going when I'm 40. I'll just find some kid on the street and say, "Hey, this is my son. I'm with him." And then I'll ask for candy.

Anyway, I got out of tutoring on Halloween night and met up with some family friends that we know here in Lawrence. They have two kids – one of them is in the seventh grade, the other is in fourth. I put on a mask I'd brought from home. I wish my buddies from Minnesota could've been there to go out with me that night. We used to come up with the most bizarre costumes. My sophomore year in high school, I was a transvestite in a toga. I put some basketballs under my toga – against my chest – and rang someone's door. A lady walked out and said, "Wow, are those things real?"

## GROWING BOY
I was 6-foot-5 in the fifth grade and 6-foot-8 as a high school freshman. I've

always been a growing boy. When I got to campus this year, my dad told Tyrel, "If he ever gets in a bad mood, just feed him." I really do love to eat. One of my favorite places in Lawrence is Backyard Burgers. Montana Mike's is pretty good, too.

### CAMARADERIE

I can't think of anyone on this team that didn't like someone else. You'd always see us out together. It was like a big family. That's why I think we really listened to each other and respected each others' comments when we got together after the Oklahoma State loss.

Darnell and I are the ones that came up with the idea of meeting at Henry T's. We were talking the night after the loss and one of us said, "We're better than this. We need to get back to having fun again. We need our swagger back. Let's do something about it." So we sent texts the next day that said, "Meeting at Henry T's at 4." I think things really changed after that.'

### HI, TYLER. MEET COLE.

Coach told me before the season that I was going to play some sort of role this year. He said, "We're going to need to play four big guys, because we all know Shady is going to get in a little foul trouble and Darnell and Sasha may get into foul trouble, too. So you've got to be ready to come in and play five minutes, 25 minutes – whatever. Just go out there and bust your butt. Grab every rebound and help us every way you can."

Luckily, I was able to do that against North Carolina. With us having to go against Tyler Hansbrough, I knew I'd probably get some minutes, because the plan was to throw a lot of bodies at him and wear him down.

I watched a lot of film on Hansbrough before the game. I knew he didn't have a ton of size, but he was still a very, very good player. The one thing I noticed was that he struggled a little bit against people that walled up on him. By walling up I mean

## 68

standing in front of him with your chest out and your arms in the air as high as they can go. I've got some crazy-long arms, so I thought I may have a chance against him.

Even when you do wall up, Hansbrough is still really tough. He'll get his shot off and, if it misses, he'll slide around you and beat you on the offensive glass for an easy put-back. You've got to try to match his effort, and that's not easy. I never thought I'd end up playing 17 minutes in that game, but when I look back at the tape, I think, "Dang, I did pretty good." I think it helped that I'd played against really good players like Michael Beasley and Connor Atchley at Texas. That helped my confidence going into the game.

### MEMPHIS

I got in for a few minutes against Memphis and, frankly, I was a little sped up, a little nervous. Joey Dorsey stole the ball from me on one play and dunked it. He gave me a little chest bump afterward – the one my friends keep bringing up. Everyone is like, "Man, you should've kicked his (butt)!" There were definitely a few things I would've liked to have said or done to him after that. But I'm not a trash-talker or a dirty player. Hopefully the millions of people watching that game saw what a (jerk) he was and didn't think bad of me for not retaliating. I just moved on and thought about the next possession.

When Mario hit his three-pointer it was the best feeling in the world. It was like, "Finally – we're going to win the game. There is no way in hell we're going to lose now." It was such an intense situation up until that point.

I remember being on the bench when Shady came over during a timeout. He said, "Dude, we're going to lose this (freakin') game because of me." He was upset because he missed a box-out on Chris Douglas-Roberts. Darnell looked at Shady and said, "No we aren't. We're going to win this (freakin') game. Just watch." Right after that is when we made our little run to force overtime.

Looking at Memphis' players after Mario's three-pointer ... their eyes looked dead. The emotions and the heartbreak of losing that nine-point lead were killing them. Pretty soon after that, the streamers were falling through the air and we were celebrating. In the locker room people were looking at each other like, "Did this really happen?" Coach Manning put it the best when we said we're spoiled freshmen. Those seniors busted their tails for four years to try and get to that point. They finally won it, but here the freshmen are, getting rings after our first year. That's not supposed to happen. We're not going to take it for granted, I can promise you that.

### CELEBRATION TIME

The whole week after we won was just ridiculous. We had the parade on Sunday, and I remember one of the coolest things ever was riding down Mass Street in that

convertible. At one point, as we were crossing an intersection, I stood up and held my hands in the air and everyone started going nuts. It was such a great feeling. One lady even yelled, "Cole, will you be my baby's daddy?" I just said, "No, but thanks for the offer." The last thing I need right now is a kid. I'm just having fun playing ball. I'm not ready to be an adult quite yet.

Jeremy Case

A few weeks after hoisting the national championship trophy in San Antonio, Kansas' seniors embarked on the annual "Barnstorming" tour. The way it works is that, each year, players who have exhausted their eligibility travel throughout the state and play pick-up games against high school teams to raise money.

This season more than ever – from Kansas City to Garden City - nearly every stop was packed with fans hoping for a picture or an autograph from their favorite player. Or perhaps even a hug.

That was the situation at Blue Valley Northwest High School, where a young girl – probably 15 or 16 – waited near the locker room door for the players to emerge. She wasn't there for Russell Robinson or Darnell Jackson, both starters on KU's history-making team. She wanted to see Jeremy Case, the fifth-year senior who averaged just 1.6 points per game. The girl waved bashfully at Case as he made his way toward the court. "Hi Jeremy," she said softly. Case leaned in for a quick hug. "How you doin?" he said with a smile and wink. That was all it took. Case didn't see it, but as he jogged away, the girl nearly crumbled. It literally reached the point where her friends had to hold her up while her eyes filled with tears.

"Oh my God – he's so gorgeous," the girl kept saying. "He's so gorgeous."

The situation was a reminder that, no matter how much air time or ink you receive, as long as you're a Jayhawk, you're a star in the minds of the fans.

Maybe that's one of the reasons Case chose to remain in Lawrence when it became clear after a few years that he'd always have trouble getting the playing time for which he so desperately yearned. Case was the best pure shooter on Kansas' team and had the ball-handling skills to be an on-court regular.

But with a guard-heavy roster that featured the likes of Russell Robinson, Mario Chalmers and Sherron Collins, Case never really got a chance. Understandable as it may have been, the situation was still a shame.

The Jayhawks will tell you that no player on Kansas' roster maintained a better attitude or a more consistent work ethic than Case. So respected by his teammates was Case that, when he unleashed a flurry of three-pointers on Senior Night, there were a few players on the sidelines who became teary-eyed because they were so happy to see him enjoy some success in his final game at Allen Fieldhouse.

Case – who redshirted in 2004-05 — was the only member of Roy Williams' final recruiting class to play his entire career in Lawrence. David Padgett

(Louisville), Omar Wilkes (Cal) and J.R. Giddens (New Mexico) all transferred. But whenever thoughts of leaving crept into Case's mind, the McAlester, Oklahoma, native remembered why he chose Kansas in the first place. "Simple," Case said. "I wanted to be a national champion."

### IN JEREMY'S WORDS

Any kid that loves basketball grows up dreaming about what it would be like to win an NCAA Championship, but once we actually did it, I'm not sure anyone knew how to act.

After we cut down the nets, watched "One Shining Moment" and all that other stuff on the court, we finally made it back to the locker room. It all happened so quickly. One minute we were standing on the court in front of thousands of fans with cameras all around us and confetti raining down. But the next minute it was just us. Just the team and the coaches - alone.

It was a weird feeling at first. I think everyone was in shock. We were trying to celebrate, but some people had this look on their face like, "Did this really just happen?" It was actually kinda quiet in there at the beginning. But eventually things just got louder and louder, and then people started throwing water. After that it got pretty crazy.

### REACTIONS

Coach Self, surprisingly, was really calm. I was hugging him and crying and

saying all this stuff in his ear, but he actually wasn't all that emotional. It seemed like he just knew that we were going to win it all along, like he never had any doubt in his mind.

For the most part, Coach Self doesn't give too many big speeches. But whenever he does they really get us going. He gave two at the Final Four – one before each game. He just talked about the tradition and how it was our time. He told us how it had been 20 years and about how KU needed this championship. He reminded us of how hard we'd worked to get there. But he also talked about how there was no pressure on us. We'd made it to the Final Four, so the pressure was off and we could just go out and play.

I think the bigger thing for Coach Self – at least as far as stress – was beating Davidson the week before and advancing to the Final Four. He got pretty emotional after that win. It was a side of him we weren't used to seeing. The first round eliminations, the losses in the Elite Eight ... all the struggles that we went through to get to the Final Four just came down on him at once. His voice was cracking and his eyes were glazed over. It was a special moment.

We all felt the tension that game. I talked to Russell and he was like, "Man, I couldn't breathe out there." We were so nervous and so tight. It was understandable. We were one game away from the Final Four. The media and the hype had worn on us. Plus, Davidson was a really good team.

### TITLE GAME

Anyway, back to Memphis: After we won we went back to the Hilton and they had a big reception set up for us on the 22nd floor. That was more for family and really close friends. I had my mom up there and my grandmother and sister and aunt and my dad. We sat up there eating chicken wings and posing with the trophy.

After that, the players and managers went down to our rooms on the 11th floor and got after it. We partied all night. I probably got to bed around 5 a.m. When I woke up ... I just can't describe how I felt, knowing that I was a national champion.

### RECRUITING

The main reasons I came to Kansas were the fans and the tradition. I came on a recruiting visit with Josh Boone - who ended up at Connecticut - and it was amazing. I went to Late Night, and I still remember all the fans that were there and how much love they showed me. I'd never seen anything like that.

Coach Williams made a great impression on me. He had me over to his house on Sunday morning for breakfast. I really respected him for inviting me into his home and cooking eggs and waffles and bacon for me.

We had a great recruiting class that year, with myself, J.R. Giddens, David Padget and Omar Wilkes. It's strange to think I'm the only one that spent his whole career here, but sometimes things just work out that way. Omar and David wanted to go in a different situation, and everyone knows about J.R.'s issues.

J.R. was my roommate for two years at Kansas and one of my best friends. When he left we weren't on good terms. I wish that weren't the case. I still respect him, and I'm proud of him for sticking it out at New Mexico and turning things around. He's a great player. It's too bad his reputation was stained because of some bad decisions. Hopefully some NBA team will give him a chance.

Obviously, I never got to play for Coach Williams, because he left for North Carolina about five months after I signed. I was disappointed at the time. But I understand why he did what he did. Given his situation, most people would've made the same decision.

I was excited when Kansas hired Coach Self. He and my father, Win, had been teammates for two years at Oklahoma State, and my dad said playing for him would be a good experience.

### LACK OF PLAYING TIME

I had a great time at Kansas. But on the court ... I won't lie. It was a struggle sometimes. I didn't expect to play a lot as a freshman, and my sophomore year I redshirted. After that it was tough because I wasn't getting many minutes. I thought about leaving, maybe transferring far away to USC. Or maybe to Oklahoma, where I could be close to home. I thought I was good enough to be playing more at Kansas. If anything, I knew I could go somewhere else and put up a lot of numbers.

It's always hard when you're on the bench, but it's especially tough at a place like Kansas, where so much attention is placed on basketball. Everyone sees me on the bench and I'm sure they're thinking, "Oh, he's not any good." It hurts your ego a little bit. You just have to sit back and take it and know in your mind that you can play. And when you do get in for those two minutes ... make it worth it.

Sometimes Coach Self would tell me to go in at the end of games and I didn't even want to do it. I didn't want the "sympathy" minutes. Plus, there wasn't even enough time to get a sweat going so I could loosen up. Think about it: I'm a three-point shooter, but I would sit there for two hours without touching the ball. When that happens your hands are all tight and stiff, and then you go in and have one or two chances to make a shot from about 20 feet. It's not easy. I tried to go hard on defense so I could get loose that way.

I decided not to transfer after talking with my dad. With the places I talked about going, I knew it'd be tough to win a national championship. That was something I'd always dreamed of and I knew Kansas gave me my best chance of fulfilling that dream.

It's not like I didn't have some good moments on the court. The best was Senior Night, when I hit those three three-pointers. I played 12 minutes against Texas Tech that night. It was a lot of fun to get into the flow and into a zone. I wish I could've played a little longer. I literally think I could've made about eight threes, but time ran out.

### FUTURE

As far as what's next, I definitely want to get into coaching like my dad. I feel like I know so many people because of my connection to Kansas. Roy Williams, Joe Holladay, Steve Robinson, Norm Roberts, Tim Jankovich, Rex Walters and all of the guys who are here now. Hopefully someday soon I'll find a spot on someone's staff. My goal is to coach at the Division I level, even if it's as a graduate assistant. I feel like I know the game. Things come natural to me. I've been around it my whole life because my father is a coach. Things pop up in my head that most people may not get.

No matter what happens, I'll always have a championship ring. That's something no one can ever take away. Even during this season there were times when I thought, "Should I have left?" But winning a national championship made everything worthwhile. All the struggles I went through made me who I am today. There's nothing I would change.

There were moments during Kansas' championship season when Brady Morningstar was the hottest player on the Jayhawks' roster. Unfortunately they all occurred during practice.

At the urging of head coach Bill Self, Morningstar opted to redshirt in 2007-08. With a backcourt that was ocean-deep in both experience and talent, the Lawrence Free State graduate realized playing time would be scarce, so he chose to spend the season improving his game in preparation for his final three years in Lawrence.

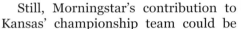
*Brady Morningstar*

Still, Morningstar's contribution to Kansas' championship team could be felt in many ways. His three-point prowess during workouts forced the Jayhawks' guards to bring defensive intensity to each practice. Off the court, he often helped lift the spirits of roommate and close friend Sherron Collins, who battled injures throughout the season.

Morningstar averaged a team-high 18 points a game for Lawrence Free State as a senior in 2005, when he was named Sunflower League Player of the Year. He spent the following season honing his skills at New Hampton Prep in New Hampshire, where he scored 22 points a contest.

Brady's father, Roger Morningstar, helped Kansas reach the Final Four in 1974. He averaged 11.7 points during his two seasons as a Jayhawk.

### IN BRADY'S WORDS

Not long before the season started I was in my room when I got a call from my dad. He said, "Coach Self wants to see you in his office." I asked him if something was wrong and he said, "I think he wants to talk to you about red-shirting."

So the next day I went to Coach Self's office and told him I would do whatever was best for the team. I think my dad wanted me to do it, too. He called all of his good friends and his former coaches like Ted Owens, just to ask them about the red-shirt experience. They all said that, hands down, I should do it. I should've seen it coming anyway. We had all those good guards coming back. The team was so deep. Regardless of how I played in practice, we had Brandon, Mario, Sherron and Russell. It'd have been tough to mix those guys up with a smaller, skinnier white guy.

Sometimes it got frustrating. I'd be sitting on the bench during the last few minutes of the game and Coach Self would look down toward the end and say, "Tyrel, all of you guys go in." I'd be like, "Put me in, too, Coach! Put me in!" He'd just laugh.

**PRACTICE**

I loved playing on the scout team during practice. Me, Jeremy or Tyrel would mimic the upcoming opponents' leading scorer – as long as that person was a guard. Coach would say, "Brady, every time you get the ball, shoot it." If I did so much as get a shot off, the starters would have to run. That's how much Coach Self preaches defense. Still, there was no way they could keep us from getting shots all of the time. Matt and Cole would set screens for me and Case and we'd just start firing. There were some days when I couldn't miss and I'd think, "Man, I could be out here shooting like this during games." But then I'd tell myself that I haven't proven myself in a game yet. Anyone can hit shots in practice.

Even though I haven't contributed a lot yet on the court, I'm so glad I chose to come to Kansas. Growing up, I used to come to almost every home game. I remember in elementary school, during the NCAA tournament, they'd pull a big screen television into the cafeteria so we could watch the games while we ate lunch. That would be the highlight of our day. On that day I'd be like, "Hey, Mom, can you bring me and my friends some Micky D's?" That was our big day. The only problem was that, after lunch, they'd make us go to recess so we couldn't stay inside and watch basketball.

**RECRUITING**

I had offers out of high school to play at Butler, Valparaiso and a few other smaller schools. I could've gone someplace like that and been an A.J. Graves type of player. But I wanted to test the waters and go to prep school for a year in New Hampshire. I had never been away from home, so I knew that'd be good for me. Plus I went up there for a visit and loved it. I got a few more good looks after playing up there for a year, but when KU became an option I couldn't turn that down. Coach Self was actually one of the people who suggested to my dad that I go up to New Hampshire for a year.

He and Coach Dooley came up there to visit for a day and I told them, "Hey, you don't need to worry about me. Don't waste your time recruiting me. Go out and get some players that I can play around because I'm coming to Kansas. I don't need you to come watch all my games and practices to try to sell me on the school. I'm committing now. I'll see you when I get to Lawrence."

**LOCKER ROOM**

One good thing about red-shirting is that I still got to travel with the team. I could suit up for games – I just couldn't go in. I was glad I could still be around everyone, because this group of guys is crazy. Every 30 seconds someone starts crackin' on someone else. Eventually, the jokes make it all the way around the room. We're always raggin' on somebody.

In the locker room, Shady usually has control of the music. He's always bringing in CDs and turning it up so loud that the room rattles. Coach Self comes in and says, "Turn that down! We can hear it in the hallway!" Shady likes Lil' Wayne, Flo Rida, Jay-Z ... all that stuff. Sherron likes to get out in the middle of

the floor and do his "My Dougie" dance. Look it up on YouTube. You'll see what it looks like.

### BEST FRIENDS

Sherron's my guy. We've lived together for the last two years. He was injured a lot during his freshman year and I just thought he was unlucky. Then it started happening this year, too, and I thought, "Man, is this ever going to stop?" I know how good Sherron is when he's healthy. Last summer he was healthy and he was killin' everybody on the court – and I mean everybody. When he's healthy he's the hardest person to guard in the country. Hands down, no question. He can handle the rock and he's quicker than everybody. That's all there is to it.

There were times during the season when his injuries really had him upset. I told him, "Hey, get that look off of your face, man." After we lost to Oklahoma State he was like, "Man, what's wrong with us?" and I was like, "Every team goes through this – even the good teams." I don't' think he's very used to losing and not playing well. He hates when he's not playing a big part in the game. So when we weren't playing well he kind of put it on himself. He thought his injuries were the reason we were losing. I told him, "This is about everybody. It's not a one-person team. You're hurt and you can't do anything about it. Just wait until you get better and you can definitely carry the team."

It's not hard to tell when Sherron is really about to turn it on. Remember when he hit that shot from the corner against Memphis? He clenched his fists and got low to the ground until he picked up his man. He gets that look in his

eye. Every time I see it, he takes over the game. In those moments, I'm just glad he's on our team.

## AFTERMATH

Ever since we won the title things have been crazy. That parade ... people around the country wouldn't believe the stories about how impressive it was unless they were actually there. I wasn't even on the court this year and people recognize who I am. I can't imagine being Mario or Brandon right now. They probably can't walk anywhere without someone saying, "Sign this. Sign that. Good shot. Good game."

Mario is probably the most grounded person on the team. He hasn't talked about his shot once. He's happy that we won, but he's never said, "Look at my shot." That's the one thing I really respect about him. He never big-times anybody. He definitely knows he's good but he doesn't act like it.

The other day my dad made a good point. He said that, as much fun as I had this year, the upcoming years might be even better because I'll have the chance to play and compete for a national championship – not just help the team in practice. Now I'll have a chance to actually go out and make big plays in big games. I can't wait.

Tyrel Reed

Before he ever gave his verbal commitment, freshman Tyrel Reed won the hearts of Kansas fans. How, you ask?

Prior to his senior season at Burlington (Kan.) High School, Reed wore a Kirk Hinrich jersey during an unofficial visit to Kansas State. Nice.

Reed learned to play basketball from his father, Stacy, who spent 19 years as a head coach at Eureka and Burlington High Schools. It wasn't uncommon for Reed to wake up at 5:50 each morning and head to the school for shooting drills. Before that, during elementary school, Reed jogged a mile to watch his father's practices each night and then hung around afterward to work on fundamentals with Dad.

With Reed – a four-time all-state selection – leading the way, Burlington went 95-4 from 2003 to 2007. Reed was named Mr. Kansas Basketball as a senior, when he also won the state title in the long jump.

Stacy Reed retired from coaching over the summer so he could watch Tyrel compete for the next four years at Kansas. Early on, it looked as if he'd have plenty to cheer about.

Reed averaged 6.8 points in Kansas' first four games, but then injuries struck. Within a two-week span Reed sprained both of his ankles. By the time Reed regained his health, it was too late for him to fight his way back into the rotation. Reed still managed to post some impressive stats. He made 11 of his 24 three-point attempts and had 21 assists and only four turnovers.

With the graduation of Russell Robinson and the early departure of Brandon Rush, you can bet Reed will be a major factor for Kansas beginning next season.

### IN TYREL'S WORDS

The college experience was a little overwhelming at first. You don't realize how well-prepared you have to be at each practice. If you show up one day and you aren't well-prepared, you're going to get embarrassed. I've never felt that way before. In high school, you could have an off day and still be one of the best players. When you get here and you have an off day, you are going to be sitting on the sidelines.

Being a freshman, I wasn't really worried about playing time or anything like that. I just wanted to keep working hard and getting better. I thought I'd get to play a little, but there were already so many great players here when I signed. My main goal was just to come in and learn from them.

In practice it was usually my job to guard Mario Chalmers or Russell Robinson.

It was a huge challenge every day. Nobody will give him credit, but Russell is probably one of the strongest guards I have ever played against. Physically, he's just extremely strong. He's not overly quick, but he knows how to get his body in a position to get you off of him.

Mario was a completely different challenge. He's so long and so deceptive with all of his moves that I was just trying to keep him in front of me every day. That was my main goal.

Another fun thing was that my sister, Lacie, works for the team as a manager. She stays and rebounds for me after practice and does a lot of different things for the team. She works in the office and I know she does a great job writing things out for our scouting report and things like that. I can always tell it was her when I see her handwriting.

Looking back on the season, one memory I have that sticks out is the feeling after we lost to Oklahoma State. I remember getting back into the locker room feeling pretty devastated. We had a little lull in our season and we just hadn't been playing great. It was a tough loss, but I really think that ended up being the turning point for us. Mentally, everything changed after that.

Having grown up as a Kansas kid – and a Kansas fan – my first NCAA Tournament is something I'll never forget. We got to Omaha that first weekend and there were cheerleaders waiting for us at the hotel when we arrived. They were doing the Rock Chalk Jayhawk chant and just cheering for us. It was just crazy how much the anticipation picks up for the NCAA tournament.

In the locker room, we were playing around the whole time, making jokes. We really weren't that nervous or tight. The young guys were just trying to follow the lead of the seniors, and they were pretty loose. They had been there before and they felt like this was their year.

When it came time for the game, though, you could definitely see a different kind of look in their eyes. They were a lot more focused. There was no more playing around. Before the Davidson game - the one that would send us to the Final Four - there was a different feel. I wouldn't say we felt extra pressure, but there was definitely a different feel. We know how big a deal it was for Kansas to get to a Final Four. We'd been trying for it for some time and kept coming up short. Luckily we survived that one, because after that, there was really no stopping us. I'm just blessed.

To play with this great team and these guys was a blast. We had so many great players on this team. Hopefully now we can find some new pieces and go out and do it all over again.

Early in the season in 2005, Kansas returned to Lawrence in the wee hours of the morning from New York, where a loss to St. Joseph's in Madison Square Garden had dropped the team's record to 3-4. Upon arriving at Allen Fieldhouse around 3 a.m., the Jayhawks got off the bus and headed for the dorms.

Well, most of them.

As coach Bill Self and his family drove home on that dark, frigid morning, they spotted a lone figure trudging up a hill on KU's snowy campus. When Self pulled over and offered the man a ride, he realized it was walk-on Matt Kleinmann, whom he'd left in the Allen Fieldhouse parking lot only minutes earlier. Self asked Kleinmann why he wasn't at his apartment getting some shut-eye.

*Matt Kleinmann*

"I'm going to the architecture school," Kleinmann said as he hopped into Self's SUV. "I've got a test to study for and this is my only time to do it."

Self dropped Kleinmann off at his destination and then turned to his young son, Tyler, who was sitting in the back seat.

"What did you think of that?" Self asked his son.

Tyler smiled. "Stud!" the boy said.

The player who says he has the "worst tan Kansas history" certainly helped the team's grade point average. But don't for a minute think that Kleinmann's on-court contributions weren't valued, as well.

Kleinmann's biggest role was at practice, where the big red-head did his best to prepare forwards such as Darnell Jackson, Sasha Kaun and Darrell Arthur for the tests they'd face throughout the season. Even though he couldn't emulate stars such Michael Beasley or Tyler Hansbrough, the 6-foot-10, 250-pound Kleinmann was big and physical enough to make workouts tough on his teammates.

Kleinmann was hardly a slouch when he arrived at Kansas back in 2005. Before his senior season at Blue Valley West High School ever began, Division I schools such as Pacific had offered Kleinmann an athletic scholarship.

Along with his height, part of the appeal – at least for Self – was that Kleinmann played for arguably the top high school coach in the Kansas City area in Donnie Campbell, who is particularly good at tutoring post players.

Campbell's biggest success story was Vanderbilt star Matt Freije, whom he'd mentored at Shawnee Mission West. Talent-wise, Kleinmann wasn't in Freije's category. But he certainly understood the game and where to be on the court in various situations. As a practice player, that's half the battle.

## IN MATT'S WORDS

When people started talking before the season about where we were being picked to finish, I told them I didn't want to know. I didn't want to hear anything and I didn't want to read anything. Friends and family tried to talk about it, but I think most of us avoided it as much as possible.

There are reasons some of us are superstitious about that kind of stuff. My freshman year, some magazine – maybe it was *Sports Illustrated* – picked us to win the NCAA championship. We were walking through the airport and Christian Moody grabbed me and said, "Have you seen this?" He pointed out that we were being picked to win it all, and all of a sudden I got a bad feeling. It's not about what people say. It's about how you play. Ever since the Bucknell loss in 2005, Coach Self talks to us all the time about blocking out distractions and not paying attention to that kind of stuff.

After we lost to Bucknell, I could hardly even watch ESPN. I lived with Sasha, and whenever someone would talk about it on TV, he'd say, "Change it. I don't want to watch this." We don't watch a lot of ESPN on the road, either. Instead we find other ways to pass the time.

## LIFE ON THE ROAD

Some guys play cards, others bring their PlayStation 3. A lot of us played this computer game called "Call of Duty." It's an online game, and a lot of the players really got into it. We'd come to practice and trash talk. Guys like Brad Witherspoon and I played about one minute each game, so "Call of Duty" was us our one chance to trash-talk guys like Darrell and be on the same level with them.

Coach Self would always refer to it as "Tour of Duty," and I think he was actually pretty mad because he found out a lot of us were staying up really late to play. But stuff like that is what really brought us together – stuff away from basketball.

When it comes to unity, I don't think many teams are as close as this one. There are so many fun stories about this group.

In Detroit, Coach Hudy - our strength and conditioning coach – rounded up all of the guys who don't play as much and dragged us to Bally's to work out. We had to walk across this big, icy parking lot in our shorts and basketball shoes. We were all wearing our bright blue shirts that were coordinated with our shorts. I'm sure we looked pretty awkward walking into this big Detroit mall. We had a police officer with us and he said it was one of the only malls in the country with its own police force.

Anyway, we walked through the mall and got up to Bally's. There were all these people asking for autographs. We actually had a group of people running after us through the blizzard and all the way up to the Bally's, but they couldn't get in because they would've had to pay.

Inside the gym, I think there were people wondering what was going on, but we didn't care too much. We did our own thing. We hopped up on the bikes and lifted for a little bit, but it was fun. I was doing an ab workout with Coach Hudy and there were two or three random guys who started doing it with us. It was funny watching them try it and hearing them say, "Man, that's a tough workout."

We did the same kind of thing a few weeks earlier in Omaha. It was fun getting away from everything for an hour or two. I also liked staying in the room, though. Me and Sasha would just watch movies.

All in all I'd say we traveled really well, although I will say that the plane you saw in *Sports Illustrated* a few years ago ... that had to have been a staged

photograph. They even had Jayhawk cheese in the picture. I've never seen Jayhawk cheese. I don't think that's the same plane. I don't think we're at that level.

Now we just fly on a regular charter plane. We have to make sure guys like Sasha, me, and Danny get the rows with the extra room. That's my luxury - being able to stretch out.

### SPECIAL SEASON

One of the things that made this team so successful is that we all bought in a long time ago to Coach Self's system. We respect him and what he has to say. He really held us together at times. Other times, though, we brought ourselves together. After that loss to Oklahoma State, everyone talked about the meeting we had at Henry T's. I'll admit now that there was about 10 times more eating than there was talking. Everybody kind of chimed in and said something when they felt like it. But really, the fact that we all showed up is what was most important.

It's not about what was said or done. It was more about the fact that we were all there. In years past not everyone would've come.

This time, everybody showed up and everybody stayed. What was said was that we are all in this together. My freshman year, we had a great senior class with Aaron, Keith, Wayne, and Mike, but there was definitely some disconnect within the team. There were the young guys, and then there were the old guys.

When I was a freshman I always had to clean up the locker rooms, I always had to pack the bags, I always had to know my place. Now that's changed a little. When Brandon and Mario got here, we accepted them as equal. When Sherron and Shady got here, we accepted them as equals. The same thing happened with Cole, Tyrel, Conner and Chase. We might tell them to clean up the locker room because no one else wants to do it, but everyone on the team is equal.

Some of these guys could star on any other team in the country, but here we are all the same. Not only are they OK with it, but they enjoy it. They enjoy being a part of this atmosphere and helping to make it better for everybody.

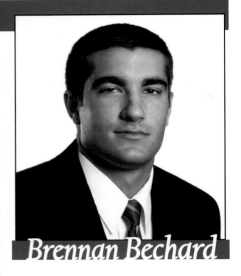

Brennan Bechard

A common saying among walk-ons is, "When you get your chance, make the most of it." Brennan Bechard did just that during Kansas' national championship season.

Bechard only played 21 minutes for the Jayhawks in 2007-08, but he scored 14 points. Five of Bechard's nine field goal attempts found the bottom of the net – and two of those were from three-point range.

That's not easy to do when you enter a game with stiff hands and a stomach full of butterflies, but Bechard – who attended Lawrence High School - found a way. A junior, Bechard is the son of Kansas volleyball coach Ray Bechard and the nephew of Harold Bechard, who covers the Jayhawks for The Hutchinson News.

### IN BRENNAN'S WORDS

Most people would never guess it, but one of the best opportunities we have to bond during the season is on the long bus rides home after some of our road games. If we win, everyone celebrates and has a good time. Usually we watch a replay of the game and then someone may pop in a movie. Road trips in general are usually a lot of fun. At night, everyone keeps their hotel door propped open.

Players go from room-to-room to hang out with one another. That was the best thing about this team – the way it got along.

I was so happy to see Coach Self finally get to the Final Four. He was so tense before that Davidson game but after that he told us to loosen up and enjoy the moment. We all had a bitter taste in our mouth from last year, because we got knocked out one game before the Big Dance. I think the memory of that motivated us all season. I got a few opportunities to play this season and, for the most part, I thought I did OK. The first couple of games I got kind of nervous. But as soon as you enter the game your adrenaline takes over and your nerves go away.

Still, as much I like to get out there and compete, the main responsibility of the walk-ons is to get the top players ready for the games. We have to make things tough on them in practice, which means we have to play great defense. I usually end up guarding Sherron or Mario or Russell. Sherron is the hardest to guard because he's so quick and so strong. It's fun to go against those guys every day to try to make them better. I think they appreciate it. Winning the championship was definitely a collective effort.

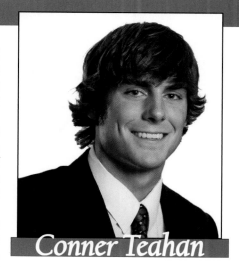

*Conner Teahan*

A television announcer nicknamed him "Cool Hand Teahan," and that was a bit misleading. After all, during the first three weeks of the season, Conner Teahan couldn't have been any hotter.

A freshman from Kansas City's Rockhurst High School, Teahan began his college career by making nine of his first 10 three-point attempts. When Teahan looked at the basket, he didn't see a rim. He saw a Hula Hoop.

Before long fans were chanting his name and students were sporting his shaggy haircut. Whenever he touched the ball – even if he was standing at half-court – folks at Allen Fieldhouse jokingly yelled, "SHOOT IT!"

Teahan eventually cooled off, making just three of his final 10 attempts from beyond the arc. Still, the 6-foot-5 guard did enough early in the year to explain why he'd been deemed as Kansas' most-coveted invited walk-on in years.

A two-time Missouri Gatorade Player of the Year, Teahan averaged 25 points during his senior season at Rockhurst, where he played for one of the area's top coaches in Mark Nusbaum. He received a scholarship offer from Wichita State and was also being pursued by Kansas State and Missouri. Teahan also had scores of opportunities to play college football.

In the end, though, the chance to win a national championship at tradition-rich Kansas was too much to pass up.

"You always want to go where you're wanted, and Kansas proved they wanted me there," Teahan said shortly after committing to KU. "They recruited me just like any other athlete. I've always loved Kansas. It's the best basketball school in the nation."

### IN CONNER'S WORDS

One of the things I'll remember the most about this season was when the fans chanted my name at Allen Fieldhouse. I started the year off by making a bunch of threes, so I guess a few fans would get excited when it was my turn to come off the bench.

I was just sitting there one game and heard this chant and I was like, "Is that what I think it is?" It grew louder and louder, and then it started to happen each game. It was a lot of fun, but I never knew quite what to do when I heard it. I kept thinking, "Do I smile? What do I do?"

I got kind of embarrassed, because I didn't know how to handle it. To play in Allen Fieldhouse is incredible enough, but to actually have people chanting your

name in there is something I never would've imagined.

Every time Coach Self heard it, he'd just put his head down. It probably put a lot of pressure on him to put me in, which is fine with me. Hey, anything that helps. The players gave me a lot of crap about it, but that was all in good fun.

In some ways it was rough after I started making those shots. At first no one knew who I was, but all of a sudden, it was a letdown whenever I missed. I remember I read a couple of times in the paper where it said "Highs and Lows of the Game." One of the lows was that I got in the game and missed. I was like, "That was going to happen sooner or later." At the beginning of the year it was fun, but once the expectations grew I definitely felt a little pressure to put on a show. That's not easy when you come in stiff off the bench.

It really wasn't a tough decision for me to come to Kansas. I had a lot of other scholarship offers, but having grown up following KU basketball, all I needed to hear was that the coaches wanted me. After that happened, I knew I was going to come here.

### TOUGH REALITY

With all the talent we had on this year's team, earning playing time as a freshman would've been tough for anyone. I told myself from the beginning that I probably wasn't going to play a lot during my first year. It was a rough transition but I got used to it and tried to make an impact on the team every day in practice. But with Brandon Rush coming back, I always felt like I was working toward next year. That was my mentality: get as good as you can so you can be ready next year.

Coach Self thinks I have the ability to contribute here. I didn't come to Kansas to sit on the bench. People keep saying, "Wow, it's got to be a great experience for you to come here and win a national championship as a walk-on." As happy as I am to be a part of something like this, I'm not going to be satisfied. People say I might be able to contribute someday like Christian Moody – another walk-on – did a few years ago. Christian was a great player, but I feel I can be more of a consistent asset to the team. No offense to him, but I just feel like I can do more. I was under the radar for most of my high school career. Not many people knew who I was, and some teams were afraid to look at me because I played football, which means I didn't touch a basketball for four months out of each year. I think I still have a lot of untapped potential.

Hopefully my minutes will increase each year and I'll become a more important part of what we're trying to do. Whatever happens, it will be tough to match the experiences we went through this season.

## LOOKING BACK

Even though I didn't get to play a lot, I still had a lot of fun. At the beginning of each game Matt Kleinmann and I would look at each other and ask what our percentage was of getting into the game. In the first half we usually wouldn't go over 45 percent unless we were really giving it to a team pretty good. It really just depended on who we were playing, but our predictions were usually pretty good. March Madness was incredible. There's so much riding on it and so many people who care. I used to always fill out brackets and stuff. When Kansas went to the national championship game in 2003 I remember yelling at the television. It was surreal to be in that spot as a player.

Our locker room was so relaxed in San Antonio, so laid back. We wanted to prove to everyone that we had the best team, because everyone was talking about Memphis and saying that we were the weak link of the Final Four. People seemed shocked that we made it. That put a chip on everyone's shoulder. We'd get asked, "What are you going to do with North Carolina? How are you going to play with them?" We were like, "How are they going to play with us? We've got just as many guys as they do." They'd say the same stuff about Memphis. "They've got so many guys." Well, our bench goes eight or nine deep, too. We all had faith that we could prove to everyone that we were the best team.

After we won, a lot of my friends said they saw me on TV, celebrating on the court. That happened a lot this year, actually. I don't know how I always ended up on the screen. I usually stay in the back and let the players that actually did a lot in the game stand up front. But I always seem to end up near the camera.

After the Memphis game everyone was in a state of mind like, "Pinch me, I need to wake up." It was like a dream come true when those streamers started coming down. You realize you're the national champion and you're hugging your family members.

The coaches were walking around after the game and telling the freshmen how spoiled we were. Our first year in college and we've already got a national championship. Stuff like that just doesn't happen. We're going to have a young team next year so it will be difficult to get back to that point, but sometime in my career I hope we can get back to where we were.

*Chase Buford*

When someone asks R.C. Buford about the night Kansas beat Memphis for the 2008 national title, the San Antonio Spurs general manager can't help but get emotional.

"What are you trying to do – make me cry?" Buford said when the subject was broached in late April. "I get choked up whenever I think about it."

Twenty years after earning a ring as an assistant coach on Kansas' 1988 staff, Buford's son, Chase, added another championship to the family resume. Chase was freshman walk-on for the 2008 Jayhawks.

Kansas coach Bill Self has a long history with the Buford family. He and R.C. became close friends while serving on Larry Brown's Kansas staff in 1985-86. Self accepted a job at Oklahoma State the following season, but the two remained close. They were attendants in each others' weddings and socialized during the offseason.

Thus, it was no surprise last spring when Self asked Chase to join the Jayhawks as an invited walk-on. Chase missed his senior season at Alamo Heights High School in San Antonio because of an enlarged spleen, but he battled back and appeared in 13 games during Kansas' championship season. Buford's mother, Beth, is a former Kansas golfer.

## IN CHASE'S WORDS

Coach Self and my dad have been close friends for a long time, but apparently their relationship changed once I started playing at Kansas. I say that because, during the NCAA Tournament, Coach Self came up to me and said, "Chase, I don't know what I've done to make R.C. hate me so much. He used to call me three times a week. But now that you're on the team and I'm not playing you very much, I hardly ever hear from him." Coach was joking, of course. He and my dad will always be tight.

Growing up, I never heard a lot of talk about the 1988 national title. My dad was an assistant coach on that team, but he's never been one to boast. He's actually a very quiet person. Still, there's no question that I was a huge Kansas fan. The YMCA teams I played for were always called the Jayhawks, and I watched them on television as much as I could. It was cool because the night we beat Memphis for the national title, Ryan Robertson and Scot Pollard came over to the hotel and hung out with us. I freakin' worshipped those guys in the mid-90s, when I was a little kid. I liked Jacque Vaughn and Keith Langford a lot, too. It's funny that both of them ended up playing with the Spurs. Before I came to school here, the last game I went to at Allen Fieldhouse was that New Year's Day win against Georgia Tech in 2005. Keith made a shot to send it to overtime – and then he hit a turnaround jumper with three seconds left to win it. I always had fun watching him play. As much as I loved Kansas, I never thought I'd come here because I didn't want to copy what my family had done. But then I got sick before my senior year. I had an enlarged spleen and had to miss the whole season because the doctors said I couldn't play. Suddenly, my list of options became very short – and at that point I was actually ready to get away from home for awhile. Kansas was a good situation. I was fortunate to have the opportunity.

### PROUD PARENTS

The night of the championship game was really special for me and my family. My dad is a train wreck during Spurs games, but other than that he's usually not very emotional. During the Memphis game, though, my mom said he was jumping around and doing a bunch of stuff he usually doesn't do. I can't blame him. I'm sure everyone was acting like that because it was such a great game.

Other than winning the championship, the highlight of the season for me was Senior Night – and the main reason for that was Jeremy Case. We beat Texas Tech by 58 points so, obviously, it was a game where everyone was hitting shots. It was really cool to see Case do so well. He's taken his lumps through the years, but he's always come back and worked hard everyday. To see him go off like that was fun to watch.

Case is like a professional. He's been here for five years. He's the resident old guy on the team. He probably didn't play as much as he'd hoped, but if it bothered him, he never let it show. He just kept his head up and worked hard in practice to help himself and everyone else get better. He's probably one of the best practice players I've ever seen.

Even though I didn't get in very many games, I still feel like I was able to contribute in other ways. We had 17 players on our team and 11 of them were guards. So a lot of times, just because of a lack of numbers, I had to play defense against our post players in practice. I'm only 6-foot-3, so I couldn't exactly match their height. But I tried to be as physical with them as I could. Hopefully that helped them during the games.

### FRESH FACES

When you're at freshman at Kansas, you have to do some things for the upperclassmen. After practice they make us take showers before anyone else so that, by the time it's their turn, the water will have warmed up. We carry their bags to and from the bus, and sometimes we have to double-up on seats if there isn't enough room for everyone to have his own row. We're also the last in line to eat. But after winning that national championship, I don't think you'll hear any of us complaining. We got spoiled.

Brad Witherspoon

When Brad Witherspoon turned down a handful of junior college and Division II offers to try to walk-on at Kansas, his friends at Humboldt (Kan.) High School couldn't believe it.

"They thought I was an idiot," Witherspoon said.

Witherspoon, though, had fantasized for years about becoming a Jayhawk. So passionate was Witherspoon about Kansas basketball that, whenever KU lost, he stayed home from school the following day because he was so depressed.

During his first few years in Lawrence, Witherspoon had to settle for being the campus rec star after being cut from walk-on tryouts in 2004 and 2005. Instead of letting the situation bother him, Witherspoon used it as motivation. His hard work paid off in the fall of 2006, when assistant coach Tim Jankovich called Witherspoon to inform him he'd made the team. "I was walking up a hill on campus when he called," Witherspoon said. "But after he told me they were keeping me, I felt like I was floating."

Witherspoon finished his KU career with just five points in 41 minutes. But you can bet he'll cherish every moment he spent on the Jayhawks' bench and in the locker room. "If I could wish one thing for every Kansas student," Witherspoon once said, "it would be the chance to run through that tunnel just once. It gives you chills."

### IN BRAD'S WORDS

It's easy for me to appreciate what's happened — especially since I almost wasn't even on the team. After I got cut from walk-on tryouts the second time, I talked to Coach Jankovich and he said he thought I was good enough to make it. The problem was that they had a full roster with Wayne Simien and Aaron and Keith and those guys. He just said, "I want you to come and watch some of our practices and see how we do things." So I did. Then, over the summer, I kept calling him to let him know how interested I was in trying out again and how much I wanted it. I worked out all summer before my junior year in 2006-07. Coming into that tryout, I thought I had a pretty good chance.

The first two times I tried out, they said, "We're not looking for players to come in here and average 30 points a game. That's why we have players like Brandon Rush." I took that to heart when I came back for my third tryout. Instead of worrying about scoring, I focused on winning all the sprints and playing good defense. I went 100 percent on all of the drills. Now, when we're sprinting, the

95

guys will make fun of me when I don't win. They'll say, "Didn't you do these drills in, like, 15 seconds when you tried out?" They're right. I did. I wanted to make the team so badly. I felt like I was dying out there.

Growing up in Humboldt, I had always been a Jayhawk fan. I loved Jacque Vaughn and Paul Pierce and Scot Pollard and those guys. I have a huge Greg Ostertag poster in my room here on campus that's signed. The first game I ever came to at Allen Fieldhouse was when KU and Ostertag were playing Louisville in 1992. I fell in love with the place.

The crowd here made me feel so good when I made the team last year. But, personally, the part of this experience that I enjoyed the most was just hanging around the guys in the locker room and all the other stuff that goes along with being a team. Coach Self said this is the closest team he's ever coached. I don't think he's lying. From one to 17, we're all best friends.

### PRACTICE

One of the neatest things for me is when we go out and win big games, like Florida last year or Texas in the Big 12 Tournament. I think I speak for all the walk-ons when I say that we feel proud when those guys are out there performing well, because we play against them in practice every day and try to get them prepared.

In practice, one of the main jobs of the reserves is to run the offense that the opponent is going to run. We played Colorado at home this year, and they run that weird Princeton offense with all of those cuts. We had to come in a couple of days early and get it down so we could run it against our starters in practice. We got it down so good that we joked about how Coach Self should put us in the game to run it against Colorado to see what they would do.

### TURNING POINT

I've got a lot of lasting memories about the season, and almost all of them are positive. But one negative thing I remember is that bus ride home after we lost to Oklahoma State. It was snowing outside so we drove about 30 miles per hour the whole way home. It was one of those times you start to realize that this is it – especially for the seniors. That was our third loss in seven games. We really didn't talk much on the bus, but I know for me personally ... I didn't even play and I was fired up after that Oklahoma State game. We were so lackadaisical out there. We didn't play with any sense of urgency.

We got back to Lawrence and, a few days later, one of the guys – I think it was Cole - sent me a text that said, "We're all meeting at Henry T's at 4." Everyone showed up and we talked things out. After that we didn't lose another game.

### HOMETOWN HERO

Ever since we won the championship I've done a lot of interviews for all kinds of papers near my hometown. They're really proud of me, I know. My coaches have been sending me text messages that say, "What's it been like? What are

you doing? Is it dying down yet?" I'm sure someday everything will sink in, but I don't think it has yet. When we won, my dad said, "It's great right now, but you'll really appreciate it five, 10 or 20 years later." Who knows? Maybe I'll come back to Lawrence and our team picture will be painted on a mural in the hallway that leads to the coaching offices. That's when I'll really look back and say, "Wow, I was on the greatest team in KU history."

the coaches:
# A YEAR TO
# REMEMBER

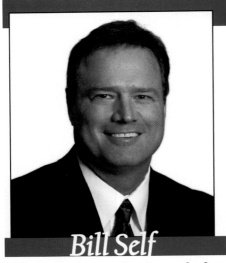
**Bill Self**

In April of 2003, while vacationing in Florida with his wife and two children, Bill Self received word that the University of Kansas was interested in hiring him as its head basketball coach.

Self had just one request.

"Bill didn't want to be one of the candidates," said R.C. Buford, one of Self's closest friends. "He wanted to be the *only* candidate."

And he was.

Oh, sure, courtesy interviews were conducted with Mark Turgeon, Tom Crean and Ernie Kent. But it was no secret that Drue Jennings – the interim athletic director at the time – had pegged Self as the Jayhawks' main target to replace Roy Williams. His reason was obvious.

"Bill Self," Jennings said then, "couldn't be a better fit for Kansas."

Everyone could sense it.

The disarming personality and down-home charm ... the respect of KU's history and tradition and the ties to Larry Brown ... the record of success at Oral Roberts, Tulsa and Illinois and the recruiting connections across the country.

As good as Williams was, some folks predicted Self would achieve even more at Kansas. They were right.

Just five years after his hiring on Easter Sunday of 2003, Self has already accomplished the one thing Williams never could during his 15 seasons in Lawrence. Kansas' 2008 national title – its first in 20 years - will be remembered not just for the dramatic fashion in which it was won, but for the coach who made it all happen.

Self recruited a team so talented and deep that an NBA-caliber center and potential future first-round draft pick came off the bench. Even more impressive is that Self was able to convince each member of his cast of all-stars to sacrifice statistics and national notoriety for the good of the team.

Not one member of the 2008 national champions was named first or second-team All-American. Heck, because of their balanced statistics, no Kansas player was even named first-team all-league by the Associated Press.

Not that that mattered to the Jayhawks or Self, who will never again have to listen to murmurs about how he's a better recruiter than a coach, or about his inability to win the big one. In what billed as the greatest Final Four in college basketball history - with four No. 1 seeds and Hall of Fame coaches and lottery picks galore - Self and his players found a way to be a little bit better than the best.

## IN BILL'S WORDS

Our record here is unbelievable, and our regular season accomplishments are unmatched anywhere in the country. But you're always judged on the tournament. Obviously, before we beat Memphis, there were a lot of people that weren't too happy with the way things had gone in March. Getting to the tournament obviously isn't enough, and losing in the first round – especially when you have a better team – was especially tough.

I'll be honest. The Bradley loss in 2006 bothered me a lot, but it was nothing like the Bucknell loss the year before. The Bradley one ... hey, that team – because of youth — wasn't prepared to win in the tournament like the 2005 team. We started three freshmen (Brandon Rush, Julian Wright and Mario Chalmers) and two sophomores (Sasha Kaun and Russell Robinson). We knew something like that could happen against a team like Bradley - which was way under-seeded – and we knew the future was bright. But the one the year before, against Bucknell, was the end of the road for a lot of guys. There was no future after the Bucknell game for Wayne Simien, Aaron Miles, Keith Langford and Michael Lee. That was frustrating. It hurt me, it hurt our players and it hurt our fans. We all felt it.

Still, the team that played Bucknell was not a great team. We had Mike Lee as our top performer in that game and we started a walk-on in Christian Moody. Keith played in that game, but he was basically non-existent because of his stomach and ankle problems. He wasn't even close to being himself that game. I knew it wasn't a great team, but the perception was that it was, simply because some of those guys had played in two Final Fours and an Elite Eight. The difference in 2005 was that guys like Collison and Gooden and Hinrich weren't around. After the loss,

I took my family to Cancun. It was the worst vacation I've ever had. All I did was lounge on the beach and mope.

## TOUGH TIMES

The loss to Bucknell in 2005 was the start of a terrible summer. The Moon Bar incident with J.R. Giddens happened two months later, and it was bad. When I heard about it, I was in Chicago recruiting. Kurtis Townsend and I had been out late that night with some other coaches. We were leaving a restaurant, and as we got in the car to drive back to the hotel, ***-4129 showed up on my cell phone. It was Aaron Miles. Obviously, with the call coming in that late, I thought, "Oh, this isn't good." I picked up the phone and Aaron told me what happened. There had been a big fight and J.R. had been stabbed and was in the hospital.

We started running down people as fast as we could. I was able to reach J.R. and talk to him for a few moments. Then I talked to some police officers to find out what was going on. I wasn't able to get all the details that night, but I found out enough information to know what we were in for. Publicity-wise, the rest of the summer was a big mess. I became very defensive.

Then, of course, we caught a big break when Brandon Rush signed with Kansas right at the start of the school year. That changed everything. We had Micah and Julian and Mario coming in, but Brandon gave us a boost of adrenaline. That was something that got everyone excited, which was nice, because we needed some momentum at that time.

## ADRENALINE RUSH

Brandon had entered the draft out of high school, but he pulled out when he realized he probably wasn't going to be a first round pick. I was at the Price Chopper Invitational in Kansas City, sitting in the bleachers, when I overheard someone say Brandon had made his grades and was eligible. With J.R. leaving the program a month earlier, I knew what a boost Brandon would be for our program. They played the same position. I had heard Brandon was already looking at schools such as Illinois and Indiana. Still, I called his former AAU coach, John Walker, and asked him to have Brandon call me. Not long after that, I was having dinner with my staff at Set 'Em Jacks in Lawrence, and Brandon contacted me. I went outside to take the call. A few minutes later I walked back in and said, "Guys, Rush is coming to Lawrence for a visit."

Before he ever came I called his mother (Glenda) and his grandmother (Jeannette Jacobs) and they were great – especially considering all of the circumstances. I knew they weren't happy with how things played out when Brandon's oldest brother, JaRon, had been recruited by the previous staff. It's been fairly well-documented. There were certainly hard feelings between the Rush family and Kansas. And there were hard feelings from the Kansas fans because a local great had chosen not to attend their university. Even though they still weren't ready to give their blessing after we talked, Brandon's family certainly felt much better about him at least visiting.

As soon as Brandon walked into the office, I thought we were going to get him. You could tell he felt at home – and he loved Mario. We were nervous because we weren't going to sign him until we knew he was on solid ground academically. There was a lot of stuff we had to look into. So there were two weeks that went by after he committed when he wasn't around because we wouldn't allow him to be. I'm sure he was still coming out here to hang out with the guys, but we didn't allow him to do anything like work out with the team or go to class. We didn't give him any aid at all. Legally, we could have done it. But if he wasn't declared eligible by the NCAA Clearinghouse, he would've had to pay us back 50 percent of the entire semester's tuition. We didn't think there was any reason to risk that.

Coaching Brandon has been a pleasure. It's been a challenge at times, but it's been a pleasure. He's done everything we've asked him to do. We knew there was a chance we might only have him one year, but we tricked him into coming back for another one. Of course, he got hurt last year and came back for a third and had a great year. He's going to have success in the NBA. He's a pro athlete with a pro body. He has the length and skills that are important at the next level. The money he makes in the NBA will be because of his defense, which is ironic, because when he came here everyone said he didn't like to defend.

### KING KAUN

Sasha, when he got here, was always nervous that he was going to screw up. We would literally say, "We're going to lift at 3:30 and then practice at 4:15." I'm not exaggerating: Five times between the moment we initially told him and before he left the building, Sasha would ask: "Practice is at 4:15 and we're lifting at 3:30, right?" He had to confirm it and then confirm it again. We made a big joke about it.

Here's another funny story about Sasha. I was getting worried about him for a while during his freshman year. I always want to make sure our guys are enjoying themselves and having a life outside of basketball. So I said, "Sasha, you've got to get out and meet some people." The next thing you know, he's strutting

around campus without his shirt on and stuff like that. I asked him if he'd found a girlfriend. He said, "No, Coach, I don't have a girl." I asked him if he'd at least met any and he smiled and said, "Well, yeah, I'm doing pretty good, Coach." He was really tan at the time, and he told me he'd been tanning with a bunch of girls on top of a sorority house. Here I am worried about him, and I find out he's been spending his free time sun-bathing with the prettiest girls in school. I better not tell you what house it was because I don't want to get those girls in trouble. They were probably sneaking him up there.

### HEY MR. D.J.

When I think about Darnell, the first thing that comes to mind is one of the times I was in Oklahoma recruiting him. I went to his high school, and his team was supposed to run eight laps around the track, which is two miles. After the first lap he was tied with the leaders, after the second lap he fell back a little bit, and after the third lap he was ready to drop. The next thing you know, he's AWOL. I knew what he had done, though, because I'd been watching him. When his coach wasn't looking, he went and hid behind a shed. At the end, when the leaders passed the starting line for their last lap, Darnell jumped right back in behind them. I never said anything because I wanted to see how it'd play out. I watched him cross the finish line and he was all bent over and stuff, breathing really hard. I'm thinking, "Good gosh." I went up to him and asked him what place he came in and he said, "I think it was fourth or fifth." I told him he'd run really well and he said, "Thanks, coach – just trying to get in shape."

At the time we were recruiting both Darnell and Kalen Grimes. We knew we weren't going to take both of them. I'm just glad Darnell jumped at the chance, because it's been great watching him grow both on the court and away from it.

Everyone knows that Darnell has experienced a lot of tragedy in his life – especially since he's been at Kansas. There was the wreck that took the life of his grandmother and injured his mother, Shawn. And then there was the cousin who was shot and killed. Sometimes it got to be too much for him. When Darnell was a junior he ditched a practice and we found him back in Oklahoma. We called to make sure he was OK, and then we talked to his mom and told her we were going to get on a flight and be down there as soon as we could. Ronnie Chalmers and I went down that evening. We had a long talk in Darnell's living room. It was a good conversation. Everybody wanted what was best for Darnell. His mom and his uncle were in the room with us, and all of a sudden Darnell said, "Hey, Coach, come outside with me." We just went outside and that's when we hugged and he broke down a little bit. The reason that whole scenario was admirable was this: Some people want to quit because it's too hard. He wanted to quit because he was doing so well and had such a good life ... you know, he felt guilty because his family wasn't experiencing the same things. His reasoning was admirable, but it wasn't logical. In his mind he was thinking: "How could they suffer and I not?"

### FROM NEW YORK, NEW YORK

Russell came on his visit and, to this day, I think his dad is one of the most positive, appreciative parents I've ever been around. It almost felt like he was trying to sell us. I knew that we had Big Russ. The question was whether we could get Little Russ.

One of the best stories about Russell happened while we were practicing before our trip to Canada in August of 2004. He was an incoming freshman, and he wasn't doing things with quite the intensity that we wanted. We were in the huddle after practice and I said, "You know what, Russell? You're nothing but a spoiled little brat boy from New York City." I was really mad, but when I said it all the guys started laughing. But, man, was he irate. He ripped off his shirt and everyone was saying, "Come on, Russ. Calm down." They were trying to grab him and he starts swinging his arms and saying, "Get off me. I'll beat anyone's (butt)." When it was all over, Aaron Miles came up to me and said, "Coach, I think we got us one here. He'll fight. He'll fight for us. We can go to war with this guy." The whole point of me saying those things was just to light a little spark under him. I'd say it worked.

### EFFECTIVE AND EFFICIENT

When it came to recruiting, Joe Dooley went to Alaska most of the time to see Mario. I only went up there twice. I loved his talent coming out of high school.

He and Greg Paulus were regarded by most people as the top two point guards in their class. I remember watching him play in high school and on the AAU circuit after he committed. I was thinking, "Gosh, he should be doing more than what he's doing. He should be playing better." It's not like he was playing poorly. He just wasn't playing like the best point guard in the country. I told him that. When he was on the AAU circuit I told him, "Hey, you're representing Kansas now. You should be kicking everyone's butt." Personality-wise, he was the type that kind of went with the flow.

When he got to Kansas, we threw him to the wolves and he wasn't quite ready. He really struggled early on with the point guard position. So we switched things up and moved Russell over there and moved Mario off the ball. Once we did that, he just took off. His mind was freed up so he could just play. He's had a great three years. The thing that impresses me the most about his statistics is how efficient he is offensively. Assist-to-turnover ratio, three-point and free throw percentages and that kind of stuff. He got a lot of credit for stealing the ball – and he was great at that – but his consistency on offense was huge for us.

I don't think Mario is cocky. He's confident. He's one of those guys who goes with the flow and then picks his spots when it counts. Everyone always asked who our go-to guy was. You could make a case for Brandon, Shady and Sherron being our go-to guy at different times. But the most consistent one was Mario. He was the most clutch player we had.

### SENIOR STUDS

We anticipated guys like Mario and Brandon and Sherron and Shady having good careers here because they were so highly recruited. But these seniors - even though they had other high-major offers - weren't as highly touted when they got here. So to see Darnell and Sasha both having great chances to play in the pros is very rewarding, because it speaks to their hard work and how they've developed. Russell will have opportunities, too. Since Russell became our starting point guard, we've gone 95-16 – and 70-8 the last two years. For a starting point guard in a league as good as the Big 12, that's tough to beat.

Our other seniors have been great to be around, too. I've known Jeremy longer than any of our guys combined because of his father, Win. We were college teammates at Oklahoma State, and I actually held Jeremy when he was just an infant. I think everyone would agree that, although he didn't leave his mark from a production standpoint, he'll always be remembered for the way he carried himself. He's going to be a good coach. He'll be the type of guy that gets a good opportunity.

### HOT ROD

When we signed Rodrick, people thought he was coming here with a lot of baggage because things hadn't gone well for him at USC. But the only baggage we were aware of was the rumor that he wasn't doing well academically. It was never confirmed. I liked him as a kid and I loved his athleticism. I said at the time that we needed a "fire-starter." We were losing Keith to graduation, and I was counting on J.R. entering the draft after his sophomore year. We thought Rod would be a great piece to have in place if that indeed occurred.

When Rodrick hurt his knee at the Final Four it rattled me for a lot of reasons. We had a rule that stipulated that the freshmen were the only people that were supposed to dunk in shoot-around. But, for some reason, Sherron took off anyway and then Rod went second. It was something he'd done a thousand times, but for whatever reason, his knee just gave out on him. I don't think he slipped. On tape it doesn't look like he slipped. It was a nasty scene. He split his knee right in half. The whole situation was very upsetting – mainly because he was a fifth-year senior. He would've gotten in the game. He would've played.

### SLIM SHADY

Shady has changed a lot since he's been here. He used to be nervous around people he didn't know. Now he's somewhat comfortable in those situations. Getting away from his home in Dallas was good for him from a maturity standpoint. His first semester (in the fall of 2006) was rough at times because he and his mother are very close. She came up to stay with him for a few days when he got homesick. You look at these kids and their bodies and think they should be so mature. Sometimes we forget that they're still just kids, going through the same struggles that other people go through. Sandra, his mother, handled things great. She gave him space but was also there if he needed her to be there. She knew it was important for him to branch off and do things on his own.

Regarding Shady's recruitment ... we thought we had him and then we thought we'd lost him. It was one of the longest recruiting ordeals ever, because we knew that he was probably going to sign late, but we had to roll the dice and convince him to sign early. When that didn't happen the whole spring became a pretty interesting deal. One day it was us and Baylor, then it was us and LSU or us and Texas. The good thing was that we were always the one common denominator. It was usually us and someone else. The problem was that we had put all of our eggs into one basket so we could sign him early, so we didn't have many bullets left in the end as far as the amount of times we could go see him and stuff like that. We had saved up a couple of things, but still, the people that were new in the game were coming at him with a full-court press, and we had already used our full-court press in the fall. We couldn't be as aggressive. At the end we just had to hold out hope. The day of his press conference, I literally had no idea if we were going to get him or not. I was in downtown Lawrence at a lunch deal when he sent me a text that said: "i'm coming 2 kansas."

### PAGING MR. COLLINS

With Sherron, we got in on him a little late, but it really didn't matter because all of the other schools hadn't done much, either. He basically didn't start the recruiting process until the summer before his senior year. He's a great story, because he's so tough, and he's one of those guys that has certain buttons that are easy to push to get him really motivated. I really want to see him do well for a lot of reasons – mainly so he can have a life that most people from his background never get the opportunity to have. I think he's starting to realize the position he's in and the influence he can have on so many people.

Winning the title will make that even more apparent – not just with Sherron, but with all of these guys. What happened in San Antonio will stick with them for the rest of their lives. And to think ... we were one shot away against Davidson from not even making it there. If their three-pointer at the buzzer goes in, who knows how different things may be today?

### KANSAS VS. ROY

As excited as I was to get to the Final Four, I knew a lot of people would look at the game as a Kansas vs. Roy Williams deal. And I knew there would be a lot of really upset people if we lost. To me, it's unbelievable that people could think that if you lose a game to somebody who's just as good as you are, the sky is falling. I can't believe people would be like that. That'd be like the New York Giants fans being ticked off that they lost to the Patriots in the Super Bowl. I mean, Carolina was the No. 1 seed of the entire tournament. I guess fans just don't see things that way, though. I even heard people say, "Hey, our national championship game is

Saturday – not Monday." I didn't look at it that way.

Roy called me the Tuesday before the game. It was a congratulatory call more than anything. If we'd have been playing Illinois, it would've been me on the other end calling Bruce (Weber). I'm sure the situation conjured up a lot of thoughts and memories of how he left things with all of our fans. We talked a little bit about how we were going to handle some of the questions we'd be getting during the week, but the bottom line is that we probably didn't need to talk about that kind of thing at all. We were going to handle the situation the same way – regardless of whether we talked on Tuesday. Neither one of us was out to get the other guy.

Most of the pre-game talks I give in tournament settings are done not the day of the game, but the night before – unless I think our team is flat. I don't give many fire-and-brimstone pre-game talks because our team is very even keel. You can usually tell when they're excited to play, but a lot of

times, we play our best when I think we're flat and our worst when I think we're jacked up. I hadn't given many fiery speeches all season, but before the game against North Carolina, Jeremy Case went up to one of our assistants and said, "Hey, tell Coach that it's time. We need one." I ended up speaking to them that night.

One of the things that stood out to me about the North Carolina game was the way Cole Aldrich played – eight points, seven boards and four blocks in 17 minutes. He was the best player in the game for a stretch – not for the entire game – but for a three or four minute stretch he was the best player on the floor. We had seen that coming. He was better than the minutes he played this season. Obviously, he would've played more, but we were so deep up front.

### FINALLY, AFTER 20 YEARS ...

I was a lot looser for the game against North Carolina than I was for the game against Memphis. When I got out there, I had to drink a lot of water because I kept getting cotton mouth. We got off to a bad start – we were down 9-3 early – so that probably contributed to my anxiousness. For the most part, though, I really enjoyed coaching in that game. I had a blast. I remember turning around a few times and talking to the members of the selection committee that were

seated on press row. I remember saying, "They told me these guys couldn't make free throws," after Memphis started out so good from the line.

It almost got away from us when they went up by nine with two minutes left. We were going back and forth, but then we had a couple of bad possessions and they threw in a couple of shots. All of a sudden they're up by nine points and it's like, "Wow. We've almost let this get away from us." Luckily, we were able to come back.

To me, if you're going to evaluate the entire game, I think Darrell Arthur, hands down, played the best. He made the hard turnaround jumper when we cut it to two, and then he had the big 18-footer. Had Mario not made that shot, Shady would've been the Most Outstanding Performer. Mario made some unbelievable plays and Sherron made some unbelievable plays. Darnell and Sasha were solid. Brandon didn't score all that well (12 points), but he did such a great job defensively on Chris Douglas-Roberts. There aren't many players in college basketball that slide as well as Brandon. But again, the best player in the game was Shady.

### THE AFTERMATH

Once we finished up our media responsibilities, we went back to the Hilton and there were a lot of fans outside. The security was so tight that nobody could get into the hotel unless you had a room key.

We immediately went up to the 22nd floor and had a reception. Not a dinner, just a reception with snacks and drinks. It was a big, open-room reception for administrators, coaches, players and their families. It was so cool, because it was just like Senior Night all over again. Everybody was hugging everybody. Everybody was taking pictures with everybody. Coach (Larry) Brown came up there and everybody wanted to get a picture with him. It was so much fun walking around to the different areas and seeing all the families and how happy everybody was. That's the thing that sticks in my mind - just how happy everybody was. We've had a lot of families go through some tough times, so it was good to see everybody beaming.

I had also rented out a suite across the hall from my room, where I hosted all my family and friends. It was all my boys from Oklahoma and their families, plus guys like Norm Roberts and Tim Jankovich and Barry Hinson. I hung out with those people until about 5 a.m. All of our coaches came up there with their families, too. So we probably had about 50-70 people in that little suite. We had to be at a press conference at 9 the next morning, and President Bush called at 8. I was on the Mike & Mike radio show at 8:20. It was a pretty rough morning, but I certainly didn't mind.

### THANKS, BUT NO THANKS

Once we got back to Lawrence I had to deal with the Oklahoma State issue. I'd said all along that I would talk to them – that I owed that to them. And I certainly owed it to myself to visit with them. It definitely pulled on my emotional strings, but it didn't change how I felt about where my family wanted or needed to be. I didn't talk to anybody from Oklahoma State during the tournament. I didn't talk to anybody that called on their behalf. So they were very professional. I had said all along that they should do what's best for Oklahoma State and not be concerned about me, because I couldn't see myself making a move.

When that situation was over, it was time to celebrate. One of the cops at the parade told me we had 100,000 people there. It was one of the most overwhelming things I've ever seen. I heard one lady got her foot ran over. People were running right up to the cars. It's amazing no one got hurt. The police did a great job of being friendly and still monitoring the situation, because things could've gotten out of control. Again, the numbers were staggering. It just shows you what a special place this is and how lucky I am to have this job. I knew that before, but I really know it now.

**Joe Dooley**

A few hours after defeating Memphis for the national title, Kansas' coaches and players were celebrating with their families on the 22nd floor of the Hilton Palacio del Rio in San Antonio. At one point Bill Self approached assistant Joe Dooley and smiled.

"Isn't this unbelievable?" Self said.

Always no-nonsense, Dooley gave a quick nod.

"Yeah," he said. "Now we've got to figure out a way to win another one."

The Jayhawks' chances of bringing another trophy to Lawrence will certainly be greater as long as Dooley is on KU's staff. The former East Carolina head coach recently completed his fifth year at Kansas. Along with helping the Jayhawks improve on the court, Dooley's biggest impact is felt on the recruiting trail.

He made countless trips to Alaska to help land Mario Chalmers and was relentless in his pursuit of Sasha Kaun. Dooley's main recruiting territory is the East coast. But considering he's also had stints at Wyoming and New Mexico, Dooley is versatile enough to mine any area because he's established ties in all parts of the country.

Prior to the 2007-08 season, a handful of publications tabbed Dooley as one of the top assistants in the nation.

### IN JOE'S WORDS

One of the most humbling things - not just this year, but every year - is when they show the highlight video before each of our home games. All of a sudden Coach Naismith pops up on the screen and you start thinking about the history and tradition of the program. You see clips of all the old players like Wilt and Clyde Lovellette and Danny and then some of the more recent guys like Drew Gooden and Wayne Simien. We watch it game after game, but it never gets old. I've been here for five years and it still makes the hair on the back of my neck stand up every single time.

Another neat thing for me is that, when we're watching the video before pre-game introductions, we're standing on the opposite end of the court from all of the retired jerseys. So while the video is playing, in the background I can see all those great names hanging up there in the rafters. There really is no place in college basketball quite like Allen Fieldhouse.

This year, at the last home game, the video was really neat because they changed the ending. They always have the countdown that goes 50 conference championships, 12 Final Fours, two national championships and 16,300 Kansas fans. But this time the countdown ended with "Five Great Seniors." The place went crazy. I thought that was a neat thing.

### REFLECTIONS

Speaking of videos, I saw one on YouTube that had the scene at Allen Fieldhouse the night we won the title. Can you believe they estimated the crowd at more than 10,000 that night? Wow. The funny thing is, one of the facilities guys said with only a few seconds left in the game – when it became obvious that we were going to win it - he told the security guards to get the hell out of the way because there weren't enough of them to stop everyone from rushing the court.

Another part of the season I'll never forget is the very last practice we had in San Antonio the morning before we played Memphis. Everyone knew that that would be the final time our team was ever together on the practice court. We were in the Alamodome – this big, huge building – and in a little while it was going to be filled with thousands of people and lights and cameras. But at 11 a.m. that morning, we were the only people in there. Just the players and the coaches and the janitors. It was sad in a way to know that that was the last time we were going to be together in that setting, but we were also proud to have put in all the hours and hard work to make it to one last shoot-around.

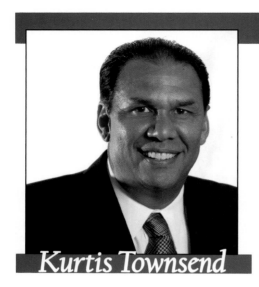

*Kurtis Townsend*

There aren't many assistants in the country with a resume quite like Kurtis Townsend's. Stops at Cal, Michigan, USC and Miami have allowed him to coach such players as Jason Kidd, Shareef Abdul-Rahim, Lamond Murray, Jamal Crawford and Tony Gonzalez.

Yes, that Tony Gonzalez. The Kansas City Chiefs tight end also played college basketball.

Nothing, though, makes a resume sparkle quite like a national championship – and now Townsend has one thanks to the players he helped lure to Kansas.

Townsend joined Kansas' staff in 2004 after Norm Roberts left for St. John's. He played a pivotal role in the recruitment of Sherron Collins and Darrell Arthur and was also one of the main reasons Rodrick Stewart left USC for Lawrence.

An honorable mention All-American at Menlo (Calif.) Junior College, Townsend transferred to Western Kentucky in 1978 and played guard for two seasons. He spent one year in the CBA before entering the coaching profession.

### IN KURTIS' WORDS

Seeing the smile on Sherron Collins' face as he dribbled out the clock was the highlight of the Memphis game for me. Actually, it may have been the highlight of the season.

Mario's three-pointer will be talked about for years but, if anything, the two plays that brought us back were the long jumper that Darrell hit and then the steal and the three-pointer by Sherron. I helped recruit Sherron to Kansas, so as I watched him celebrate, I couldn't help but think about all the stuff he's had to deal with and battle. Sitting out with his foot injury, trying to come back with a bad knee, his weight issues, the death of his son and all of the other things he's been through.

I went to give him a hug and he hugged me back. His eyes were almost full of water. Neither one of us had to say anything. Nothing that had ever happened to him in the past mattered at that moment. He'll never forget that day.

I played a big part in Darrell's recruitment, too. He's improved so much. You know, he always told us he had that dream about coming here and winning the national championship. So for him, it was also a great feeling. Twenty points and 10 rebounds on college basketball's biggest stage ... wow, he was impressive.

The crappiest part about the whole thing was the situation with Rodrick hurting his knee at shoot-around the day before the North Carolina game. You

never want to see a kid get hurt, but in some strange way it worked out pretty well for him. Had that not happened, he wouldn't have been standing front-and-center on crutches during the nationally-televised interview after our win. They announcers pulled him up there and started asking him questions and I thought, "That would have never happened for him had he played the three or four minutes he'd been averaging in the tournament."

The day he hurt himself in San Antonio, I said, "Rod, I know you can't see it right now, but everything happens for a reason." Turns out he didn't have to wait very long to find out what that reason was. That whole weekend his teammates kept saying, "Let's win it for Rod." They were obviously using his situation as motivation. I'm not saying it took Rodrick hurting his knee for us to win the tournament. But you never know.

Danny Manning

The day before Kansas' national title game against Memphis, a press release was issued announcing that assistant coach and former Jayhawk All-American Danny Manning had been elected to the College Basketball Hall of Fame.

Hoping to score a few quick comments from Manning, a group of reporters gathered outside Kansas' locker room prior to its Sunday practice at the Alamodome. Manning, though, informed an administrator that he wouldn't be granting any interview requests.

"I'm not going to do anything," Manning said, "to detract attention from this team and what it's accomplished."

An admirable gesture, no doubt. Still, as hard as he tries to avoid the spotlight, Manning can't escape it. One of the top college players of all time, Manning became one of the country's most high-profile assistants when he was promoted prior to the 2007-08 campaign. Bill Self will tell you that he's also one of the best.

With Manning offering invaluable instruction, Kansas' post players all showed remarkable improvement during the season. That was especially the case with Darnell Jackson and Sasha Kaun, who finally developed the consistency they had lacked throughout their careers.

### IN DANNY'S WORDS

For the rest of their lives, there's not a day that will go by when these players won't think about winning the title. There's not one time when they won't smile when that thought pops into their head. We're all faced with difficult and trying circumstances in our lives. Still, regardless of the situation, thinking about being on this national championship team – even if it's only for a quick second - will always bring a smile to their face.

### THE POSTMEN DELIVERED

I got a lot of gratification from working with our post players this year. With Sasha and Darnell, it's fun to look at those guys and think about where they started and where they finished. It's definitely a feel-good situation. To see what Shady has been able to do as a player also makes me happy.

Sasha has always been a reliable, dependable safety net for us throughout his career. Darnell has always had that high-energy burst to his game. This year he was able to show it a little bit more. A lot of that is because, mentally, he's at a good place in his life. When it comes to skill, Shady is one of the best guys out

there – and he's only going to get better.

Then there's Cole. The body of work that we put in this year was a wonderful piece of art when it was all said and done. But for the big guys, it was Cole's play against North Carolina that symbolized what the word "team" is all about. Everyone was happy for Cole. Everyone was proud. The three other post players made that moment happen, because Cole played against them everyday in practice. They got him ready for that situation, so they took a lot of pride in his performance that night. He had always shown glimpses of that type of play. If we didn't have the guys playing in front of him that we had, we'd have seen a lot more of him. It's just a freshman learning phase that you go through when you have some upperclassmen ahead of you that command a few more minutes.

### SENIOR STUDS

Each one of the seniors had a special thing that gave them their identity. Whenever you think of Russell, you always think of the fans chanting, "New York, New York" during the introductions. When you talk about Sasha, it's always about his effort and intensity. Darnell battled through so much adversity and Rod had that unfortunate injury. Jeremy accomplished something big by graduating in four years. He went through some tough times, so it was great to see him stick it out and get rewarded for his hard work and perseverance.

### GREAT PLAYER, GREAT COACH

My first year as a full-time assistant was a lot of fun. I'm learning from a great head coach and a great staff. These guys are always willing to share information and warn me of any pitfalls that could be coming along the way. They tell me what to look out for. I feel very fortunate to be working with a group like this.

Is this position my end-all? No. But I'm in no hurry to see what else is out there. You always listen. I'm in a very blessed position to be back here working and to also have the financial security to be able to do what I want to do.

Mario Chalmers' historic shot against Memphis tugged at his mother's heartstrings – and his father's pocketbook. Magazines, t-shirts, posters and commemorative books. Walk into a store in Lawrence these days and you're certain to find countless items bearing Mario's image.

"I'm trying to collect them all," Ronnie Chalmers said.

Ronnie is probably the proudest papa in Kansas – and who can blame him? His son's clutch three-pointer in the NCAA title game was the crowning moment of one of KU's most memorable seasons ever. And the best part was that Ronnie was there to take part in the journey.

Ronnie Chalmers

Ronnie joined the Jayhawks staff the same year Mario enrolled at Kansas. As the Director of Basketball Operations, he does everything from coordinating team travel to tutoring sessions to postgame meals. Even more important is Chalmers' role as a mentor to the Jayhawks off the court. Sometimes that involves talking to his son after a tough game. Other times it may mean flying to Oklahoma to help console a despondent Darnell Jackson.

Prior to his arrival at Kansas, Ronnie posted a 109-28 record in five seasons as the head coach at Bartlett High School in Anchorage, Alaska, where he won two state titles while coaching his son.

### IN RONNIE'S WORDS

By the time I got back to the locker room after we beat Memphis, I probably had 20 text messages waiting for me on my cell phone. I probably had another dozen or so voice messages from friends. High school buddies, the guy that coached me at Air Force, friends that I was stationed with in the military, relatives ... you name it, they called about Mario's shot.

Probably every household in Alaska was tuned in to the game. I received e-mails and phone calls from the superintendant of schools. The governor sent Mario a letter. Former Senator Frank Murkowski – one of the most powerful men in Alaska – sent a letter saying how proud people are of Mario. This is the biggest thing to happen in Alaska since Scotty Gomez, a great hockey player, helped New Jersey win the Stanley Cup in 2000.

Mario's shot was truly one of those moments where a dream became a reality. This was something that Mario had talked about wanting to accomplish for years. It was extra-special for us, because Mario and I were actually in San Antonio for the Final Four in 2004. It was the spring of his junior season of high school.

Connecticut beat Georgia Tech in the finals that year and, afterward, Mario told me that one day he would be playing in the national championship game, too. For it to happen in the same city and in the same arena ... that's what's so amazing. He did it. We did it.

I got a little worried when we were down 59-51. But I had written down a scripture on a piece of paper. At that moment, I took it out and read it, and then I got confident that we were going to win the game. Mario knew it, too. None of the guys ever gave up. They kept fighting.

Later that night, after everything settled down, we finally got to spend some time alone as a family up in our hotel room. Just Mario, myself and my wife, and his sister, Roneka. Before that the team had a postgame get-together, so it was nice to finally be able to spend time with one another and unwind while we reflected on what happened that night.

### FROM ALASKA TO LAWRENCE

It's been an eventful three years for Mario. He struggled during the early part of his freshman year – mainly because the game was coming at him so fast. One of the setbacks that Mario had when he got here was that he wasn't challenged everyday in Alaska, because he was the best player. Then he showed up at Kansas, where the ninth, 10th and 11th guy on the team challenged him day in and day out. I don't think he was ready for that.

My advice to him was: "Slow down and let the game come to you. Slow down and learn the system. Basketball is still basketball, but you're playing at a higher level now against guys who know the system, so they have an advantage over you right now. You just stick to what you know and listen to what Coach Self is saying – not how he's saying it, but what he's saying – and you're going to be OK."

The thing I hang my hat on is the maturity of Mario's game. When he came in as a freshman, he probably didn't take care of the basketball as much as he should have. From his sophomore to his junior year, his assist-to-turnover ratio made almost a 180-degree turnaround. He's never been a selfish player. One quality he has of mine is that I can make adjustments and work within any system. Mario can do the same thing on the court. He can play with anyone. He doesn't care who scores the points. He just wants to win and be successful.

### DAD'S LEARNING, TOO

For me, the job at Kansas has been both exciting and overwhelming. I've learned a lot. Coach Self is a great coach. Just to see your son develop into a young man is amazing by itself – especially when you're able to walk that journey with him. The biggest challenge for me was being able to balance everything. I could never put aside the fact that Mario was my son. But I couldn't let any of the other guys feel that he was being given the edge.

Away from the court, I take on more of a "father" role for these guys. One of my responsibilities involves academics. I push the classroom on these guys to make sure they're going to class and tutoring. I talk to them a lot about what's

going on in their lives.

I also coordinate all the travel. It's less complicated because we charter all of our flights. I basically just have to contact the airlines to make sure we have a meal or a snack on the plane, depending on where we're going. We have to get the configuration of the plane, because we want our tall guys to be comfortable. We don't want to spend more time on the ground than we do in the air. So we arrange ground transportation that will pick us up as soon as we land. We work closely with hotels to make sure they can accommodate our meal requests.

Learning this side of the business has been invaluable, but I want so badly to get back onto the floor and to teach the game. Being in this environment and watching Coach Self and his assistants is going to be a huge benefit down the road. A lot of times, I stand on the sidelines and think, "Man, if only I known that little trick, maybe I would've won four or five state titles as a high school coach instead of two." I've got a little notebook that I write stuff in. It's going to help me one day.

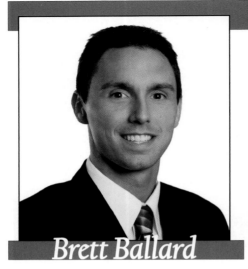

Brett Ballard

A few years ago, as he ate lunch with about 10 reporters, Bill Self predicted that graduate assistant Brett Ballard would be a great college coach someday.

"Stud – absolute stud," Self said of Ballard. "He knows the game, he's smart, he's organized and he's got a great personality. Brett's got a heckuva future ahead of him."

In the meantime, Ballard is enjoying his role as the video coordinator for his alma mater while shadowing one of the top head coaches in America.

"This experience," Ballard said, "has been invaluable."

Even though he was a walk-on for the 2001-02 squad that lost to Maryland in the Final Four, Ballard played a big role for one of the best Kansas teams in history. Two moments involving Ballard stick out from that season.

The first came when he put a forearm into the chest of Iowa State guard Jamal Tinsley when Tinsley began jawing at Ballard during a regular season game in Ames. The second occurred a few weeks later, when Ballard provided the assist on Keith Langford's game-winning three-pointer at Nebraska. The victory was significant because it enabled Kansas to become the only team in Big 12 history to post a 16-0 conference record.

Ballard will undoubtedly tell his young son, Kaden, those stories someday. And after the 2007-08 season, he's probably got a few more.

### IN BRETT'S WORDS

One of the best days of our year happens each winter when we host a group of athletes from the Special Olympics. In 2007, we did it the day after we lost to Texas A&M. Even though it was supposed to be for them, it ended up being a great pick-me-up for our guys, too. This year we did it coming off of a win and it was just as rewarding. It's unbelievable how fun it is for our guys. I know they take a lot from the experience.

Usually we bring in about 100 athletes from the Special Olympics. They're so excited to see our players. We set up a bunch of different stations and our guys are the ones running each station. The most popular station is the one where we lower the goals so the guys can dunk. We let the seniors run that station, and the Olympians love it - and I mean they *really* love it. Some of them start talking trash and joking with our players. It's great.

It's really neat to sit back and watch some of our guys interact with the Olympians. Sherron is really good with them and Jeremy Case is great in those situations, too. In the past, it hasn't been unusual for our freshmen to be a little tentative, because most of them have never been in that position before. But this season's freshmen were great – especially Cole.

## NATIONAL CHAMPS

I've got so many great memories from the night we beat Memphis for the title, but there's one thing that really got to me. About two minutes after the game I saw Jacque Vaughn sitting near the baseline. I was still shaking from winning, but I went over to him to say something to him, and I could just see in his eyes how excited he was that we won. That was really special for me to see, because he'd been on so many teams that could've won a championship – and probably should've won a championship – but didn't. So for him to be there and experience it and to get so much joy out of that ... I think it was one of the coolest things that could've happened. He was sitting down there on the baseline by Coach Mangino. As a matter of fact, you could almost see him in that *Sports Illustrated* picture.

The other thing I thought was really neat was the fact that Coach Williams came to the game and cheered for us from the stands. I wouldn't be sitting here talking to you today if it wasn't for Coach Williams, so for me, it was really cool to have him there. I was also glad to see Coach Self react the way he did. Some coaches win the big one and act more relieved than happy. But I don't think he was like that. I think he was really able to enjoy it.

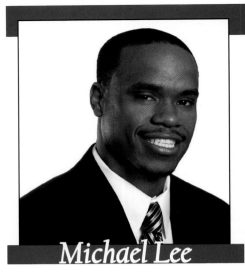

**Michael Lee**

He's played in the CBA, overseas and even with the Harlem Globetrotters. Still, when Michael Lee looks back on his basketball career, nothing was better than being a Jayhawk.

"One season I'm taking chartered flights and eating catered meals," Lee said, "and the next I'm sitting through five-hour bus trips with stops at Arby's. I never realized how good I had it.

"Playing at Kansas and being in college was the best four years of my life. Even the pro players come back and say, 'Man, I sure do miss Lawrence. I sure do miss Allen Fieldhouse.'"

Too old to be a college player anymore, Lee decided last summer to try his hand at the next best thing: college coaching. Turns out he may have been the Jayhawks' good luck charm, as Kansas won the national title in Lee's first year as a graduate assistant.

It didn't take Lee long to reap the rewards of being on KU's championship staff. Just one month after the season, Lee was hired as a full-time assistant at Gardner-Webb.

Lee played for Kansas from 2001 to 2005 and was a key contributor in the Jayhawks' march to the 2003 national title game, where they lost to Syracuse. During his career, Lee, a Portland native, competed in two Final Fours and an Elite Eight.

### IN MICHAEL'S WORDS

The best part of the season for me was Senior Night. For one, it was great to see Jeremy Case have his little breakout game. I've been a teammate of Jeremy's, so I know him a little better than some of the others. Everyone knew he was capable of doing that, but to see him go out and perform like that with his mother and father in the stands was really something special. I was so happy that I got teary-eyed just watching it.

I remember looking over at Russell before the game and seeing the tears running down his face. The thought that went through my mind was, "These guys are starting to figure it out."

There's something special about Kansas – something besides what happens on the basketball court. It's more than that. You see teams become families, you see kids become men. Take Russell, for instance. He came here as a wide-eyed, 18-year-old from New York. He was tough and confident, but he didn't have a clue. Russell had some hard times. I remember rooming with him on the road, and he was really down about the way things were going with Coach Self. He'd

spread his hands apart and say, "When it comes to messing up, Coach Self gives most of the guys a rope this long. But he only gives me a shoelace." He was so upset. So to see him four years later on Senior Night – and to think about how far he's come – that's what's special to me. When I look at these guys, I'm thinking about the story behind each one. I'm thinking about what they've been through. Especially this senior class.

Those seniors did everything anyone could've asked of them. They were scholar athletes. They stayed four years. They represented their school well and stayed out of trouble. All the stuff they've done ... people don't get to see the process. They just see the finished product. They don't see all of the blood, sweat and tears these dudes went through just to get out on that court. Practices, boot camps, staying after a game until midnight to sign autographs and then getting up at 8 a.m. – dead tired – to go to class. After that it's right back to practice. It takes a toll on you. Being on the road, lifting weights at 6 a.m. in the summers when you don't want to be there ... it's not easy being a Kansas basketball player, but it all pays off in the end.

When you leave here you're part of a network of people that is second to none. You've set yourself up for life. We saw examples of it at the 110-year reunion. All of the former players talked about their time here and how much it meant to them. They talked about all the opportunities they had in life, and at the end of each story, they'd say, "... because I was a Jayhawk."

I mean, Russell Robinson ... people love that guy. He epitomizes hard work. Even if he never steps foot on the court again, in the grand scheme of things, he's fine. He can come back here, talk to some people and probably end up with a good job. A lot of people would love to have Russell Robinson work for them because they know what he stands for. That's a tribute to him sticking it out.

*jayhawk nation:*
## A YEAR TO
## REMEMBER

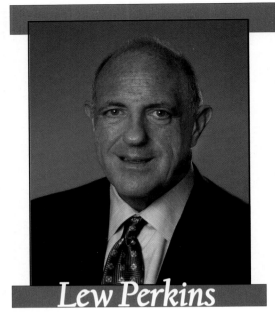

**Lew Perkins**

*When he was hired as athletic director in 2003, Lew Perkins promised that Kansas would get its "swagger" back. Five years later, no athletic program in the country enjoyed a school year quite like the one KU experienced in 2007-08. The Jayhawks' football team capped off a 12-1 season with a victory over Virginia Tech in the Orange Bowl, and then there was the basketball squad's national championship. The $23 million budget he inherited in 2003 has more than doubled during Perkins' tenure. Still, to quote The Kansas City Star, Perkins is known as more of a grandfather than a godfather around the Jayhawks athletic department. The athletes love him and so does the staff. Among Perkins' biggest supporters is basketball coach Bill Self, who said Perkins was a big factor in his decision to turn down the head coaching job at Oklahoma State.*

The situation with Bill Self and Oklahoma State didn't catch us off-guard. It's not like the issue just came up overnight. Everyone had been talking about the possibility of it happening for a long time. Both Bill and I like Sean Sutton an awful lot. We were hoping they'd retain him as their coach. But we were realistic enough to think that it could potentially happen, which is why we'd been talking about it and preparing for it for a long time. At the end of the day, as much as you try to talk and plan, you never know what's going to happen.

Obviously, the timing of it wasn't in anybody's best interest – especially ours. But Bill is a professional, and I like to think I'm a professional. We agreed that we weren't going to talk about Oklahoma State until after the tournament was done. The problem was that, as much as we wanted to ignore it, I kept getting asked about it by reporters at the Final Four.

All I kept trying to ask of people was, "Just let us get through the tournament. One or two days is not going to make a difference." Mike Holder, the Oklahoma State athletic director, did a great job with us. He really respected what we were trying to do. I've got nothing but compliments for Mike and how he handled it.

Once we won the championship, Bill knew he'd have to deal with it. Bill had said all along that he didn't think it was going to be an issue, but I encouraged Bill to go speak with them because it's his alma mater. I thought it was important that he do that. You never know for sure that it's all done and you've kept him until he walks in and says, "I'm staying."

I wasn't over-confident by any means. I didn't take him or his situation for granted. The minute you get complacent and think you have everything wrapped up ... that's not a smart way to handle business. We felt like we were working hard on our end, but we gave Bill a lot of room to make his own decision. When he walked into my office less than three days after the Final Four and said, "I'm staying," I was so relieved.

I have great respect for Bill. I obviously feel he made the right decision. Through conversations with Bill and with the way he talked about things, I felt like he was going to stay, but you've got to remember, this is business. I understand things happen sometimes. No one thought I'd ever leave Connecticut. Even when I announced I was leaving, people thought it was a joke. You can never take anything for granted. You just can't do it – and we didn't.

### GREENSBURG, KS

One of the best things our players did this season happened a few weeks after we won the national championship – and I'm sure there are a lot of people that don't know about it. CBS was airing a special from Greensburg, the Kansas town that was ravaged by a tornado. They called and asked if we could fly some of our players in to surprise all the students at the high school. Obviously, we thought it was a great idea.

Sasha Kaun, Jeremy Case, Darnell Jackson, Danny Manning and I left Lawrence on a plane at 4:30 in the morning and flew to Pratt. They picked us up there and drove us to Greensburg so we could be on the show, which started at 7:30.

They literally snuck us into town. They didn't want anyone to know that we were coming down. They had a ceremony in the gym because they were doing a piece on the basketball team there, since they had such a great year. We sat outside and waited for a while, and then they finally opened the doors so our guys could walk in and make a grand appearance. They played our fight song and then Danny and Sasha said a few words. Our kids were just great. They shot baskets with the kids and signed a zillion autographs. We brought t-shirts and hats and passed them out. The kids couldn't put them on fast enough. We heard so many positive comments. Everyone said that was the best thing that happened to them in a long time in terms of support.

From there we drove over to the site where they were building a new park. We visited with the construction guys. They only had five days to build this park. They were really working hard. Our guys went over and shook hands and talked to them. They were all big KU supporters.

After that we went and saw a group of Kansas architecture students who have been living in Greensburg since St. Patrick's Day. As their final project before graduation, they're building a museum to commemorate the town and its history before the tornado hit. They started the project on campus and then moved their

work to Greensburg. The only days they had had off were for the Final Four. They went back to Lawrence to watch the Saturday game against North Carolina. If we'd have lost they were going to have to go back to Greensburg the next day. But since we won, they stayed around and watched the championship game with their classmates. The following day they were back in Greensburg, because they have a deadline to get this project done.

### TEXAS TWO-STEP

One other memory that sticks out is the Kansas-Texas game in the championship of the Big 12 Tournament. I don't think I've ever seen a better half of basketball played by two teams. To me, it was as good as it gets. You almost got lost in the fact that you were rooting for one team. It's what college basketball should be. It's what college basketball is. I got immersed in the game itself. I was drained – mentally and physically – by halftime.

*Cindy Self*

**Photo:** Cindy, Lauren, Bill and Tyler Self at Wayne Simien's wedding in 2006

*They're both Oklahoma State graduates but, ironically, Bill and Cindy Self were introduced in Lawrence, Kansas. It happened on March 6, 1984, following the Jayhawks' victory over Self and the Cowboys at Allen Fieldhouse. Cindy, a cheerleader, was familiar with Bill from watching him play. And Bill, of course, had noticed Cindy. So when Oklahoma State's players and cheerleaders opted to remain in Lawrence that evening, the stage was set for the two of them to meet.*

Winning a national championship is fun but, for Bill, it's also been crazy. I told him the other day that he needed to change his cell phone number. His mailbox has been full for a month. There are people pulling at him from 20 different directions. He's got charity things going on and all of these letters and e-mails to return.

Sometimes I don't know how he still has the energy to walk around. I couldn't do it. I can't even begin to imagine how he keeps his motor going sometimes. He drinks a lot of Diet Coke and Dr Pepper. Still, I think he's going to come down pretty soon and crash. He can't keep going at this pace. The other night he took our son, Tyler, to his baseball game and they didn't get home until 11 – and that was after spending the day fulfilling a bunch of commitments.

That's not to say Bill isn't enjoying all of this. He loves it.

Bill knew he'd have a good team this year, but once he found out Brandon (Rush) was coming back, he realized that it could really be special. I think he probably had less stress this year than he's had in the past – mainly because the kids knew what they were doing because they'd been around awhile. I know practice is still practice, but when Bill came home, he didn't seem worried about whether they were "getting it" or not. Two years ago, when it was all freshmen and sophomores starting, there was a little more pressure. There was pressure this year, too, though. When everyone in the country is talking about how good you're going to be, there's a lot to live up to when it comes to expectations.

Bill and I talk about those things a lot. I like talking about basketball with him because I've always loved sports. I don't know that much about basketball, but I always like to know what's going on with the kids. One good thing about Bill is that, when he has a bad day, he's good about not being too down when he comes home. He stays pretty upbeat around our children.

That's not to say there haven't been some down times. Believe me, there have. When Kansas called Bill about the job, we had some pretty unhappy kids. They didn't want to move, but they've eventually grown to love it here.

Things went great during our first year here. The team got to the Elite Eight. But our second year here, reality kind of set in after we lost to Bucknell. It was not a good year, not a good feeling. The expectations were so high. The coaches did everything they could do. They worked their tails off. Things just didn't work out.

To be honest, I was a little bitter at that point because we were hearing a lot of backlash from fans and media. Sometimes people can't accept that things happen to teams – things like injuries. I don't know if everyone knew everything that was going on with the team at that point. We had a bunch of kids, like Keith Langford, that had to have surgery immediately after the season. We just weren't healthy.

Plus, sometimes the ball just doesn't go in the basket. Most of Kansas' fans are pretty understanding and pretty knowledgeable. But in most people's minds there was no excuse for us to lose that game – and there probably wasn't. Still, that doesn't mean that the coaches weren't doing the best job that they could. It doesn't mean they weren't working as hard as they could. As coaches, they're not any different today, after winning that championship, than they were then.

People just got so out of control. I was thinking, "Why did we come here?" Plus, the Illinois team that we left was doing fabulous at that time. Seeing them advance to the national title game was like pouring salt in the wound.

People can be so critical. They seem to forget that these players are just 18- or 19-year-old kids. A lot of the stuff I read ... some people don't know anything. People on the radio get on their high horse and decide that they know it all about basketball. Bill is real good about not listening to talk shows and reading the paper. I read the paper and tell him if there's something he needs to know about. I'm not as thick-skinned as he is. I also don't like our children to hear negative feedback from people. But they did (after the Bucknell loss), and that's part of it.

I realize that things like that happen with different sports in different towns all across the country. But people are so much more passionate here, and that's a good thing, because it shows you how much they care. That's why we absolutely love it here. Along with winning the championship, the best thing about this year was that we had five great young men – five seniors – who stuck with it through thick and thin. I think I'm happiest for them. Kids today ... a lot of them won't stick with it like that. They're really good kids, good individuals. To me, that's what this season was all about. It was about their leadership and how they took control. All of them had such moving stories. There was Darnell and everything he went through off the court, and Sasha, whose mother had the courage to let him move to the United States from Russia at 16. Seeing all those kids with their families on Senior Night was a real tear-jerker.

The national championship game is pretty much all a blur. When we got down on the court it was like, "Pinch me. Wake me up." It was like a dream that I couldn't believe was happening.

The best part was going back to the hotel and celebrating with all of our friends and the families of the players. They were so happy. After it all ended and everyone was gone, I was finally alone with Bill. I could see how emotional he was about the whole thing. He was just so happy for those boys. It was cool. It's funny how you can be in the cellar one day and the cream of the crop the next.

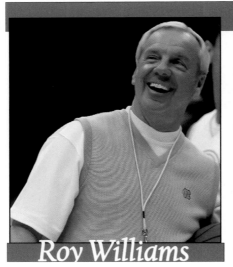
Roy Williams

*Roy Williams went 418-101 and reached four Final Fours while coaching Kansas from 1988 to 2003. To this day, some Kansas fans remain livid with Williams for his decision to leave Kansas for North Carolina, his alma mater. Williams was replaced by Bill Self, whose Jayhawks defeated Williams' Tar Heels 84-66 in the NCAA semifinals in San Antonio. At one point Kansas led 40-12. Despite the loss, Williams returned to the Alamodome two nights later to watch his former school defeat Memphis for the 2008 national title.*

It was difficult the week before the game because the Roy Williams-Kansas stuff dominated the headlines when it should've been about the teams and what great years they'd had. For the most part, though, it wasn't as bad as I thought it would be once I got to San Antonio. I saw so many great friends from Kansas. I went down on the Riverwalk on Friday night to eat at Boudro's. I saw huge throngs of Kansas fans. They were all great. Connie Friesen, my real estate agent from Lawrence ... I saw her walking by. She came over and we hugged. Ray Bechard, the volleyball coach, came by. I had a chance to visit with him. All the other fans were nice, too. That made it easier to focus on the game.

A real thrill for me came Thursday night. At the end of the Salute dinner, I was walking out of the men's room and Jeremy Case, Russell Robinson, Brennan Bechard and little Morningstar walked up to me, and Russell Robinson asked if they could all have their picture made with me. That was one of those neat experiences that will always be special to me. You know how corny I am, though. It might not have been special to someone else, but it was to me. It showed me that, with the kids, it wasn't about what happened five years ago. They said they had a great deal of respect for me as a coach. I've known Brennan and Brady since they were kids. I recruited Jeremy. They know how I feel about Kansas. And Russell Robinson is probably the best player in the country to average seven points a game. I told him that. Those kids really made me feel good.

Once I stepped onto the court, I didn't pay any attention to the hoopla surrounding the game – just like I didn't in 1991 and 1993, when I was at Kansas coaching against North Carolina and Dean Smith. Once the game starts and you go out on the court, it's about who you're playing. It's not about all the stuff on the periphery. I just wish we'd have played better. We picked the biggest stage to play our absolute worst game of the season.

I was still really confident when we were down by 28 points. I thought we

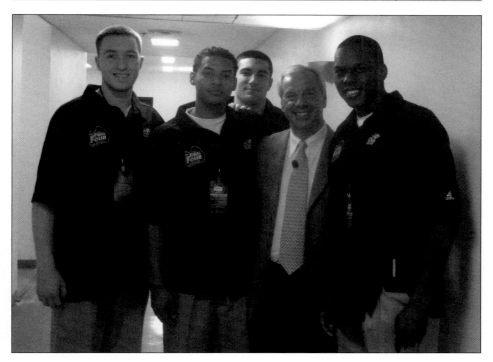

could come back and win the game. I was really that confident. But you can't come back from that big of a deficit against a team as good as Kansas. During the last month of the season I stated publicly many times that I thought Kansas was playing better than anybody. They proved me right in San Antonio.

We didn't play well at all. But give them all the credit in the world. They were playing great. They came out ready to play from the opening tip. We came out and had these looks on our faces like, "Oh my gosh, look at us, we're in the Final Four." They hit us right between the eyes. It's like the boxer who gets stunned and has trouble getting his senses back. We never got them back until they had us down by 28. I was really disappointed with the way we ended the half because we gave up a dadgum lay-up at the buzzer to Collins. We had cut it to 15 and that made it 17 – and it gave them the momentum.

I promised our team at halftime that if we just came out and played the way we were capable of playing that we'd get back in the ball game. I think we did. But it's like that little engine that says, "I think I can, I think I can, I think I can." We almost got to the top of that hill, but then we just ran out of gas.

There were two plays in my mind that really hurt us near the end. Danny Green shot a three-pointer that basically went all the way in the basket and then came out. We were down by five points and that would've cut it to two. We got the offensive rebound and then fumbled it out of bounds. If we'd have scored there it would've made it a one-possession game, and that would've put a whole

different kind of pressure on Kansas. Then we got it to four, but we never got it to four with the ball in our hands. They got a couple of lob dunks and that was pretty much it.

Kansas was a really fun team to watch – or at least they were when we weren't playing them. Russell Robinson did so much for that team, and I loved watching Mario Chalmers play all year. He can beat you in so many ways. He shoots 47 percent from the three point line and he can take it to the basket. I don't know of many guards in the country that play as well as he does defensively.

Brandon Rush is so confident out there. I go back a long way with Brandon and his family.

I didn't bring that stuff up in the handshake line. Part of what I said to him I'll keep private. But the thing I said consistently to all of those kids was,

"Congratulations. Now win the whole blessed thing Monday night."

It was an easy decision to stick around a few more days to watch Kansas play in the final. Scott, our son, lives in London now. He was in San Antonio and couldn't get out until Tuesday and Kim, our daughter, couldn't either. That was the first part of the decision. I wasn't going to go home and pout. I was going to stay in San Antonio and pout with my kids. But just as important was the fact that I wanted to stay and watch Kansas. I knew who I was going to cheer for. That was the easiest decision I've ever made in my life. I had nine former players there – guys like Scot Pollard, Jacque Vaughn, Rex Walters, Kevin Pritchard, Mike Maddox and Steve Woodberry. Brett Ballard and Michael Lee are on the Kansas staff.

I didn't sit in the Kansas section. I sat with the North Carolina parents who were also stuck in Texas until Tuesday. I know I got criticized for wearing that Kansas sticker, but I was glad to do it. I saw Ryan Robertson and stopped to exchange hugs with him. He said, "Thanks for being here tonight." Someone across the aisle leaned over and said, "Coach, do you want this sticker?"

He handed me the sticker and it was still on the little piece of paper. So I took it off and put it on my chest.

I didn't go by the locker room after the game to say anything to Bill. He knows I'm happy for him, but doing something like that ... it wouldn't have been my place. Someone would've accused me of trying to get attention. I pulled for them. I cheered for them and then I got out of there.

I left with the feeling that my second favorite team won the national championship. There's no question that I enjoyed that. I was sitting there after the game thinking about the exhilaration we felt after we won the title at North Carolina in 2005. I was thinking about the satisfaction that those Kansas players would always feel and the relationships that they're going to have for the rest of their lives. I couldn't have been any happier for them, knowing that they were going to experience that.

I was also thinking about other people, too. I saw Roger Morningstar sitting across the way. I saw Bud Stallworth. There are so many former Kansas players that have so much pride in their program. They're all going to have good feelings about this, too.

As sweet as this championship is for the town of Lawrence, I'm not sure it will do much to change it. I say that because they already had so much pride and passion for the Jayhawks. They take a backseat to no one with their support of the team. In 1993, I was coaching Kansas and we lost to North Carolina in the semifinals. I stayed around and waved my North Carolina-blue pom-pom and watched them win it all two nights later. I remember going to the stadium when we got back to Lawrence for a big celebration. I told the people, "Folks, last night I watched my alma mater win a national championship. One of these days I'll be sitting there watching your alma mater win the national championship." At that time I was thinking and hoping it would happen with me as the coach. We tried as hard as we could try. We did all we could do. We had great teams, but we were never fortunate enough to get it done.

I know that probably frustrated some people, but I'm just glad those people are happy now. They had a great season with a great team and a great coach. I've heard folks saying that the moon must've been full for Mario to hit that shot and for Memphis to miss all of those free throws. But that's not fair. Mario may have made the biggest shot in Kansas history, but before he did, those players made plays to put their team in a position to win that game. They weren't lucky to win that game. They earned that win.

Forever and ever, it's going to say that Kansas won the national championship in 2008. Those kids are going to remember that for the rest of their lives.

*JaRon Rush – the oldest brother of KU standout Brandon Rush – is arguably the top player in the history of Kansas City high school basketball. Rush led Pembroke Hill to back-to-back state titles in 1997 and 1998 and finished his career with 3,387 points, which ranks second all-time in Missouri. Rush appeared to be Kansas-bound, but former coach Roy Williams stopped recruiting him because of some remarks Rush made in The Kansas City Star. Rush played two seasons at UCLA before entering the NBA Draft. He was not selected. These days Rush is an assistant Penn Valley Community College coach and also works at Quest Diagnostics.*

JaRon Rush

When Brandon was growing up, he was always referred to as "JaRon's little brother." Now the role has reversed. Now I'm "Brandon's older brother." People are always asking me to get Brandon to sign stuff for them. It's weird, but I'm enjoying it. I'm happy for him. Brandon isn't in anyone's shadow anymore. If anything, he's creating his own shadow.

Each time I went to watch Brandon play at Allen Fieldhouse, the people there treated me great. It didn't feel awkward at all. Tons of strangers used to walk up and to say hello and congratulate me on my basketball career.

I was worried about it at first, because things got a little messy years ago when I was considering Kansas out of high school. I referred to Coach Williams as "Roy" in a newspaper article and said that I was concerned about playing for a coach that subbed so much. The whole thing led to a big misunderstanding and we ended up going our separate ways.

When I said that stuff, I had no intentions of things turning out like they did. Howard Richman and I had developed a relationship over the years. He had covered me for The Star since I was in the seventh grade. He came up to me at a game and asked me some questions. I was comfortable opening up to him – plus, I was just young and running my mouth. It was my mistake. I didn't know what I was saying.

The article came out and Coach Williams called me the next night and said, "Are these things true?" He wasn't mad about me calling him "Roy" or anything like that. He was more upset about me questioning the substitution patterns he had at that time. Coach Williams liked to sub a lot back then and I wasn't sure what to think of it.

It's unfortunate that it happened. When he called me, I basically owned up to saying everything. I just told him how I felt. If I would've denied the things that were in that article, I think he would've continued to recruit me. But I didn't deny making the comments, because that's how I was feeling at that time. I was a high school senior just talking a bunch of nonsense. Anyway, after I told him I really

**139**

said those things, he said, "OK, Kansas is no longer recruiting you." I just accepted it and decided to go to UCLA. It's unfortunate that it happened like that.

It was hard, because I had a bunch of friends that were going to KU. I thought that going there would put me on the right track. Coach Williams is such a strong coach. It would've been great to play under him.

I don't have any animosity toward Roy Williams. That whole situation had nothing to do with him. It had everything to do with me. It was my decision to come out and say those things. I wish I could take back everything I said. He would've been a great coach for me. I needed a good disciplinarian. Instead I just went out to California and ran wild.

### LIL BRO

I'm glad that Brandon made the decision to go to Kansas. Things couldn't have worked out any better for him – both on the court and off of it. I'm very proud of him because he's grown up so much.

It's tough when you're a good basketball player and getting all of this attention. I went through the same thing in high school and at UCLA. People are coming at you from every direction. You never know what their intentions are and you don't know who to trust. Eventually, people start asking you for things, and you feel like you've been burned by someone you thought was a friend.

The good thing about Kansas is that the coaches there have taught Brandon to look at life in a different way. They've shown him how to pursue basketball as a career and how to be a man and take control of things. You could see examples of that at the end of the season, when he actually started to become a leader. People thought he was joking at first when he started barking orders at people. But to me, it was an example of confidence that he hadn't always shown before.

I still can't believe that they won a national championship. I know how tough that is to do. Kareem and I were talking the other day and we said, "Man, Brandon has a championship on us now." We can't ever say anything about it. No one can take that away from him.

### FAMILY LIFE

When Brandon was little, Kareem and I never really talked to him about the pressures that come with being a Rush. The main reason was because we didn't know if he was going to be good. He was just out there playing, and all of a sudden people started realizing that he could be really good. I had never seen him play, so I didn't know if they were serious or not. Apparently they were.

It's funny to hear all the reporters ask Brandon about the advice he got from Kareem and I when he was younger. Honestly, back then, Brandon wasn't that close with Kareem and I. It's not like there were any problems or any tension. It's just that, when Brandon was young, Kareem and I were never in town because we were traveling around the country playing AAU ball. It was hard to have any influence on him or to be there for him given that situation.

One of my goals is to keep improving my relationship with Brandon. Our relationship has been pretty good for the last few years – ever since he came out to California for a visit. Now he's returning texts and returning phone calls. We're joking with one another and things like that. Everything just keeps getting better.

## HOMEBOUND

I can't tell you how much I regret not being able to be in San Antonio when Brandon helped Kansas win the national championship. Kareem was able to make it, but that Monday (April 7) was the first day of my new job at Quest Diagnostics. I couldn't miss it.

That night I sat at home and watched the game with my son and his mom and her parents. We ordered some chicken from the new Stroud's on Shawnee Mission Parkway. I'm very animated during the games. I sit there and sweat, just like I would if I was in the game.

Seeing Brandon play defense like he did against Memphis is what impressed me the most. Everyone says he slides so well, and you could really see that in the second half against Chris Douglas-Roberts. I knew Brandon would be back to his old self a month or two earlier, when he got his brace off. If you look back at the stats, that's when his numbers really started to improve. He never would admit it, but I'm sure his knee affected him at times throughout the season.

## BROTHERLY LOVE

I remember my mom calling me last May to tell me that Brandon had hurt himself. She said that he was really down about it and that he was crying a little bit. I couldn't reach him because he didn't want to talk to anyone. I was pretty upset about it, too. I actually shed a few tears for him, because I had been through knee injuries before and I knew it was a long road back. To this day, I still don't know how he came back so fast. Coach Self and his staff deserve a lot of credit for monitoring his rehab and keeping him on track.

I haven't played against Brandon since the summer of 2006. He was a sophomore and he came out to Los Angeles. I was out there working out with Kareem to see if I could get back into the league or back into the flow of playing basketball. We played a little pickup. It wasn't that physical. We're more finesse players that like to do everything by the book. But we had some pretty good battles.

People always joke that my mom must have some good genes, because all three of her sons ended up being good athletes. I don't understand how it happened, because she's never picked up a basketball or baseball or anything like that in her life.

Almost every week someone asks me, "Who is the best Rush?" They know that I had a lot of talent, but that it kind of went down the hole with all my partying and everything. Kareem, right now, is the best Rush. He's having great success in the NBA. Brandon is No. 2 because of what he did in college – and, as we all know, his book is still being written.

*Drew Gooden earned first-team All-American honors at Kansas in 2002 after leading the Jayhawks to the Final Four, where they lost in the semifinals to Maryland. The Memphis Grizzlies selected Gooden with the fourth overall pick in that summer's NBA Draft. He has played for four organizations and is now a standout forward with the Chicago Bulls. He is also a teammate of Kirk Hinrich, the point guard with whom he starred at Kansas.*

Drew Gooden

The thing I noticed most about this Kansas team was the way these guys matured over the years. I remember coming back to Lawrence for the alumni pickup game in the summer of 2005. Coach Williams had been gone for two years at that point.

Anyway, in the locker room, there's always been a Jayhawk logo in the middle of the floor, designed into the carpet. We always tried to keep it as clean as possible. The myth was that stepping on it was like a curse. Everyone always knew the rule: "Don't step on the Jayhawk."

That's why I got so upset that summer I came back. I went into the locker room and looked at the floor, and the Jayhawk was dirty. I sat there and watched as guys walked all over it. I was like, "Man, these guys don't even know." I realized they had a new coach and that some things were different. But there were still a lot of things that had been a part of the Kansas tradition for years – things that should never change. I didn't feel like those guys were respecting that.

That was also the summer after the Bucknell loss, when the J.R. Giddens stuff went down. The mood surrounding the program just wasn't right. Kansas was always known as a program that kept its nose clean and I didn't want that reputation to fall apart.

So I asked everyone to sit down so I could give a little speech. I told them the first thing they needed to do was to quit stepping on that bird. I told them that there were a lot of players that came before them who gave everything they had because of the pride they had in the Kansas program. I reminded them that, when they put on that uniform, they're not just representing themselves – they're representing people like me and anyone else that ever played a game at Allen Fieldhouse. I wasn't yelling at them or raising my voice too loud. I was talking to them like I'm talking to you now.

I was angry, though. I wanted them to feel the passion that I felt. Roy used to tell us all the time: "There are people out in the world talking about you guys everyday." I'm in the outside world now, and I'm beginning to understand that.

One day they will, too.

Someone told me recently that the speech I gave all those years ago really had an impact. That makes me feel good, although I don't know if I like feeling like an old veteran. I don't like feeling old. I haven't been gone that long, have I?

I watched the championship game in Miami with Kirk Hinrich and Joakim Noah. We were playing the Miami Heat the next day, so we couldn't make it to San Antonio. Instead we went to Wet Willie's on South Beach. We were probably the only Kansas fans in there. And, remember, we've got two Dukies on our team (Chris Duhon and Luol Deng), so there had already been a lot of trash-talking going on during the week.

I always tell everybody that my last year there was our year to win it, but we couldn't come through. Watching the game this year, I was like, "It's finally our turn. It's finally our time." That was one of the best college basketball games I've ever seen in my life. And I'm not just saying that because it involved Kansas. That was literally one of the best basketball games I've ever watched.

*Ed Hightower is known throughout the country as one of the top referees in all of college basketball. He's worked in 11 Final Fours and was one of the three officials on the court when Kansas won its national title – both in 1988 and 2008. In 1999, Hightower was selected as one of the Top 100 Athletes of the Century in St. Louis. He's served as the superintendant of the Edwardsville (Ill.) Community Unit School District since 1995.*

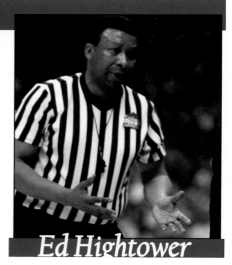

## Ed Hightower

One of the most fascinating aspects of the national championship game was the athleticism of the players from each team. A lot of the kids in that game ... they don't just have a *chance* to play at the next level. They *will* play at the next level.

The good thing about Kansas vs. Memphis was that it was a game where the athletes were the stars. Not the coaches. Not the officials - but the athletes out there on the court. They were the ones that made the plays and decided the game.

There were only a couple of times when the officials had to play much of a factor at all. We had to change Derrick Rose's three-pointer to a two and we had to put some time back on the clock at the end of the game, but beyond that, the players absolutely took over the game, and that's how it should be.

One thing that's unfortunate is that I've heard some people talking about the free throws that Memphis missed. People say Memphis "lost" the game. That's unfair. It's a disservice to one of the greatest NCAA championships ever.

Just look at the game in its totality: There was so much athleticism, so many great plays, so many great stops, so many exciting moments. There were so many opportunities for the game to be won and the game to be lost. That's how it should be when two great teams get together.

I was one of the referees when Kansas beat Oklahoma for the title in 1988. Billy Packer talked on the air that night about the excitement of the game. That was 20 years ago. Now ... try to think of a national championship game between then and now that was so close and down-to-the-wire. How many of them went to overtime? I don't think you'll find many that were as intense as this Kansas-Memphis game. You were on pins and needles the whole time. There were so many great moments. That's how the game should be remembered instead of people talking about how Memphis missed free throws.

## CRUCIAL CALL

Rose's shot was a very, very close play. Officials reserve the right to go back and fix something like that at any time. We do it a lot. In that situation, as I started to walk over, the official at the table said, "You may want to look at this again, just to be on the safe side." It was all about angles. Where was his foot when he actually started his shooting motion? That's the key thing. The first time we looked at it, it looked like he was behind the line when he started shooting. But then, when we looked at it from a different angle, he actually started his shooting motion with his front foot inside the arc. That's what instant replay is all about. You've got to give the NCAA credit for allowing officials to use replay. It's not about who's right. It's about what's right. That's the key thing. That call was right for the game. Other people may ask why we didn't assess a technical foul when the kid from Memphis slammed the ball against the court. My answer is that it wouldn't have been right for the game. He wasn't mad at the officials. He wasn't mad at another player. He was mad that he missed a couple of free throws. That's understandable. Why would we want to step in and get involved in the game at that point? Why wouldn't you just allow the great players to finish the game at that point? That's what it's all about.

There was no key moment in that game. There were just so many moments because of the electricity of 44,000 people. I'm a fan of the game - not a fan of a team, not a fan of a player, not a fan of a coach, but a fan of the game. The way things played out that night was great for the game of basketball. The greatest moment was basically when that game was over. We walked away and said, "Wow, it's over, now let's move on. We have no controversy, everything went well, let's move on." As an official, that's the greatest feeling you can have.

*Dana Anderson is one of the most influential supporters of Kansas' athletic department. Anderson, who lives in Los Angeles, is Vice Chairman of the Board of Directors of Macerich, which owns and operates shopping malls in the western United States. Anderson has 41 years of shopping center experience with Macerich and 46 years of experience in the real estate industry. At the University of Kansas, he serves on the Endowment Board and the Advisory Board of the School of Business. Anderson's son, Justin, is a well-known dentist in Lawrence.*

Dana Anderson

First the football team wins the Orange Bowl - and then the basketball team tops that by beating Memphis for the national title. I laughingly told someone the other day that my investments in KU this year paid off better than the investments I made in the market.

One person that needs to be thanked for what happened in San Antonio is R.C. Buford, the general manager of the San Antonio Spurs. He played a big role in Bill Self coming to Kansas, because he was the communicator for both sides back when we hired Bill from Illinois. He paved the path that led Bill to Lawrence.

R.C. had a get-together in San Antonio the night before the championship game at a place called The Vault, which is an old bank building on a corner not too far from the hotel. Larry Brown was there. Tim Jankovich was there. Almost everyone you saw had ties to Kansas. It was such a good group of people – and all of them have so much respect for Coach Self. I'm not sure if there's a better fit for the Jayhawks. My son, Justin, is a dentist in Lawrence and has had the chance to get to know Bill and his assistants very well. You never hear one bad thing about them – not one.

The game against Memphis was one of the most exciting nights of my life. It was almost like it was meant to be, because with two minutes left I thought it was over. I even turned to my wife, Sue, and said, "We can't win now." She looked back at me and said, "Dana, don't give up so quickly." When it was over, I was so happy for the team - and I was even happier a few days later when Bill turned down the Oklahoma State job and announced that he was staying at Kansas.

Most people wouldn't have been able to turn down the kind of money they were going to offer him. It was obvious that he had the opportunity to write his own check. I didn't think he was going to take the job, but I didn't have any basis for that opinion. Even though he hinted all along that he would stay, money can sometimes change things. After it was all over, I talked to Lew Perkins. He laughed and said, "Dana, we're going to have to raise more cash."

The other neat thing about our win over Memphis was seeing Roy Williams in the stands. Anyone who was surprised that he showed up for that game ... they just don't know Coach Williams. When I got back to California, I wrote him a letter thanking him for supporting us that night. Instead of worrying what others may say, he chose to come and support his former team. By doing that he showed a lot about his self-assurance and character.

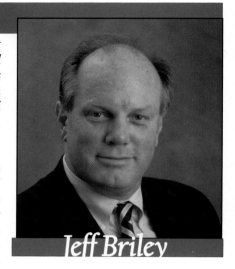

*Jeff Briley - a Kansas season ticket holder for the last 25 years – attended the Final Four in San Antonio with his wife and three children. He also serves on the national board of the Kansas Alumni Association. An Overland Park resident, Briley is an insurance broker for CBIZ.*

Our family didn't grow up with a horse or a boat, but we've always had our KU tickets. In San Antonio, we felt like we were living a dream just like everybody else. My kids were all very young when we won it all in 1988, so back then I was the one that was really into it. This time it was more for the kids.

The most memorable moment we had in San Antonio occurred about 10 steps into our first stroll on the Riverwalk. We ran into Larry Brown and asked him to pose for a picture with us. He was as cordial as he could be. He was happy to do it. The kids had taken a picture with him in 1988, so for this one, they got into the exact same pose. Just like the picture we took 20 years ago, Coach Brown was in the middle and the kids were on the side. It's neat now to hold the pictures up, side-by-side, and look at how much everyone has changed.

The thing I noticed in San Antonio was that our fans completely infiltrated the town. For every Memphis or UCLA or North Carolina shirt, you'd see seven KU shirts or hats. I think the people there were overwhelmed by the way our fans support the school. It made us proud to be Jayhawks.

Usually you don't walk into a restaurant and stop by every table to start up conversations with strangers or exchange high-fives. But at the Final Four, you do. Even if we didn't know one another, we were all there for the same purpose: To support our team and our school. Basketball really brings people together. I'm not sure people outside of Kansas realize just how deep this is.

It was great winning in San Antonio, but then you get home and there are all of these parades and banquets and national attention. It's so much bigger than it was back in 1988. The championship touched so many people in so many different places. I heard from pals and business associates all across the country. They all sent notes that said, "Congrats on the win," or "We watched the game and were thinking of you, because we know you're celebrating right now."

I sit on the Board of Directors for the National Alumni Association, and I can see first hand how monumental something like this is for your university in terms of applications, enrollment and contributions. The front page headlines we're getting have brought an enormous amount of attention to our university, all the way down to the biology labs.

# 148

Winning the national championship in basketball is pretty good for a football school (laughing). We really had a wonderful 90 days at KU.

**Above:** Greg Gurley, Bob Fitzpatrick, Jeff Briley and Scot Pollard at Rita's on the Riverwalk Sunday, April 6
**Below:** Brooke Briley, Larry Brown and Jason Briley on the Riverwalk Friday, April 4

*Larry Brown was Kansas' head coach when the Jayhawks won the 1988 national title. He is also close friends with Bill Self, who served on Brown's KU staff during the 1985-86 season. Brown is the only coach in history to win championships at both the collegiate and NBA level, as he led the Detroit Pistons to the 2004 title. In the fall of 2008, Brown will begin his first season as the head coach of the Charlotte Bobcats. Brown spent Final Four weekend shadowing the Jayhawks.*

**Larry Brown**

I went to the Final Four with my kids. During the Saturday night game against North Carolina, my daughter looked over at me and said, "Dad, why are you a pro coach? This is much more fun." I just said, "Madison, not everybody gets to the Final Four. Not every game is quite like this." She shook her head and said, "I don't know, dad. This is pretty special." She was right. I don't think that a Final Four could be any better than that one. I was connected with all four schools in some way. Bill and John Calipari both coached with me. I think so much of those guys. It's not like I don't think a lot of Roy and Ben Howland. I have a tremendous appreciation for what they've done in their careers.

I told my wife this: I've had a lot of special days as a basketball coach, and I care a lot about Roy and North Carolina. But on Saturday night, I don't think I could've had a better day in my life than watching John and Bill get to the finals. It was a pretty incredible feeling for me. I had a chance to be around Kansas during some of their practices in San Antonio, and that was a big thrill for me. It was obvious that this wasn't a group of individuals – this was a team. They cared about each other. I've had the opportunity to go around and watch a lot of teams practice, and that team I was watching work out ... it had a purpose.

When Rodrick Stewart got hurt at the shoot-around on Friday, I couldn't believe it. I just thought, "Wow. Here's a guy that had worked his whole life for a moment like this, and he goes down the day before the Final Four." It was so tough to watch. Then there was the whole issue of Bill having to go through all the questions about Roy. He kept trying to tell people, "Kansas is playing North Carolina – not Roy Williams." I couldn't fathom the pressure he must've been under in that circumstance. He handled it really well.

I stayed at the same hotel as the Kansas people. Kansas is such a unique place. When you're around those fans, you realize how much they love that program and the tradition and what's been accomplished there. It's pretty compelling. I've been away for awhile but, as soon as I got back around it, I realized why I loved it so much.

This championship has made me think a lot about the one we won back in 1988. It was pretty unlikely, but we had the best player in the tournament (Danny Manning) and a lot of other special kids that were a part of that. I smile each time I think about that team. There are days when I'm driving my car and I can remember it like yesterday, and that's what I told Bill.

There is no job that's any better than Kansas. There's no greater group of fans and no place where there's more interest. If you're lucky enough to be part of it then you've got a lot to be proud of. If you're lucky enough to win a championship ... that's icing on the cake.

**Above:** Kansas City radio personality Marty Wall (left) interviews Larry Brown during the NCAA Final Four.

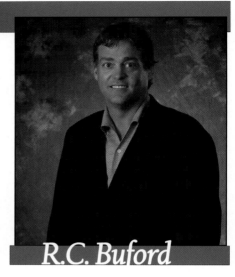

*R.C. Buford has been the general manager of the San Antonio Spurs since 2002, but his resume also includes a stint as an assistant coach at Kansas when the Jayhawks won the 1988 national title. Buford counts KU coach Bill Self as one of his closest friends. His son, Chase, joined the Jayhawks last fall as an invited walk-on.*

R.C. Buford

Every time I start talking about Kansas' national title, I can't help but get a little misty-eyed. The reasons for that are obvious. My son, Chase, is a freshman on the team, and Bill Self is one of my very best friends. We were in each others' weddings.

I was one of the go-betweens when Kansas hired Bill back in 2003. Kansas was trying to make its hire at the same time Bill was on vacation in Florida with his family. To this day, I'm not sure a lot of people realize just how tough of a decision it was for Bill to leave Illinois. Everyone thought it was a slam dunk that he'd take the Kansas job, but as I talked to him during that process, it was obvious that he was very torn. He had so much love for those players at Illinois. He had recruited an excellent team there, which was obvious considering they went to the national title game two years after he left.

Bill didn't want to be part of a beauty pageant, where they marched a bunch of high-profile coaches through Lawrence before settling on someone. In other words, he didn't want to be a candidate. For Kansas to get Bill, they needed to tell him from the start that he was the only guy that they were interested in, and that as long as they could work out a deal, they were ready to hire him on the spot. I felt the same way. If Kansas had any other intentions, I wouldn't have gotten involved. There didn't need to be a "search."

**A VIEW FROM THE STANDS**

The team was so focused when they were down nine with 2:12 to go. That team never appeared to be defeated. There was a lot of skepticism and disappointment in the stands at that point, but the team never acted or played that way. Once Mario's shot went in, there wasn't even any celebration. They got right back on defense and made sure Memphis didn't get a good shot with two seconds left. Then, when that horn sounded and the game went into overtime, there was such a positive vibe. They never lost sight of the saying, "the game's not over until it's over."

Bill was on top of his game all weekend. Every time he walked into a room, the place lit up. He was himself the whole time. At no point was there any sign of anxiety other than just normal preparation.

As far as Chase ... I don't know what greater joy a dad could have than to see his son so happy. We live in San Antonio, and having Chase leave home was a very difficult thing for me to deal with. But for him to be a part of something as unique and special as Kansas basketball makes me happy and it makes him happy. The memories he's made with this team and the coincidence of it happening 20 years after our championship ... it's going to be something he'll never forget. Now, when the 1988 team has its 30-year anniversary, it will be this team's 10th. When we have our 50th it will be their 30th. Chase and I will be able to share those moments, which is the greatest gift a dad can have.

*Tom Devlin graduated from Kansas in 1993. He is part-owner of three of the most popular nightspots in Lawrence: The Yacht Club, The Hawk and The Cadillac Ranch.*

At the Hawk, we had 30 people from Kansas City waiting in line before the North Carolina game. By 2 p.m. we were at capacity and the game didn't start until 7:30. At the Yacht Club, two people slept in tents that had signs on them that said, "Wake me up when you open." We were full by noon.

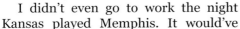

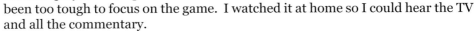

Tom Devlin

I didn't even go to work the night Kansas played Memphis. It would've been too tough to focus on the game. I watched it at home so I could hear the TV and all the commentary.

I went downtown with some friends after we beat Memphis. We left about 10 minutes after the game ended, and traffic was already lined up on Sixth Street all the way from Mass to Monterrey Way. That's probably about three to four miles. I took back roads the whole way there.

There was a sea of people rushing downtown. It was like nothing I'd ever seen. They estimated that 40,000 to 50,000 people were there, and that definitely seems accurate. The alleys were like latrines. It was unbelievable. I heard someone describe it as organized chaos. It wasn't out of control. It was just a bunch of happy people running around celebrating.

About an hour after the game, there was a truck that was trying to back out from one of those metered parking spots on Mass Street. That was around 11:15. He was probably there until three in the morning.

We didn't have any problems with basketball players this year. They didn't come by that often. I'm usually up at The Ranch. When they did come up you really didn't see them drinking. In the past, Kansas had guys that went out and really partied hard. I'm not sure these guys are like that. Some of them go to The Hawk sometimes. They just blend in. They don't get out of control and cause a scene. They basically just hang out and dance with girls – just like any other college kid.

I think winning the title has breathed life into the town. Everywhere you go, people are still talking about it. There is still a lot of electricity in the air. I've witnessed so many close calls over the years. To finally win one ... not only was there a lot of electricity in the air, there was also a sigh of relief.

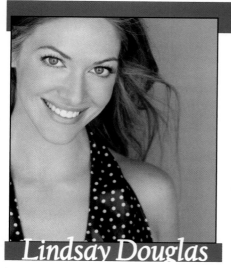

Lindsay Douglas

*Lindsay Douglas graduated from Kansas in 2002 with a degree in communications. That same year, she was named first runner-up at the Miss USA pageant in Gary, Indiana. Douglas worked at the Yacht Club during her college days and was a member of Chi Omega sorority. She's also famous for having her purse stolen – allegedly - by former Kansas football players Mario Kinsey and Reggie Duncan, who were charged with ordering pizzas with Douglas' credit card. Upon graduation Douglas moved to Los Angeles, where she's pursuing opportunities in the television and film industry.*

Even though I'm thousands of miles away in Los Angeles, there are plenty of moments when it almost feels as if I'm back in Lawrence. This town is swarming with Jayhawks fans – especially during the NCAA Tournament.

There's a big group of us that call ourselves the LA Jayhawks. We have a page on myspace.com and a committee member that coordinates all of the watch parties. For almost every game we meet at El Guapo, a really big bar on Melrose in West Hollywood. The night of the NCAA title game it was absolutely insane. There had to be at least 150 people in there wearing Kansas shirts. People who had come in there just to hang out were like, "What's going on? Kansas has taken over the bar." And we all said, "That's right!" They said they had never seen a group of such loyal fans. We were screaming and yelling. It was like that almost every single game.

In December, the group got together and went to the USC game. Once again there were about 150 – or maybe even 200 – of us and we were so much louder than all of the USC fans. People were booing us because they were so mad that we were taking over one of their sections. We were a huge distraction.

I love all of Kansas' players, but my favorite is definitely Brandon Rush. You can see on his face that he's such a competitor and you can tell that he has a lot of passion toward the sport. And I think it is neat that he was able to step out from his brother's shadow. I know Kareem Rush because I grew up in Lafayette, which is in central Missouri. I have a lot of friends that went to Mizzou and one of them used to date him. He's a super-nice guy. I'm also good friends with the Kroenkes, so of course I had to give Josh Kroenke (a former Missouri player) a really hard time after Kansas won. My parents went to Mizzou and my other sister went to Mizzou, so I was the darkhorse, the black sheep of the family because I went to KU. My cousins live in Lawrence, so they basically brainwashed me when I was little and I watched Jayhawks basketball games all the time. I was in Lawrence when they won the 1988 championship. I still have the t-shirt they gave me, the one they made me wear when I was, like, eight. I really had no idea what was going on, but I remember Lawrence was going crazy. We went down to Mass Street and from that moment on, I was always like, "I'm going to KU."

Clyde Lovellette

*One of the greatest players in Kansas history, Clyde Lovellette averaged 28.4 points in leading the Jayhawks to the NCAA title in 1952. He later became the first basketball player ever to play on an NCAA, Olympics and NBA championship squad. Lovellette ranks fourth on Kansas' all-time scoring list with 1,979 career points. Still an ardent Jayhawks fan, Lovellette resides in Munising, Michigan with his wife, Judy.*

I follow the team as much as I can, but here in upper Michigan, we don't get many Big 12 games on television. It's mainly the Big 10. Luckily I've got people down in Kansas that keep me informed. I try to talk to some of my old teammates as much as possible – guys like Bill Hougland and Bill Lienhard and Charlie Hoag. They go to games and keep me up to date.

It made me very happy that Kansas won another national championship. I stayed up and watched the game on television. I thought we had it wrapped up and then, all of a sudden, things turned around. You could tell by the way Memphis came out in the second half that it was going to be a very tight game. I knew when Kansas hit that Hail Mary – that three-pointer – that they'd win in overtime. But I can't understand why the Memphis coach, John Calipari, didn't foul before Chalmers took that shot. They had a three-point lead, so even if KU had made both free throws, it would've still been a one-point lead. But I guess no one likes armchair quarterbacks.

One of my favorite players to watch during the tournament was Sasha Kaun. One reason is that he plays the same position as I played, and the other is that I've always thought the guys on the bench are just as important to the team as anyone. If a reserve can come in and play just as well as a starter and get some key points and rebounds, he becomes as valuable as anyone. I watched Sasha all through the tournament, and Kansas never lost anything when he was in there. He actually lifted them up at times. Sometimes the guys that come in are even more valuable than the guys they replace. The freshman, Aldrich, was another example of that – especially against North Carolina. You have to have a deep, well-rounded ball club to win a championship – and Kansas certainly had that.

The thing that was most pleasing to me about this title was that there was not a lot of bragging or boasting or taunting from Kansas once it was over. They were like, "We did it. We won. We're the champions of the NCAA Tournament." And that was fine. That should be expected. Other than that, though, they were very humble about their victory. There was no arrogance about them. They just walked around with big smiles on their faces, hugging one another. They were very grateful. I'm sure the way they handled themselves that night made a lot of alumni like me proud.

The best thing about a championship like that is that no one can take it away from you. You hear about it or think about it every single day. You don't want to dwell on the past, though, because you can't do that and live your life the way it should be lived. I still remember 1952, but I don't dwell on it. That's not to say I don't enjoy going back to Kansas with the 1952 team. I'd love to go back there and hang out with friends like Max Falkenstien and guys that are still around like Jerry Waugh. I'd just want to sit down, have dinner together and spend the night reminiscing. We wouldn't need to be on the court in front of the fans. We enjoy each other's' company because we played together for four years. We lived and died basketball and went through the same joys and heartaches. Experiences like those are ones you never forget.

*Max Falkenstien*

*After 60 years behind the mic, legendary Kansas radio personality Max Falkenstien retired in 2006. But that's not to say the 84-year-old Basketball Hall of Famer is no longer involved with the Jayhawks' basketball program. Read on.*

On Senior Night, I've always been the guy that comes out onto the floor and introduces the players. They usually give me a big hug and thank me. I've always dreaded the one night when we didn't win. Knock on wood, that's never happened. We've won every single Senior Night that we've ever had.

Every year has some sort of special moment. Wayne Simien gave a sermon in 2005 when he talked for 25 minutes. Jacque Vaughn told Roy Williams that, if his wife ever had a child, he hoped Roy would be standing next to him in the delivery room.

This year, with five seniors, Bill Self told each of them to keep their speeches under five minutes and they all did. Bill had an exact order in which he wanted them to be introduced. Rodrick Stewart came out first and gave me a big hug. A picture of it ran in one of the local papers and it looked like we were in love with each other.

After each guy gave their little talk, someone came up to me afterward and said, "Max, you haven't lost it." Two years after I retired, that really made me feel good.

I almost felt sorry for Texas Tech that night. They lost 109-51 and, after the game, Pat Knight had a funny quote. He said, "I feel like someone wrapped a meat necklace around my neck and threw me into a lion's den." Any school that plays Kansas on Senior Night probably feels that way.

I don't get nervous about my speech in the same way that the players do – mainly because I don't have to talk a lot. I just always try to come up with something personal to say about each player.

People always ask me if I get emotional listening to those great speeches on Senior Night. Some of them have definitely touched me, but I've always managed to hold off on the tears. When I used to do Roy Williams' television show, the stories about KU's players helping out with the Special Olympics kids always got to me. Both of us would tear up over that.

I also got to introduce the players at Memorial Stadium the day they came back from San Antonio. There were 28,000 people there. Kathleen Sebelius, the governor, was there, too, and she gave me a kiss on the cheek after I announced her name just like she always does.

It had been so nice and warm in San Antonio, but when we got off the plane in Lawrence, it was 45 degrees with a 15-mile-per-hour wind out of the north. We went straight to the stadium and all we had were the light jackets we'd taken with us to Texas. I was shivering so badly as we walked into the stadium that I was afraid I wasn't going to be able to talk. Luckily, I was able to block it out and everything went fine.

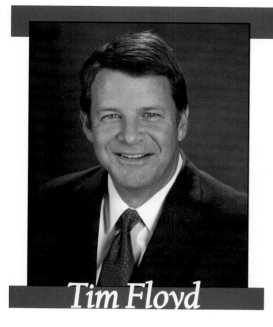

Tim Floyd

*One of Kansas' toughest non-conference games was a 59-55 victory at USC on Dec. 2. Stalking the sidelines for the Trojans that day was Tim Floyd, who arrived in Los Angeles in 2005 with a resume that includes NBA head coaching stints with the Chicago Bulls and New Orleans Hornets. Floyd said he couldn't have been more impressed with the Jayhawks.*

We played Kansas in each of the last two seasons, and it was obvious that all of their starters were capable of being 20-point-per-game guys for most any team in the country.

The thing I admired about them the most was their willingness to make the extra pass to get the best shot. I think that was dictated by how much they gave on the defensive end. They played so hard defensively. It was like they were out there thinking, "We worked so hard to get the ball back, there is no way in the world we're going to take a bad shot." They valued the ball so much.

We played them when they were missing one of their key components: Sherron Collins. He was out that game. Having seen him the year before, I knew what a game-changer he was. He has a level of speed and an ability to penetrate and create that their team lacked when we saw them in December.

The other thing that jumped out at me was this: Everyone was aware of what great talents Rush and Arthur were. But the guys that impacted the game both times we faced them – last year and this year – were Chalmers and Darnell Jackson.

Chalmers was the best, most non-talked-about great player in college basketball this season. If I was a pro coach again, he'd be a guy that I'd want on my team. He's rarely mentioned as a first-rounder but, in my opinion, he's a pro guard who will play for a long time in the NBA. He impacts games defensively. He makes the open shot. He penetrates. He does it all. Everyone knew he was a good player. I just thought he was even better than advertised.

People talk about how they didn't have a single player make first-team All-Big 12. I actually think that's a tribute to all of them. Obviously, the votes were split because people couldn't decide which star to vote for. They're getting their just due now.

I think a lot of the credit should go to Coach Self. For a team to be that selfless, it always goes back to the coaching staff. For one thing, they recruited winners. They also got those kids to understand that they're not any different than any other player in the country as far as their desire to play in the NBA. He got them to understand that their reward would come from winning at a high level.

It's rare in these times to find players who were as highly recruited as those young men were who really didn't care where the credit went.

*Ed Fritz*

*Ed Fritz is the head boy's basketball coach at Blue Valley Northwest High School, which was the site of Kansas' first Barnstorming stop on April 17. Barnstorming is a yearly event that occurs when Kansas' graduating seniors raise money by touring the state and playing pick-up games against various high school teams. Pre-game autograph sessions are also a part of the festivities.*

The Barnstorming event at Blue Valley Northwest couldn't have worked out any better – mainly because we hosted it nine days after Kansas won the national title. We weren't allowed to advertise for it until the season was over because of NCAA restrictions, but that didn't matter. We put our tickets on sale on a Tuesday morning and a Thursday morning. Each time, we sold every ticket available within 90 minutes. The demand was unbelievable. We could've sold 6,000 or 7,000 tickets if we'd have had the space.

The gym that night was standing room only. There were people lined up on the baseline against the walls. There were so many people that we had to lock the doors to the school so that no one else could get in. The autograph line was so long – about 1,200 people – that we actually had to cut if off. There were some people who got upset, and that's understandable. But with the turnout we had, it would've been impossible to accommodate everybody.

All the KU seniors were there that night: Russell Robinson, Jeremy Case, Darnell Jackson, Sasha Kaun, Rodrick Stewart and Brad Witherspoon. They couldn't have handled the situation any better.

I watched those players sign autographs for an hour and 45 minutes. Not once did they take a break. There was no screwing around. They looked every kid, every parent and every grandparent in the eye. They were just really, really classy the whole time.

Once the game started, those guys did everything they could to make sure people had fun. They were throwing their wristbands into the stands and giving away their warm-up jerseys. There was a group there from an inner-city church – Hope Church – that came to the game. They brought about 20 kids from the inner-city. Darnell Jackson ran up into the stands and talked to them awhile before the game. The way he dealt with them was something special. Coach Self talked a lot about character all season, and those guys really have it. The other cool thing was that the game was a really big thrill for my players. They'll never forget having the chance to get up close to Kansas' players and interact with them. In their eyes, it was the most important game they played all season.

Alex Galindo

*Alex Galindo averaged 4.3 points as a freshman at Kansas in 2004-05 before transferring to Florida International, where he's led the Golden Panthers in scoring and rebounding each of the last two seasons. There are more than a few Jayhawk supporters who wish Galindo would've never left Lawrence, as he was a fan favorite who came up huge in down-to-the-wire victories against Texas A&M and Georgia Tech.*

I'm happy at Florida International but, basketball-wise, it's hard not to wonder how things would've turned out for me if I had never left Kansas after my freshman year.

I'd have a national championship, ring to put on my finger and I could've been a part of this great senior class. Who knows how I would've fit into the rotation here? I mean, everyone needs a shooter, right?

I wish I could've been in San Antonio the night Kansas won the title. Instead I watched the game from home in Miami. When Mario hit that shot, I jumped out of my bed and started screaming. I felt so good for all of the guys I played with: Russell, Darnell, Sasha and Case. It just felt good to know that, at one time, I was a part of that team.

I still keep in touch with Russell. I talk to him twice a week. I talked to him right after the Memphis game and he said it was the best feeling he ever had. I came back to visit Russell in May. He's leaving and the other guys I played with are leaving. I figured this might be my last chance to come back.

When I was in Lawrence, I went over to The Fieldhouse to shoot with Case and Mike Lee and some of the guys. A lot of feelings and memories came rushing back. Coach Dooley started talking about the shots I made to help beat Georgia Tech and Texas A&M, and I could picture the fans in the stands with the "Salsa For Galindo" signs.

It made me realize how much I miss Kansas basketball. I miss the fans and all the love that they showed me, and most of all I miss the winning. It's tough at FIU. We've lost a lot of games, and it seems like every night I'm facing box-and-ones. I'm a three-point shooter, but some nights it's tough to get a good look because so many teams center their game plan on me. I'm playing 35 minutes a game – 40 some nights. There are times when I get tired and don't have my legs.

Don't get me wrong. I'm happy there. It's just totally different.

I talked to Coach Self when I came back. He's not mad at me. He couldn't have been any nicer with the way he welcomed me into The Fieldhouse and into his office. Coach Self understands why I made the decision I made. One of the main reasons I left was because I wanted to get my family back together. My mother and father moved to Miami from Puerto Rico. I'm living with them now. I just graduated and I've still got one more year to play. Everything worked out well for me. Everything worked out well for everyone.

Billy Gillispie

*It's no secret that Kentucky head coach Billy Gillispie is one of Bill Self's closest friends. Self hired Gillispie as an assistant at Tulsa in 1997, and Gillispie followed Self to Illinois three years later before landing his first head coaching gig at Texas-El Paso. Gillispie and Self faced off three times during Gillispie's head coaching stint at Texas A&M from 2004-07, with Self winning twice. The SEC co-Coach of the Year in 2008, Gillispie was in the stands during Kansas' victory over Memphis in San Antonio.*

I never had a brother, but Bill Self is certainly the closest thing to it that I can imagine. That's why I was so excited to be at the Final Four this year. I felt like I was rooting for a family member. Bill is one of my best friends, and he's the guy who's most responsible for any success I've ever had. Now here he was, playing in a game for the highest stakes. It was long overdue, really. Bill has done a great job from Day One with that team, so for him to have a chance to climb that ladder and cut down that net was gratifying to watch.

Because Bill and I are so close, the games at the Final Four were really nerve-wracking for me. Everyone around me was pulling for Bill, and when they got up so big against North Carolina, you couldn't help but think, "Wow." Then all of a sudden, Carolina started playing well and whittled away at the lead, so everyone was on pins and needles again.

I saw Bill after the game that night. He was excited but ready to move on. He was eager to get prepared for the championship, but you could also tell he was grateful and relieved and overjoyed just to have the chance to play in it.

Bill deserved to win that Memphis game. He's a good coach and a good person. He gives you confidence about anything and everything you do and makes you feel like you're good at what you do. He allows you to do your job and to be an individual. He gets good people that he has confidence in and lets them do their job. He gets you prepared for that next step, because he wants you to have an opportunity to be a head coach. He's fair and he's honest. He's just a joy to work with. You don't ever really feel like you work for him. I always thought that we were working side-by-side, together. That's the mark of a great leader.

It is awkward having to recruit against him sometimes. Sometimes you're going to win and sometimes you're not. It's never become personal, though. And it never will.

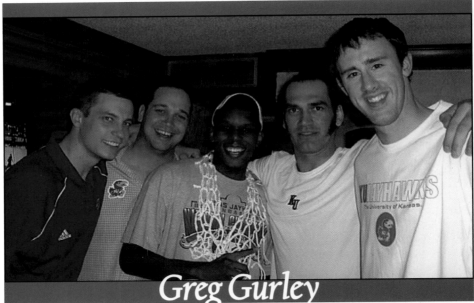

**Above:** Hours after winning the National Championship, Russell Robinson (center) celebrated with former Jayhawks (from left) Ryan Robertson, Greg Gurley, Scott Pollard and T.J. Pugh.

*Greg Gurley etched his name into Kansas history by helping the Jayhawks reach the Final Four in 1993. An alumnus of the KU school of business, Gurley currently owns Collegiate Marketing Services, a manufacturer of corporate and collegiate apparel.*

Before I ever committed to Kansas, Coach Self and Eddie Sutton came to my house on a home visit back in 1990. Bill was an assistant at Oklahoma State at the time, and I can honestly say that, if I hadn't picked Kansas, I would've gone to Oklahoma State because of him. He was a young guy who was really sincere, and he seemed like a lot of fun.

During that visit my mom, Carole, made a batch of cookies. Thirteen years later, Bill got hired at Kansas. I was excited about it, so I drove to Lawrence for the press conference. Bill saw me and said, "Hey, Greg. How are Jim and Carole? Do they still live in that house with the big basement? Tell your mom to make me some more of those cookies." I just couldn't believe he remembered that. He'd probably done 500 in-home visits since then.

I know he's never had any formal public relations training. But he's as good with people and the media as anyone I've ever seen. Just watching him operate ... he always handles himself so well and says the right things. It's by no means phony. It's just the way that he is. The guy just knows how to handle people.

The other thing that people really appreciate is the way Bill treats all of Kansas' former players. He treats us like we played for him. He has no reason to hang out and do anything with us. But he includes us in a lot of stuff. A lot of it is stuff like us being able to call the basketball office and get tickets for the game. Or being able to stay in the team hotel, which we did at the Final Four. He could've just as easily said, "Our players have a lot of family members to take care of," or "I've already promised the tickets to someone else." Instead he found a way to help everyone out.

We all got great seats. We all got to sit together with our wives. After the North Carolina game, we all got to go up in his room. He took the time to hang out with Scot Pollard, Ryan Robertson, T.J. Pugh and myself and our wives. It was around midnight or so. He was just shooting the bull with us for about 20 minutes. We basically talked about everything except basketball. It was the kind of casual conversation you'd have with someone at a bar.

Bill realizes it's important to keep former players involved. Kids want to feel like they're part of a family. That's what builds tradition and longevity. There are teams out there that will have a few good years and make a run at a Final Four. Cincinnati, for instance, had a few good years, but now they've dropped off. I really doubt they have a reunion every five years. There are very few schools that have done it consistently like Kansas has. That has a lot to do with keeping everyone involved, whether it's donors or former players or whoever.

I think the current team was able to see that camaraderie during the 110-year reunion. Players from each decade stood up and talked – guys like Darnell Valentine and Jeff Gueldner and Ryan Robertson and Wayne Simien. They really did a good job of engraining in these guys' heads that these will be your friends for life and how important it is to cherish these moments. Kansas basketball isn't just about your teammates. It's about the coaches, managers, trainers and academic support staff. Hopefully those guys took a little bit of that to heart and carried it over onto the court. Considering they won the national championship, I'd say they did.

**Above:** Scott & Mindy Pollard, Greg & Amy Gurley and Ryan & Andrea Robertson at the Final Four in San Antonio.

*Doug Holiday may not know much about the Jayhawks' practice habits – but he can certainly tell you about their eating habits. As the owner of Bigg's Barbeque in Lawrence, Holiday has catered plenty of pre-game meals for Kansas the last few years. Bigg's has also become a favorite of the sportswriters who cover the team, so here's a tip: Stop by Bigg's on Monday for the wing special or on Tuesday for the ribs special. You'll leave happy. Honest.*

Doug Holiday

For years now we've catered a lot of Kansas' pre-game meals. Whenever someone asks me to name the biggest eater on the team, I tell them it's Sasha Kaun. The guy is a riot. We usually have about three choices of meat and then some sides, and he piles up on everything. Ribs, pork, chicken, brisket. Whatever we have, he usually takes something of everything. One time he had a little bout with the flu and he wasn't very hungry, but other than that, he always puts on a show in the buffet line. He just loads up.

The biggest thing these guys like is hamburgers. One of the best things at Bigg's is the ribs, but if we have burgers out, the players will take those before anything. The coaches are the ones that like the ribs. Danny Manning is big on our banana pudding.

Before he left for Illinois State, the coaches used to always give Tim Jankovich a hard time. I don't know if he was watching his weight or what, but he'd come up to the dessert line for some banana pudding and say, "Just give me half – just a little taste." But then he'd end up coming back about six times, so he basically had three full servings of it.

Usually we have three different sides. Cold or hot potato salad, cole slaw or barbeque beans. Sometimes they want something special, like fried chicken. Darnell really enjoys our wings, but Wayne Simien used to be the big wing-eater of the bunch. He came in and bought about 100 of them for his graduation party. And keep in mind, our wings are big.

One of the funniest stories ever happened years ago when I worked at the Hereford House. We had just opened, so we had new plates – and new knives. Apparently our butter knives were still a little sharp, because Eric Chenowith cut his finger with one. I went downstairs to the medicine cabinet and got him a Band-Aid. I come back and he's standing there, and he's just so tall. I'm looking up at him as I'm helping him clean up his finger. I started to put the Band-Aid on him and he says, "You think I'm going to need stitches?" I told him I thought he was going to be just fine. Then he asked me if I was a doctor.

It's kind of interesting to sit back and watch the guys interact during meals. In years past, you could tell there may have been a little division. When J.R. Giddens was here he'd always sit at a table all by himself. Other guys would spread out, too. But with these guys ... they all sit together and joke. You could tell it was a real cohesive group and that everyone really got along. I'm sure that really made a difference on the court.

Cole Aldrich was a freshman this year so, naturally, he was kind of shy at first. One time, for whatever reason, things were kind of quiet and Coach Self screamed out, "Hey, Cole – you got a girlfriend yet?" Cole turned beet red and didn't say anything. Self just said, "You've been here long enough now. I hope you have one."

Coach Self and his staff are so personable. Coach Williams was a great guy, too, but he was a little tenser than Coach Self. He's so relaxed. Every player always thanks me and stops to say "Hi." Everyone is just really genuine, really nice.

It never fails. Each and every time Kansas plays a basketball game, the island at Arizona's Sports Bar in Overland Park is occupied by the same five Jayhawk fans: Brett Hunter, Mark Wittlinger, Mike Blair, Ben Vargas and Rick Blowey.

## Arizona's Sports Bar Crew

**Above:** Brett Hunter and Mark Wittlinger

"Grape bombs for everyone," has become the popular battle cry following a Kansas victory. And after a loss, well ... "Grape bombs for everyone."

### BRETT HUNTER

The guys I watch games with at Arizona's are some of the best friends I'll ever have. But when you really step back and look at it, we really are a strange mix. The ages range from 27 to 50, and each of us takes on a different personality when it comes to watching the Jayhawks.

You've got Mark, the 50-year-old who hardly says a word until something crazy happens at the end. He's the kind of guy that sits back and analyzes things without ever getting too up or too down. If people start complaining and worrying when Kansas has a bad stretch, he just takes a sip of beer and says, "It's early. It's early."

Rick is the glass-half-empty guy, the guy who's always preparing for the worst and waiting for the game to turn against us. He has a hard time just letting himself go and getting excited. Part of that is understandable. There have been a lot of heartaches in the past, and some people remember those more than they do the big wins.

Then you've got Ben. He's a nervous wreck during every freakin game. He was so uptight the night of the Memphis game that he refused to drink anything but Diet Coke. He said his stomach was in knots. I know the waitress was upset, because Ben was there all that time and probably had a six dollar tab. She didn't make anything off him that night. For about a week after the game, Ben kept complaining about how he hurt his shoulder by pounding on the bar whenever he got excited during the Final Four.

Mike and I are the young, crazy guys – the ones who yell and scream at the TV and jump around giving high-fives.

We've also got a few other buddies named Wildcat (Tony Fankhauser) and Jim West. One's a Kansas State fan and one is a Missouri fan. They pretty much hate KU, so they drink with us up until tipoff – and then they leave.

### MARK WITTLINGER

I've known these guys for five years now. Back when I first met them, they'd spend the whole afternoon running from television to television throughout the bar so they could watch all the different games and keep track of the $3 bets they made on the internet.

**Above:** Ben Vargas, Mike Blair and Rick Blowey

Back then Arizona's was called "The Fieldhouse," which was owned by Randy Buhr. Randy runs a bar in Lee's Summit now called "Sharkeez," which is another great place to watch a game.

Arizona's, though, has become our home away from home because most of us live really close by. It's almost like Groundhog Day when we're up there. We always order the same drinks – I'm a pitcher kinda guy – and most of the guys usually eat the same things. A barbeque sandwich for Blair, a patty melt for Brett and, for me, wings that are cooked just a little bit longer, to make them crispy.

Brett and Mike get the most excited during the games. They're the loudest. If someone makes a great play, it's always, "Did you freakin' see that?" Or if the ref makes a bad call, it's "Did you freakin' see that?" I'm 50, and these young guys are making my hands sore with all of their hard high-fives.

There was obviously a lot of that going on this season. It was extra-special for me because I've got two kids that go to Kansas. Ray graduated this spring and Jackie will be a senior. I wanted so badly for them to be able to experience something like this in their lifetime. I watched Kansas win it all in 1988. I watched the Chiefs win a Super Bowl and the Royals a World Series. I know how fun it is to be a fan when something like that happens. I would always tell them about it, but there's nothing like living through it first hand. They called me from Mass Street after Kansas beat Memphis and part of me really wanted to be down there with them.

The morning after the game I bought as many copies of *The Kansas City Star* as I could find. I put the front page in frames for them and bought books and t-shirts and everything else I could find. I even took down the big, over-sized NCAA Tournament bracket that was hanging on the wall at Arizona's and had Kayla – one of the waitresses – fill it out so it would be in good penmanship. I gave it to Ray. Hopefully it's something he'll keep forever.

*Kansas' victory over Memphis in the national title game created an amazing sight in downtown Lawrence – especially from a retail standpoint. Just ask Ryan Owens, a 28-year-old Kansas grad who works at Jock's Nitch, a local sports apparel store. Owens said the rush of fans in search of NCAA commemorative gear was unlike anything he ever imagined, with t-shirts and hats flying off the shelves as if they were free.*

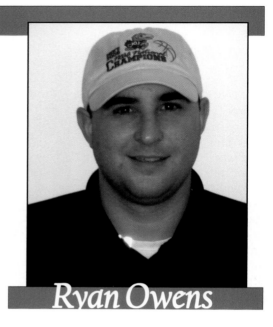

Ryan Owens

Crossing our fingers that we'd beat Davidson, we had some shirts pre-made for the Final Four. So as soon as the Davidson game was over, we opened the doors. The atmosphere down here was incredible. Mass Street was packed. We sold all of our shirts within 90 minutes. We didn't realize it at the time, but that was just a preview of things to come.

The buildup to the North Carolina game was amazing. We had a crazy – but phenomenal – week. Everyone was so anxious to play North Carolina so we could beat Roy Williams, but there were obviously even bigger things at stake. It was probably the most enjoyable week I've had since I've worked here, because a lot of fans walked through that door, and all of them were excited.

We didn't think anything would be able to top the reaction after the Davidson game. But after the Carolina game, the fans went nuts. We figured we should be open that night for retail purposes, because you only have one day of sales in between the national championship game and the semifinals.

We had people buying stuff right up until tipoff of the North Carolina game, and after we beat Memphis, people were flocking in here to buy things so they'd have memories of such an amazing night, an amazing event.

After that, it kept building for a couple of weeks. It was a great environment and fun to be a part of. You just don't know how often something like this is going to happen, but hopefully, it happens again soon.

*One of Larry Keating's main responsibilities as Kansas' Senior Associate Athletics Director is scheduling for men's and women's basketball. It's a pivotal role – especially considering how heavily a team's RPI plays into its NCAA Tournament seeding - and Keating is regarded as one of the best in the country. Keating's resume includes a 12-year stint as athletics director at Seton Hall. His son, Kerry, was an assistant coach for the UCLA squad that defeated Kansas in the 2007 Elite Eight. He's now the head coach at Santa Clara.*

## Larry Keating

We knew going into the season that this team had a chance to be special, so we wanted to make sure we played a schedule that would help us on Selection Sunday. When you're scheduling at Kansas, you're not as concerned about getting into the tournament – we know that's going to happen – as you are about where you're going to be seeded.

A few years ago this schedule would've looked strong, but we caught some bad breaks because some of the teams we played – teams that had been good in the past - struggled a little bit this year. The result was that we didn't have a very good RPI. Even though we won a lot of games, the most important factor when it comes to determining the RPI is strength of schedule.

Because of that, we literally had to fight it out until the very last game to wrap up that No. 1 seed. If we'd have lost any of those games in the final week of the regular season, or if we had dropped a game in the Big 12 Tournament, I don't think we would've been a one-seed. Even with only three losses, we were still the fourth No. 1.

Georgia Tech and Boston College were two teams we fully expected to be a lot better than they were. Loyola-Baltimore was picked in the preseason to win their league because they had a bunch of good transfers. They figured they'd win 20 games, but instead they ended up around .500.

Because of that, by the time conference play rolled around in January – and as good as I knew we were – we were struggling in the RPI. We started off 20-0, but then we lost a couple of games that I thought might kill our chances of being a No. 1 seed. I literally thought we might have to go 34-1 to get a No. 1. I don't think the RPI is a true reflection of how good you are. The same thing happened in football, when people ripped us for our non-conference schedule being so weak. But we knew we were good, and I think that was proven in the Orange Bowl. The best teams come through in the end.

## The Leek family

*David and Mud Leek graduated from Kansas in 1982 and have had football and basketball tickets ever since. They have three girls who are also big fans. Lanie, 14, has been ball girl for KU games the last three years. Anna, 17, will most likely be attending Kansas, where her 18-year-old sister, Ellie, is a freshman. David runs a dental insurance company and Mud is a preschool teacher. They love to attend home games and always try to make a few road trips, too.*

### DAVID

I was in San Antonio for the North Carolina game, and the thing I'll never forget was seeing Roy Williams on Friday - the night before the semifinals. I was with some friends at Rita's, which is the bar on the Riverwalk where hundreds of Kansas fans met each night to hang out and catch up with one another.

At one point I looked up and saw Roy walk past the bar – and he was all by himself. It happened about three times during the course of the night. He kept walking back and forth outside, and he wasn't with anyone. He would pause near the edge of the crowd and just look at everyone. It was like he was thinking, "Boy, it sure looks like they're having fun in there." A few people went up to him and asked for pictures, and he didn't seem to mind. One guy was even wearing a "Got Roy?" shirt. It was all kind of strange.

**Above:** Ellie Leek (white shirt) celebrates KU's victory over Memphis with friends in Lawrence.

Rita's was unbelievable. You saw people you hadn't seen in years and you saw people you had seen last week. It was the perfect place for everyone to congregate.

Rita's was overwhelmed by the business. They ran out of beer by about 9:30. Somehow they eventually found some extra somewhere, and they started selling beer for five bucks apiece. Everyone was mad, but they didn't have any choice but to buy it. The management there told me that the KU alumni totally overwhelmed them. They said they'd never seen anything like it. They couldn't keep up with it. They had no idea what they were getting into. The place was just jammed. It was the greatest time ever.

We saw Mark Turgeon there, and he was by himself, too. I talked to him for a long time. He was like, "This is why you go to Kansas. This is what it's all about." I couldn't believe the head coach of Texas A&M was there by himself, but he just wanted to be a part of it. He's a fan of Kansas who just wanted to hang out and support his university. You've gotta admire that.

Greg Gurley was with Scot Pollard, who somehow knows Jared from Subway. Jared was hanging out with them at a private party Sunday night. I had gone home by then, but my buddy was with them. They called me up and put Jared on the phone to talk to me. It was pretty funny.

I went to the game with some friends – David Duncan, Joanie Wilkerson and Brian Wilkerson, all from Lawrence - on Saturday night and sat in the front row, just to the side of the band. John Thompson was sitting on press row. He

**Above:** Ellie Leek (far left) attends Kansas' Welcome Home rally with friends on April 8th.

was wearing this beautiful suit, but then I looked down at his feet, and he was wearing Crocs.

Rodrick Stewart walked by on his way to the court, and he got a standing ovation. You could see how moved he was by the reception that he got. He got a little emotional and welled up a little bit. I was watching Mark Teahan, Conner's dad. Seeing the look on his face when his son got in the game was a neat thing. There was just so much pride in his eyes.

I had tickets to the championship game. It would've been a great setup. But I couldn't get a flight back until Wednesday, and I had to get back for work. Plus, I wanted to be with my family. My oldest daughter, Ellie, goes to Kansas, so she was in Lawrence experiencing it all with her friends. But my youngest daughter, Lanie, was with me.

When it got to the point where it seemed like we might lose, she started in with all these superstitious rituals – anything she could do to help change the mojo and the karma.

### LANIE LEEK, 14

I was mad when they got down so big with about two minutes left, so I walked out of the room. When I was in the hallway, I heard everyone cheering because KU made a big shot, so everyone yelled at me to stay there. I put my thumb in my mouth and leaned my head against the wall and spread my feet apart. I ended up staying in that position for the rest of the game. I'd hear everyone cheering, so I'd run into the TV room and celebrate with them for a few seconds. Then I'd run back into the hall and get back into my position for the next play. I was shaking and biting my thumb. By the end of the night my nail was down to nothing. I didn't get to see Mario's shot live but, trust me, I've watched it plenty of times since then.

**ANNA LEEK, 17**

I watched the game with a bunch of friends. Most people were really into it, but there were also some people who just wanted to be a part of the party and hang out. There were so many ups and downs during the championship game that you felt like you were on a roller coaster. Our family went to the Final Four in Atlanta in 2002 and we lost the first game to Maryland. We still had so much fun. I can't imagine how fun it must've been to be in San Antonio.

**ELLIE LEEK, 18**

I watched the game at The Bull in Lawrence with some close friends of mine. As soon as we won, we sprinted onto 14th Street and headed toward Mass. I looked back and there were hundreds and hundreds of people behind me running down the hill. Most of them were from The Hawk and The Wheel. I had to move to the side of the road because I didn't want to get trampled. Our designated meeting place was Fatso's. We got there and everyone was standing on the tables and loud music was playing. Outside, the cops were being really cool. They were just letting things happen as long as we were safe.

By the time we made it to Mass, people were dancing on tops of cars. I saw a bunch of people dancing on top of this brand new Lexus SUV. The hood was completely caved in. There were at least 10 people on top of it.

There were tons of little kids there. It wasn't just college kids. There were a lot of families, too. There were also a lot of random shoes strewn all over the street. I guess they came off people's feet as everyone was running down there.

As big of a fan as I am, I haven't gotten to know many of the basketball players, but a bunch of girls from my high school (Shawnee Mission East) know Conner Teahan really well because they grew up with him. When we were waiting to greet the team at Allen Fieldhouse after they beat Davidson, Conner was texting them from the bus and saying, "We're five minutes away."

We see the players out at the bars a lot and get pictures with them. They handle it really well. I think they know it's going to happen whenever they go out. They're nice and don't act annoyed by all the attention. I'm sure they're enjoying it. Lawrence is a fun place to be right now.

## Roger Morningstar

*Roger Morningstar never misses a Kansas game – partly because he's a fan, and partly because his son, Brady, is a member of the Jayhawks' roster. Roger was a standout on the 1974 Kansas squad that reached the Final Four. He now owns Planet Construction in Lawrence.*

I'm usually not a big "jump-up-and-down-guy" when I watch games. I don't pump fists and stuff like that. I normally just like to sit there and enjoy the game. Every now and then, I'll focus on the little individual battles between players and some of the other things going on within the game, but I'm not so much of a rah-rah type of person.

The Final Four was different, though. There were a couple of times during the tournament that my emotions got the better of me and I had much more of a reaction to certain plays.

We are close with Shawn Jackson, Darnell's mom, and we usually sit with her during games. Anytime Darnell pounded his chest three times after a play and looked toward our section, it was a pretty emotional time and feeling.

Going through what he has gone through - with all of the tough times during his career – it's pretty moving to see him recognize his family like that. When he did it in the North Carolina game especially, it was just such an incredible feeling. On that stage, in that big of a game, it just doesn't get better than that.

During that same game, I was sitting next to Cole Aldrich's parents. I'll always remember the play where Cole got an entry pass and loaded the ball in his hand like a grapefruit. He was going to throw it - and whatever was hanging on to him or that ball - through the basket with as much force as he could.

The dunk actually missed. But you know what? He still pounded his chest as if to say, "Hey, this is Kansas." I jumped to my feet and out of my chair on that one and, at the same time, his dad did the same thing. I hammered his dad with my forearm in celebration. I didn't mean to, but I actually hit him right when he was in the air. He ended up flying into Cole's mom, who was standing next to him, and Cole's mom fell into the aisle of the bleachers.

She looked at him and said, "Walt, what are you doing knocking me down?" Then Walt looked at me like I was crazy. It was a total accident, obviously.

The other thing that stands out is that, from the very beginning, this team's mental focus was strong. Starting in Omaha, we didn't see them in the lobby of the hotel at all. In fact, we never really saw them outside of their games. They had a job to do.

It was the same way throughout the whole tournament. In San Antonio, the Riverwalk was right there, but you just never, ever saw the players messing around or wasting time.

In the final seconds of the Memphis game, there were a lot of parents, fans, and former players out of their seats. There were guys who played in the 70's and guys who played back in '52. It was just an incredible thing. Everybody was hugging and chest bumping and high-fiving. People were just overwhelmed with emotion.

**Kevin Pritchard**

*Kevin Pritchard had 13 points and four assists in Kansas' 83-79 victory over Oklahoma in the championship game of the 1988 NCAA Tournament. He played in the NBA from 1990-1996 and is now the general manager of the Portland Trailblazers.*

When Bill first took the Kansas job, I told him, "You'll win a championship here. There's no doubt about it." We were sitting at dinner, and I remember him laughing a little bit. He said, "Yeah, I think you're probably right."

The thing is that, now, I don't think it's just going to be one. I think it's going to be many. He's got everything that it takes to be successful. He can recruit. He can coach. He's got a great school behind him with a great athletic director. It's a program that's long for success now.

No matter what Bill does, though, he'll probably have a tough time assembling a team as good as this one. They truly were a "team." They were so fun to watch because they played unselfish and they played hard and they defended on every possession. I saw that early on and felt they'd have a great chance of winning it all. There are at least eight guys on that team that will have a shot to play at the NBA level.

A lot of people have asked me to compare this team to the one I played for in 1988 – the one that won the championship. I really don't think there are many similarities at all. The 1988 team was completely different. We really struggled at times. We kind of put on that glass slipper, in terms of being the underdog. This 2008 team had so much more talent. They had a good chance at the title from the get-go, from the beginning of the year. Anyone could see that.

I tried to follow them as much as I could. I did see them live a couple of times this year, because I wanted to watch them in person. I try to make it to at least a few Kansas games every season. Along with giving me the opportunity to scout, it's a chance to come back home.

Twenty years after winning the title, it still feels great to walk into Allen Fieldhouse. With each passing year, these guys will learn to appreciate it more and more. The last time I was at The Fieldhouse, Kansas was playing Oklahoma, which was somewhat nostalgic for me because that's who we beat in the championship. It was a great feeling. It's a special place. People want to get caught up in the building and the floor and the rims. But it's the people that make it special.

The team that just won this title ... they'll always be remembered in Lawrence. They don't realize it now, but it's something that will follow them for the rest of their lives. Every year they'll look back at the tournament and be amazed - yet somewhat humbled - at what they were able to accomplish. They'll realize they were lucky to be part of a team that made it to the pinnacle of their sport.

Michael Pulsinelli

*Michael Pulsinelli, though born in Manhattan (the real one on the East Coast), has been slowly but surely sucked into Jayhawk Nation since he moved to Kansas and married Molly Imber (KU MD '05), daughter of Mickey Imber, KU Education Professor. Michael currently teaches English at Shawnee Mission East High School and hopes someday to earn a graduate degree from Kansas. He is proud to say that he was there with his wife on Massachusetts Street to celebrate the North Carolina and Memphis wins. In the college basketball offseason he still gets heckled for backing the New York Yankees.*

I have to start with a confession: I have only been a Jayhawk fan for seven years. It breaks my heart to say it, but I did not care when Danny and the Miracles cut down the nets. I was a nine-year-old kid in New York getting ready for Don Mattingly and company to start the new season. College basketball for me was limited to a fleeting thought about St. John's from time to time. Unlike some of my friends, I can't name all of the KU starters throughout the 80s and 90s, and I can't tell you what it was like to have Ted Owens and Larry Brown around. But I am a convert, and I'm sold for life. Though I realized it for sure when Mario's shot defied all odds and went in, my red and blue romance has been slowly developing since I moved here in 2001. I've been to Yankee Stadium, Fenway, and Wrigley. Allen Fieldhouse can tangle with any of those giants. I love the chants, I love the band, I love calling the players by their first names, and I love Lawrence. I know I'm just an adopted son in Jayhawk Nation, but I feel like part of the family. And it's not just because they won (although it certainly helps).

That Monday night, I drove into Lawrence with my wife Molly and we watched the game at my in-laws' house. I remember that I had been feeling vaguely sick to my stomach all day. I told myself that beating North Carolina was good enough, but I didn't really believe it. I called my parents in Memphis before the game and gallantly (but hollowly) wished them luck. I'm not a calm sports viewer, but I was good through the first half, mostly because it was an absolutely incredible 20 minutes of basketball on both ends of the floor. In the second half, when Memphis pulled ahead by two possessions, I attempted to go for my characteristic "stress-release walk," but I had to come back inside because of the rain and lightning in the area. I thought it was a bad sign. I survived the crucial Memphis pull-ahead, and I was preparing for the worst. But then it all happened and - long story short - Kansas 75, Memphis 68.

After the sheer shock wore off, I went outside. I know Lawrence is not a big town, but it ain't small either. I realized that as I listened to a collective, low roar throughout the whole town. Not an isolated few screams, and not a few honking horns — a constant rumble coming from the whole city.

It took us about 40 minutes to walk downtown, but it was one of the best walks of my life. Grand Canyon? Fine, I suppose. The beaches of St. John? Pretty, I guess. Westdale Road to Massachusetts Street? Pure heaven. Then the car horns really got started. I must have slapped 300 hands on the way, and though I have sort of a weird germ thing, I couldn't have cared less that night.

When we arrived, I knew it would be crazy, but as it had when I first saw it years ago, Lawrence exceeded my expectations. Mind you, we had been there just two nights earlier after the North Carolina game. I figured no party could surpass the one after defeating Roy Williams, but I was dead wrong. I saw eight-year-olds, 80-year-olds, and everyone in between - all with shock, joy, and wild abandon on their faces. I've never been to Mardi Gras, and I'm sure it's a great scene, but the thing is, Mardi Gras is going to happen every year. A national championship in a small college town is something entirely different, because nobody takes it for granted. The band arrived to play a few numbers, and the thousands on the street joined in. I teach high school, and it was pretty surreal to run into a former student and hug him spontaneously. I'm sure it was weirder for him, thinking back. There were some shady and scary moments too. The booze was flowing and some nut had climbed about a hundred feet up the bank flagpole, but he made it down without incident. By and large, though, the craziness stayed positive. I remember thinking to myself that the rain had even stopped, as if it were moving aside for the night-long party.

After the long walk back, I stayed up until dawn watching the game again (God bless DVR) with my father-in-law and brother-in-law, and we all grabbed a couple of hours of sleep. For once in my life, I had thought ahead and taken a personal day from school on Tuesday, so all was well. I must truly be a Jayhawk fan for life, because it didn't really bother me the next day as I sat through freezing drizzle and watched my beloved Yankees lose to the Royals. I still felt like I was in paradise.

PS- The parade was pretty incredible, too. That's me, the Jayhawks' adopted son, on the front page of the Lawrence Journal-World about to congratulate Darrell Arthur!

*Former Kansas star Wayne Simien earned first team All-American honors after leading Kansas to the Big 12 championship in 2005. Even though his career ended with a disappointing loss to Bucknell in the NCAA Tournament, Simien still averaged 20.3 points and 11 rebounds during a monstrous senior year that ended with him being selected by Miami with the 30th overall pick in the NBA Draft. Simien was waived by the Minnesota Timberwolves prior to the 2007-08 season. He plans to return to the league in 2008-09. Simien and his wife, Katie, have a daughter (Selah) and are expecting a second child.*

The other day one of the seniors from the championship team came up to me and said, "Hey, I hope you know that you played a part in this championship. You guys made us better. Going up against you in practice and learning from you when we were freshmen helped get us to where we are today."

I can't tell you how good it made me feel for those guys – amid all of this hype and all of these celebrations – to say something like that about me and Aaron and Mike and Keith. It's great to hear we helped them in some capacity. Back when I was younger, Nick Collison and Drew Gooden played the same role for me.

Knowing these guys personally – especially the seniors - made the whole season so enjoyable to watch. It's amazing how far they've come. I remember the days when Russ was just a young kid from New York, homesick and not really knowing what was going on. Darnell persevered through all of his off-court problems, and Sasha ... man, what a player he became. Jeremy Case stuck it out for five years. All those other guys left and he chose to stay. It's great to see that his decision paid off for him in the end.

This was a complete team from top to bottom. They had the senior leadership, great bench play and a good staff with Coach Self and all of his assistants. It all just came together.

## BACK ON TOP

What these guys did symbolizes a new era in Kansas basketball. Coach Self has a legacy here now, and we've solidified ourselves, once again, as one of the top programs in college basketball history. Not that it should've been questioned before. The school and the city and the fans would've loved this program just the same whether they had won or lost against Memphis, but the fact that we came home with the title has given Lawrence a whole new energy.

## IT'S THEIR TIME

A lot of people have asked me how I think some of our great teams with Nick and Drew and Kirk and Aaron and Keith would match up with this one. But I don't think about that at all. Because you know what? I had my time here. The guys that played before me had their time here, too. We had some incredible teams that made some great runs and hung plenty of banners in the rafters. But it's this year's team that won the championship. They're the ones that deserve all the glory. By no means do you look back and say, "What if this?" or "What if that?" This team deserves all the praise it can get. Part of me feels as if I were out there on the court with them.

*Bud Stallworth still holds the KU record for most points in a conference game, as his 50-point outburst in 1972 propelled the Jayhawks to a victory over Missouri. After playing in the NBA for five seasons, the Kansas Hall of Famer returned to his alma mater, where he serves as business manager for KU's design and construction management department. Stallworth also co-hosts "Rock Chalk Sports Talk" weekdays from 3:30-6 on 1320 AM in Lawrence.*

**Bud Stallworth**

Being a member of the media has its advantages. I enjoy having a chance to be on the radio during the week so I can take part in the analysis of a game, and it's great to be in a position where I can be around the team and the players to get some insight. But when a game is going on, I'm too emotional to be sitting on press row. That's why I'm not a full-time member of the press. When I'm at a game, I want to be a fan.

That being said, I loved everything about our team. I've spent some time around them. A lot of times I'll see them at the barbershop or as they're leaving the practice floor. I just try to talk to them about how important it is to keep their grades up, because everybody's not going to be an NBA player. If they have questions, they know I've got an office on campus. I've got an open-door policy. I told Coach Self that if he wants me to visit with some of his guys and give them some insight, I'd be more than happy to.

One player I've really become a fan of is Sherron Collins. He's got such focus and such drive. He's one of those guys that can really take over a game – and I'm not just talking about scoring. I'm talking about the emotional part of the game. That's one of the main things he brings to the table. I thought him being hurt for so much of the season could've really hurt us as a team. But his mindset is so tough that, even when he's not 100 percent, he kind of wills himself to play as well as he can.

I went to the Final Four, and it seemed like a University of Kansas Centers Convention. There were so many guys there - in one area - that played center for the Jayhawks at one time or another. And they were all from a different era, so it was pretty impressive to have that many guys down there. Greg Ostertag was there. Scot Pollard was there. You had Walt Wesley and Greg Dreiling and David Johanning. Lots of tall guys jumping up and down and getting excited during one of the best games any of us had ever seen. When Chalmers hit that shot ... if you could've seen the reaction in the stands you'd have thought someone just won the lottery.

*Kansas junior Abbey Stockstill recently completed her third season as a member of the Jayhawks' Cheer Squad. An Exercise Science major, Abbey was a two-time state champion in the pole vault at McPherson (Kan.) High School. Her career aspirations include personal training and nutrition studies.*

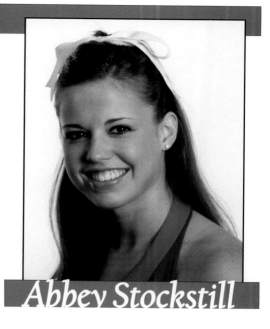

Abbey Stockstill

Obviously, the best part of being a cheerleader is getting a free ticket to every game. There's nothing like being right there on the baseline watching all of the action up close. I'll never forget being able to run onto the court after Kansas won it all and take part in the celebration.

As much fun as things were at the Final Four, it was also a lot of work. For the most part, the cheerleaders were busy the entire time. When we weren't cheering at games, we were either on the Riverwalk talking to people or doing pep rallies – and there were a ton of pep rallies. We did some where all four schools were involved, and there were plenty of KU-oriented pep rallies, as well – probably five or six before each game, so that kept us busy. One of our biggest responsibilities was just going around and taking pictures with kids and fans. We got to meet a lot of really nice people and see a lot of friendly faces.

One time, I was with my parents and a guy pushed them out of the way just so he could take a picture with me. My parents weren't too happy about that but, for the most part, everyone was as nice as they could be.

I know there are some people that don't think cheerleading is a sport, but we work hard to keep the crowd positive and yelling throughout the whole game. And just like the players, there are times when we get nervous, too. We're right down there where all the action is, so there are a lot of people watching to make sure we do the right things and hold up signs at the right times. We have coaches that are constantly saying, "Do this," or "Do that." So it's not like it's just a free-for-all. There's a lot we have to know.

Even though there's a lot to remember, you're so close to the players that it's impossible not to get into the game. Our mind is on cheering, but we still watch what's going on and get excited just like all of the fans.

My parents do a pretty good job of taping the games. When I went home after the Final Four, my dad turned on the game. He knew every moment when I

was going to be on the screen. We must've watched it more than 10 times, just because they love it.

As far as the players go ... I don't really know them personally. We don't see them that much on the road, and when we do, we're not allowed to go up and talk to them. We can talk to them on campus but, during the NCAA Tournament, they're under enough pressure. The last thing our coaches want is for us to go up and bother them.

We've never been told not to date the players. I know it's frowned upon. None of the cheerleaders on our squad right now are dating any of the players. It's probably happened in the past. We can hang out with them, but I'm sure if the administration ever found out one of us was dating one of them, they probably wouldn't be very happy.

*Marty Watson*

*There aren't many Lawrence residents who are as close to the Jayhawks as Marty Watson. For three years now, Kansas basketball and football players have stopped by Watson's barber shop on Ninth and Mississippi to shoot the bull while getting a quick trim. As talented as Watson and partner Tim Nelson are with the shears, the Jayhawks like them because they're good friends – not just good barbers.*

I always look forward to the days when the basketball players stop by to get their hair cut. They're just cool kids. They come in and laugh and joke like any normal 18 or 19-year-old would.

The best thing about them is that they're humble. They don't get any special treatment here. They wait in line just like anyone else, although sometimes I have to stay open late for them because of their practice schedules or travel schedules during the season. I'll stay open until 8:30 or 9. They'll come in and we'll order pizza, and some of them end up falling asleep. That was especially the case when I used to have a couch in here. There was always a fight for that. A lot of them are jokesters – especially Mario. They'll put shaving cream on one another when they're sleeping, or maybe some powder.

### HI, MY NAME IS ...

All of the players have nicknames. I try to think of something fun to call each and every one of them. Cole Aldrich's nickname is "Fly-Swatter." Brandon Rush's nickname is "Bart Simpson." I call Mario "Fabulous." Russell Robinson is "The Blimp" because, in the beginning of the season, he caught one off the rim and dunked it. He thought he had hops after that so we called him "The Blimp." Sherron Collins is "Eddie Winslow" from the TV show Family Matters.

Sasha Kaun is "Screech" from Saved by the Bell. Coach Chalmers, Mario's dad ... we call him "Colin Powell." Darrell Arthur is "Bert" from Bert and Ernie on Sesame Street because his eyebrows are so thick and he doesn't want to trim them.

### STAYIN' IN STYLE

The haircut trends changed a little this year. Last year the players were more into designs. Julian and Sherron did all this crazy stuff. Now, they mainly try to stay clean-cut - all even, with a taper. Darrell Arthur usually got a shadow fade. Darnell would grow out his beard for one game and then cut it off before the next. That was the extent of it. We tried to keep them looking clean and professional. We don't want them looking like they're involved in a bunch of riff-raff. The tattoos are enough (laughing). We want them looking at least halfway decent.

I don't cut Teahan's hair because he's letting it grow out. But even he still comes in here and hangs out. They do everything as a team. Whether they're walk-ons or all-stars ... there's no division. A few years ago everyone had different attitudes and different styles. It's not like that anymore.

### HOME AWAY FROM HOME

Even when they're not getting their haircut, the kids come around and kick it. We throw barbeques before the football games and the basketball players come down for that. Sometimes we sit out here and play cards. I'm the therapy guy. If they want to get away from campus they come over to my place. I've got a big basement where they can play video games or watch basketball games without being disturbed.

I'm closest with Mario and Darnell. They come by a lot – especially Darnell, when he was going through some stuff. We hang out together and eat together and go to church.

With Mario ... everyone wants to talk about his shot against Memphis. He jokes about it sometimes. He gets a little cocky and says, "Man, when I let it go I knew it was going in. It felt great." But we all know he was praying just like everyone else. It hasn't changed him, though. He's still the same guy. He handles success well. All of them do.

### FUN WITH FANS

Sometimes people come into shop and voice their opinions about basketball to them - people who wouldn't normally have the chance to talk to them. They pose for pictures and sign autographs. They'll sign anything. It doesn't matter.

I know they're appreciative of all their fans. They didn't want to let them down in San Antonio. They actually said they didn't get as nervous as you may think. They said everyone was in bed by 9 – kind of like camp. They didn't go out and celebrate after the first game, but once they came home with that title, they started celebrating and haven't stopped since.

Richard Roby

*Former Colorado star Richard Roby was always one of the Jayhawks toughest opponents. Although his team often struggled, Roby ended his career in March of 2008 as the leading scorer in school history with 2,001 points. That mark ranks fourth on the Big 12's all-time list.*

I was definitely rooting for Kansas the night they played Memphis. I had them winning it all in the bracket I filled out for fun. They had more chemistry and firepower than any team in the country. I'm not surprised they won.

I've gotten to know a couple of those guys. There are good people on that team. Me and B-Rush have been going at it for a while. We competed hard against each other. He's a good defender, long and athletic. He can really shoot the ball, especially when he sets up and has good balance before he takes his shot.

More than any opponent, I always got up to play Kansas. You knew there was going to be national attention on the game. They're always among the top five teams in the country. Whenever you're in the spotlight like that you can't help but be a little more juiced.

The best game of my career was probably the time I scored 30 points at Allen Fieldhouse. It was 2007 and I was a junior. I was 10-of-15 from the field and had seven rebounds. Anytime you can do something like that in one of the toughest environments in the country, you can't help but be proud.

They were a good team then and an even better team during their championship season. It's impossible not to respect a team like that. They're all so unselfish. They play together and always make the extra pass. There were no egos on that team. No one cared about being a star. More than anything, I think that made the biggest difference when it mattered most.

**Danni Boatwright**

*Danni Boatwright is an avid Kansas fan who was awarded $1 million for winning the hit TV show "Survivor" in 2005. She attended Kansas' NCAA championship game victory over Memphis with her husband, Denver Broncos offensive lineman Casey Wiegmann.*

When I was at the game and we were down by nine with 2 minutes left, I kept saying, "I believe, I believe." I was like, "I know we're going to win this. We can't make it to the championship game and lose again." Then it all came down to Mario's big shot. He and his parents go to our church - Lenexa Christian Center in Kansas City. So I knew he'd be blessed when the ball ended up in his hands at that key moment. When he hit that three-pointer I fell to the floor and started bawling. It was ridiculous. I knew once he hit it that we'd win in overtime, because we had all the momentum. We had waited 20 years for that. It was the biggest sigh of relief.

For me it felt even better than winning "Survivor."

I saw Mario Chalmers' parents at church a week or two later. I had to leave early, which was unfortunate, because I wanted to go talk to them and thank them for meeting and getting married and having Mario.

I couldn't even go out on the Riverwalk after the game. I wouldn't have been able to handle it. I had to go straight back to the hotel. I was just overwhelmed. Casey was like, "I've never seen anyone act like this in my life." I couldn't stop crying. I called home and my brothers were on Mass Street. It was so loud. I could hardly hear them. They were saying, "There are people climbing in the trees. There are people running around half-naked." I wanted to fly back right then and celebrate with everyone.

I told people before the year that there was something special about this team. You could see that they were hungry. Russell Robinson got criticized a little bit near the end of the conference season when he said the team was less worried about the conference race and more focused on the NCAA Tournament. I could absolutely understand that, though. These guys had the championship on their mind since November.

Everyone always asks me to name my favorite player on the team, and that's tough. It was hard for me to find a favorite player because they were such an

unselfish team. I guess if I had to pick one it would be Sherron. I like the fact that he's so gutsy. He's not afraid to take the ball to the basket and make something happen. Of course, I could've killed him for going in for that lay-up with two guys on him near the end. I love his confidence, though. He's a shorter guy but he plays like a big man.

I thought it was funny that all the analysts were saying that Kansas wasn't going to win because we didn't have a true go-to guy. Don't we always preach to everyone how important teamwork is, and how "teams" win championships? Those opinions never made sense to me.

A few weeks after the tournament I went to the Bon Jovi concert. At the end, while they were performing their last song, they were showing parts of Kansas City on the big screen and saying "Thanks for coming out, Kansas City!" They had a video clip of the Chiefs and then the Royals and then the Brigade. Then they showed the Jayhawks. The crowd just erupted. It was louder than any part of the concert. Bon Jovi started laughing and everyone just went nuts. They didn't show the Kansas State Wildcats. They didn't show the Missouri Tigers. Only the Jayhawks.

I've already bought Bo, our little baby, some new Kansas gear. I'm a little upset at Coach Self, though. The University of Iowa, where Casey played football, has already sent Bo a recruiting letter. But coach Self hasn't sent us anything about basketball. Casey is big, white and square and I don't jump too well. But you never know.

*Piotr Zygmunt*

*There aren't many Kansas fans as passionate as Piotr Zygmunt. Need proof? Just read how he reacted to the Jayhawks' victory over Memphis in the NCAA championship. Piotr (pronounced "Peter") has also become a fixture on Kansas' pre-game radio show. He almost always wins a free pizza by phoning in the correct answer to the nightly trivia question. Piotr lives in Olathe with his wife, Jenny, and dog, Toby.*

I watched the game against Memphis at Allen Fieldhouse. When Mario made his big shot, I was probably the only person in the whole arena that didn't go crazy. If someone would've taken a picture from the rafters of all the fans, I'd have been easy to spot because I was sitting down. I had no reaction whatsoever – mainly because I was in complete awe. It was like I was in a trance or something. It didn't seem real. My friends, Big Jon and Mike, were saying, "What's wrong with you? This is the national championship game and you're just sitting there." But I didn't have any expression on my face. I was so overwhelmed and overcome by the moment that I didn't know how to act.

Once the game was over, I came to my senses and started crying. My friends actually shot video of the tears rolling down my face. That's a little embarrassing to admit, but it shows you how big of a fan I am.

I wanted to do everything I could to soak up the moment. I went to mid-court and bent down and kissed the Jayhawk. Then I sprawled out – right there on the floor – and looked up into the rafters. I started thinking about how good the 2008 national championship banner was going to look in Allen Fieldhouse, and I imagined Mario's jersey hanging up there, too.

### TOLD YOU SO

I remember telling people two years ago – after we lost to Missouri in Columbia – that Mario would have his jersey retired someday. They were like, "You've got to be kidding me, right?" But I knew that day that he'd be special.

Mario has been my favorite player from the start. My wife, Jenny, bought me his blue No. 15 jersey for Christmas. It's a limited edition that says 12 Final Fours, four national championships and 50 conference championships. I also have a picture of Mario that I got signed. It's of him dribbling a basketball, and in

the background it says, "Mario Chalmers: Leading Kansas to the National Championship." It's crazy how all the cards lined up, because he ended up doing exactly what that picture said.

### NO TIME FOR REST

After the game, we went out to the parking lot next to Robinson gym, which is where my car was parked. Most everyone was down on Mass Street by then, and you could hear all of the screaming fans and horns. I looked up in the sky and saw fireworks. The noises overtook the entire town. We took it all in for a few moments and then headed to Mass Street ourselves.

I got home around 4 a.m. and set my alarm for 6:45. After I woke up I drank a few cups of coffee and got into the car with my shih tzu, Toby, and headed back for Lawrence. I wanted to make sure I got as many newspapers as possible. I stopped in DeSoto. No papers. I got to Eudora and stopped. No papers. All the paper bins in Lawrence were empty, too. I called the *Lawrence Journal-World* and, luckily, they said they had about 1,000 newspapers left, so I booked it over to their office and bought 15 copies. It was weird driving down Mass Street just hours after the big celebration. It was empty except for the workers cleaning up the roads. It was rainy outside and kind of messy, which I'm sure made their job tougher.

Before I headed back home, I thought, "Man, I really need to get some copies of the *Kansan*, too." So I drove onto campus and stopped at Stauffer-Flint. I was in hog heaven, because there was a freakin' huge stack of papers. I grabbed about 25 copies. I'm glad I have something to remember this season by.

### MR. MULTI-MEDIA

I just knew that this year was going to be special, which is why I recorded every single game. I just had that feeling. My wife asked me why I was recording games vs. schools like Eastern Washington and Yale. I didn't want to tell her the real reason because I didn't want to jinx the season. I'm so glad I ended up doing it, though, because now I have something I'll cherish forever. I made these sweet DVD cases with awesome covers that highlight the NCAA Tournament journey. They look phenomenal. I've watched the National Championship game four or five times already. Each time, I get emotional. My hands get clammy and I still get nervous as hell at the end.

The other memorable thing is that, after Kansas won the Big 12 title, I made a highlight video. I posted it on all the message boards and everyone loved it. So, naturally, after we won the national championship, I got all of these requests to do another one. I was like, "All right, I'll do it." So I worked until the wee hours of the morning – until 3 or 4 a.m. – putting this video together with music and audio footage from both the Jayhawk radio network and TV announcers. It ended up being a 19-minute video. I posted it on the message boards again, and I received some of the nicest compliments that you'll ever hear. People have said that watching it makes them cry. I've even been offered a job working in the video industry. Right now it's just a hobby that I enjoy, because it gives me a chance to relive this special season all over again.

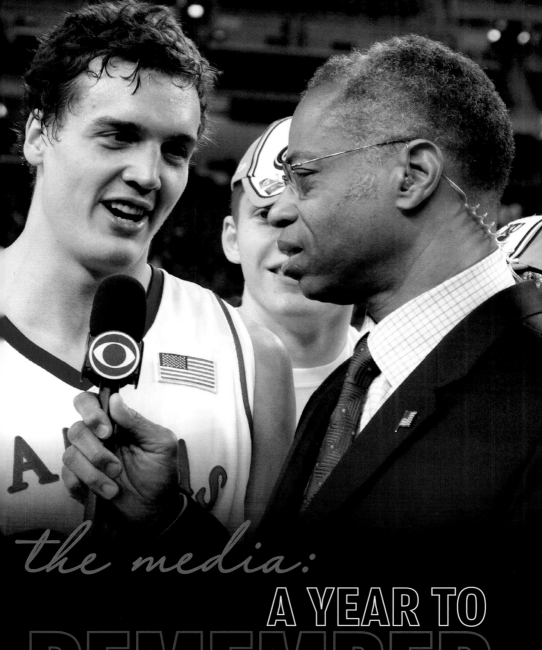

the media:
# A YEAR TO
# REMEMBER

Dick Vitale

*ESPN color commentator Dick Vitale is one of the most recognizable names in all of college hoops. He'll be inducted into the National Basketball Hall of Fame in the fall of 2008 - just a few months before he begins his 30th season behind the mic.*

I couldn't help but smile as I watched Bill Self cutting down the nets in San Antonio. Everyone likes to see class guys win, and Bill Self is pure class. Here's an example: A day or two after they won the national title, I got a phone call from Bill. He wanted to congratulate me on getting into the National Basketball Hall of Fame. He went on and on about how deserving I was. This was right at a time when his team was getting ready for a big celebration, a big party. But he said he just had to call to tell me these things. That showed me what kind of guy he is.

Another example: We had a big fundraising event for cancer research on May 16 in Sarasota, Florida. Bill came down and took part in it. He didn't allow winning the national championship to give him a big head. He could've said, "I've got to back out of it. I've got all these other things going on after winning a national championship." Instead he stood by his commitment. That meant a lot to me.

**SELF VALIDATION**

No one can question now whether Bill can coach - not that they ever should have. The fact that he'd taken four teams to the Elite Eight speaks volumes of his ability. People would say, "Yeah, but he's never been to the Final Four." Well, let me tell you something: It's not easy. With single elimination, one bad night and you're done. But to get to where he did with Tulsa and Illinois and twice with Kansas shows you the guy is a well-equipped leader.

He obviously did a phenomenal job of convincing his players that they have to share the basketball and play together as a defensive unit. Most of all, he helped them develop the tenacity that displayed itself when they came back from nine points down against Memphis with two minutes left. It also helps when you have the strongest set of guards in the country - especially in terms of depth.

### BRAGGIN' ABOUT BRANDON

More than any player on that team, I really enjoyed watching Brandon Rush. I like him because of the multitude of things he can do. He can beat you with the three-point shot. He can beat you going to the rim or defensively with a steal and a jam to give you momentum. His versatility separates him from a lot of collegians.

I know some people thought midway through the year that he wasn't being aggressive enough, but I didn't see it that way. He played within the confines of the team concept. He bought into the team concept and sacrificed his numbers so his team could win. That says a lot about that kid and what's really, truly important to him. Also, you can't forget that he played part of the season with a very serious knee problem. The fact that he was able to come back from that as quickly as he did is a tribute to him and the hard work he put in during the rehab process. I wouldn't at all be surprised if he had a long, successful career in the NBA.

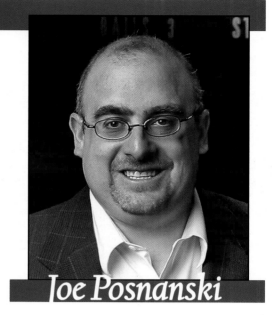

*Joe Posnanski - twice named the best sports columnist in America by the Associated Press Sports Editors - has worked for The Kansas City Star since 1996. Joe has covered Olympics, Super Bowls, World Series, Final Fours and every major golf championship. His book, "The Soul of Baseball, A Road Trip Through Buck O'Neil's America," was published in the spring of 2007. Joe and his wife, Margo, have two daughters: Elizabeth and Katherine.*

The moment that will always stick with me from this remarkable Kansas run happened in Detroit, just after Kansas edged Davidson to go to the Final Four. The last strands of confetti were still falling, and coach Bill Self was being dragged from interview to interview while fans yelled, "Way to go, Coach!" Self looked absolutely dazed.

"We got lucky," he told one coach, John Thompson, on his radio show, then he went across to the Kansas radio broadcast and said, "We got lucky," then he saw some fans from Lawrence that he knew, and he mouthed, "We got lucky."

They had gotten lucky, of course. The Jayhawks had not looked like themselves all game. They played scared, and anyone could understand. Davidson was this tournament's charmed team, led by the nation's charmed player, Stephen Curry. It was like shooting baskets against karma. As it turned out, the Wildcats had a final shot to win the game. A whole nation of college basketball fans wished that ball in the basket. It missed anyway.

There was another story here, something more than the clock striking midnight on Davidson. Self is one of America's best college basketball coaches. The coaching resume is pretty remarkable - he started at Oral Roberts, when that program was lost, and coached them up into a 20-victory team. He went to Tulsa and took that team to the Elite Eight. He went to Illinois and guided them to a Big 10 title and a No. 1 seed his first year. He went to Kansas, took Roy Williams' players on one more tournament run, then reshaped and refocused the program. It's hard to imagine any coach doing more.

The one thing Self had not done, though, was take a team to the Final Four. He was hard on himself about it, both in public and in private. He wondered what the heck he was doing wrong. Self coaches confidence more than he coaches the pick and roll; he gets in players' faces and shouts, "Nobody can block you out!

Nobody can pick you! Nobody can keep you from getting to the basket! You are unstoppable!" This is his basketball style; to get his players to believe in their own invincibility. His teams won a lot of games that way. But they had been stopped at the Elite Eight four times, and Self's own confidence waned.

"You just have to get lucky," he told me more than once. That was his final determination. The NCAA Tournament is a crapshoot. The games turn on crazy shots, missed free throws, out-of-position referees. Self wondered when he would get lucky.

Then he got lucky. The final shot missed. The Jayhawks were going to the Final Four. And Bill Self was up on the ladder, cutting down the last strands of net while the Kansas band still played and fans cheered, and Self still had that great look on his face, that "I cannot believe how lucky we are" look. I told people right then that Kansas might just win this national title.

The final two games were startling in their own ways. The Jayhawks ran over Roy Williams' North Carolina Tar Heels and then withstood the inevitable comeback. And finally, they came back in the final seconds against Memphis. The Tigers missed those free throws in those final seconds, of course. By then, though, it was clear that something was different about this year. Bill Self had turned lucky.

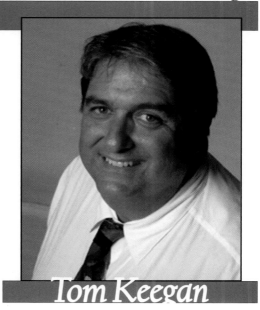

*Tom Keegan is the sports editor of the Lawrence-Journal World. Prior to his hiring in 2005, Keegan covered Major League Baseball for publications such as The New York Post, The Baltimore Sun and The Orange County Register. In 2005, he was named "Communicator of the Year" by the alumni association at Marquette University, his alma mater.*

Anonymity sometimes empowers cowards. Nowhere is this more evident than on sports-focused message boards, the bathroom walls of the Internet.

It hurts to get slammed on them, especially when there is no way to talk back, face-to-face, to a screen name. You know what hurts even worse, though? To see a college kid belittled on them, a likable student-athlete who gives his best effort every day in basketball practice, then watches from the bench during games.

Since he brought his soft touch to the University of Kansas from McAlester, Okla., Jeremy Case drew rave reviews from teammates for his long-range shooting ability. Yet, for the sin of not being as quick or as strong as the guards who played in front of him, Case sometimes was treated on the message boards as if he were a rec center hack.

Watching Case shoot during warm-ups, you knew he had a big game in him. His shot was just too pure. In the nick of time, in his final game at Allen Fieldhouse, Case grabbed the spotlight by the neck, shined it on himself, and treated 16,300 basketball nuts to one helluva shooting exhibition.

Case buried a trio of threes in a two-minute flurry on a night the five Kansas seniors combined for 50 points. For me, the biggest thrill of the season came not when Mario Chalmers swished that three-pointer in San Antonio, but rather when Case made three of them in his Fieldhouse finale. He showed the skill everyone had heard so much about but seldom had seen, and in doing so showed just how talented a player has to be just to sit the bench at Kansas.

Afterward, a five-word sentence was all the Internet posters had left to say to Case: "Thanks for the memories, Jeremy."

Soren Petro

*Soren Petro hosts one of the highest-rated shows in Kansas City from 11-2 each weekday on Sports Radio 810 WHB. A Syracuse graduate, Petro made an on-air prediction before the season that the Jayhawks would win the 2008 NCAA championship.*

Kansas' 2008 national title couldn't have come at a more perfect time. Even though it wasn't true, there were actually Kansas State fans that believed their program was getting close to being on the same level as Kansas'. The Jayhawks had the two first round losses, they hadn't won a championship in 20 years and people were still walking around town with an egg to fry with Roy Williams.

By winning this championship, though, Kansas re-established its spot in the hierarchy of college basketball's elite.

Someone should take Kansas' season and turn it into a movie. The Jayhawks ended up being one of the more interesting stories in the history of college basketball. They were a tribute to the word "team."

Seriously, can anyone think of a more compelling script?

-They claim their fourth straight Big 12 title in the last game of the regular season.

-They win the conference tournament - in Kansas City, no less - in one of the best games of the season against a Texas team that beat them earlier.

-Self drops to his knees in relief after advancing to his first Final Four, where Kansas beats Roy and North Carolina in the semifinals.

-Mario Chalmers helps them win their first NCAA title in 20 years with the biggest shot in school history.

-More than 80,000 people show up a week later to watch the team parade through downtown Lawrence.

-And, oh yeah, Self gets a big-money offer to return to his alma mater to coach (sound familiar?), and he chooses to ... stay.

Some people were starting to think that Bill Self's time at Kansas was going to be just like Roy's time at Kansas. The team was always going to be very good, but it was never going to win it all. That was truly the mindset of a lot of people in Kansas Land and across the country, too. Even when they started 20-0, people were looking for ways to knock them. Who have they beaten? Who is their go-to guy? It was always something.One thing that really impressed me before the season was when ESPN's Doug Gottlieb - who played at Oklahoma State and knows the Big 12 as well as anyone - picked Kansas to win the national title on my radio show. Everyone in the country had them in the Top 5 or 6, but no one was really picking them to win it all. Well, I picked them. So I guess I'll go ahead and pat myself on the back. Then again, I also picked them the previous year. Hey, one-for-two still isn't bad.

The other thing that gets lost sometimes is that - with all the talk about Rush and Chalmers and Arthur - people sometimes forgot how special this class of seniors was. You just don't see that in college basketball anymore. Think about how some of those guys embraced their roles. You've got a guy like Rodrick Stewart, who was the 54th-ranked recruit in the country coming out of high school. He was only a five or 10-minute per game guy for Kansas. But he embraced that situation. Sasha Kaun, frankly, is a guy I think is going to play in the NBA. And if he doesn't, he's going to become a millionaire playing in Europe. He was a starter for two years and then got moved to the bench. Instead of pouting, he actually got better.

The fact that no one on this team averaged 14 points a game was a great statement about the players and their coaches. I'm blown away by what Bill Self did with these guys. I think this opens the floodgates for Kansas basketball to be re-established. I don't think they'll have to wait another 20 years for their next title. They could win four or five more in that span.

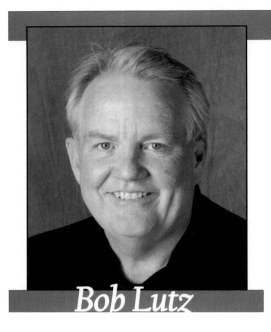

Bob Lutz

*Sports fans in the Midwest know that columns by The Wichita Eagle's Bob Lutz are a must-read. Lutz was 19 when he landed his job at The Eagle in 1974. He's been there ever since. Along with his newspaper gig, Lutz hosts Sports Daily - a radio show that airs each weekday from 9-11 a.m. on 1240 AM and 98.7 FM in Wichita.*

Impartiality is one of the most important components of journalism. Maybe the most important. Which, in some people's eyes, makes us less than human.

What the public doesn't need, though, is a bunch of journalists with agendas. That would throw the whole Earth off its axis and create problems bigger than the oil shortage and Paris Hilton combined. So, for my entire 33-year career at The Wichita Eagle, I have done my best to remain unbiased.

As a columnist, though, I'm able to walk that ledge with a little more leeway. It's OK to like people. And I like Bill Self.

I don't know Coach Self that well, except through our professional lives. I know this: I ask him a bunch of questions during his NCAA Tournament news conferences. And, without fail, he answers every one of them - even the ones that are less than astute - with thought, patience and candor. We in the business call Bill Self a quote machine, because he always has great and even colorful answers to our questions.

Bill Self comes across as a guy it would be fun to play croquet with, and that's the highest compliment I can give a coach. Come to think of it, I haven't played croquet in decades, but if I ever decide to play again, I'm going to call Bill Self and see if he'll come over.

He fits in like one of the guys. He doesn't have that air about him that says: I'm the head coach at Kansas and you're whatever you are and there's really nothing we should be talking about. I'm not saying most coaches come across that way, but there are some who do. And it's hard to work with them.

Self has never been hard to work with. I'm sure he hasn't appreciated everything I've written about him or about his team over the years. In fact, after the Jayhawks lost in last season's Elite Eight to UCLA, Self asked me point blank why I wrote what I did after the defeat. I told him and he accepted my answer and there was never anything else said about it.

It can be so tough to go into those long NCAA news conferences and listen to coaches and players who simply have no interest in being there. I'm not sure Self enjoys being there, either, but you would never know it from the answers he supplies.

I was happy for Self when the Jayhawks beat Davidson in the Midwest Regional Elite Eight game this year in Detroit. I watched him as the last shot by Davidson, a shot that would have won the game, missed. He was on his hands and knees and he just fell forward, catching himself with the palms of his hands. It was the first time Self had led a team to a Final Four after four near misses, and the celebration that followed was something to watch. Self's wife and two children looked so happy. And so did everybody else who surrounded the celebration. Including, even, the journalists who are supposed to be unbiased.

Most of the time, we are.

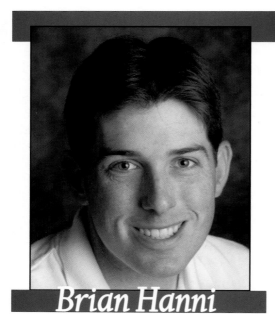

**Brian Hanni**

Brian Hanni has covered the Jayhawks for the last nine years for KLWN and the Jayhawk Radio Network. In 2002 he launched "Rock Chalk Sports Talk," a daily radio show that airs weekdays from 3:30-6 PM in Lawrence on 1320 AM. A 2002 Kansas graduate, Hanni has called several KU men's games on the Jayhawk Radio Network and serves as a full-time announcer for KU women's basketball and KU baseball. In addition to his broadcast work, he's written for "Jayhawk Illustrated" magazine since 2003.

My favorite memory of the Jayhawks' run through the tournament didn't take place on the court and didn't even involve a member of the championship team. Instead, it was a hug and a chat with a member of the KU basketball family who might have been wearing the biggest grin of anyone in the Kansas locker room right after the win over Memphis.

I've always had a strong rapport with Julian Wright - dating back to his high school days at Homewood-Flossmoor High in Illinois - so it didn't surprise me when, immediately following the title game, he brushed off my attempt at a handshake and offered a hug instead.

We've long had a mutual respect based on a shared faith. During his sophomore year at Kansas, Julian told me that he was just trying to use his platform "for God's cause." I remember being so wowed by his selflessness when he said that. It's so rare to hear things like that coming out of the mouth of a 19-year-old future millionaire.

Just as he did so many times at Kansas, Julian amazed me again on the night of the national championship.

After celebrating with his former teammates on the floor immediately following KU's 75-68 win over Memphis, he made his way onto the platform at mid-court to watch CBS' "One Shining Moment" with the rest of the guys. It was as if he'd never left.

Then, 30 minutes later in the locker room, as his former teammates basked in the glory of the first Kansas men's basketball national title in 20 years, Julian was right there with them, celebrating as if he had hit the big shot instead of Mario Chalmers. Honestly, he looked like a kid on Christmas morning that just got everything he'd hoped for and more. No one appeared to be soaking up the moment with as much sheer joy and jubilation as Julian.

"It's a great feeling coming back," he uttered, almost out of breath from all of the jumping around he'd been doing in celebration. "This was the only time in my schedule that I could come here and make it to a game. I wouldn't pass this up for anything in the world."

As it turns out, Wright had to really scramble to get a flight into San Antonio on the day of the game. Monday's title game was the only possible time he could get away in the midst of his busy schedule with the New Orleans Hornets. Then, in order to rejoin his team on time, Julian had to leave in the middle of the night. It was worth it, though, because of a love for his former teammates and the University of Kansas. Plus, he said he knew KU would win it all the moment it got past Davidson.

Following the game, Julian was elated for his teammates, especially the guys he came in with: Mario Chalmers and Brandon Rush. He said the title win was a culmination of a lot of success and several failures of the previous three seasons.

"Everything happens for a reason," Julian told me. "Looking back at the Bradley game and everything else that led up to this point ... it's just so amazing."

So was Julian's unselfishness. After all, that night, he could've easily been thinking about an opportunity missed. Yes, Julian is now a millionaire forward on one of the NBA's best young teams, but despite New Orleans' surprising success, his former team had just won a national championship. His old teammates would soon be fitted for title rings that they'd wear for the rest of their lives and one day pass on to their grandchildren. By leaving early, Julian was in line for none of that. But on that night, he didn't care one bit.

I asked him if any thoughts of disappointment, buyer's remorse or jealousy had crept into the back of his mind and made him wonder, "What if...?" He quickly shot that down.

"No, it would be really selfish of me to say that," Julian said. "You have to make the decision that you feel is best for you. All I wanted for this team was for it to do well, because once you're a part of KU, you're part of a family. I just wanted to come here and support them. I really knew they were going to do it."

Surely, somewhere deep inside, Julian wonders about what might have been. I can't imagine at least a small part of him didn't want to climb that ladder and cut down a piece of the net. It's only human nature to covet something so sweet, but in Julian's case, I really believe the overwhelming sentiment was one of great joy for the players he'd come to love, a coach he respected tremendously and a university and town that he misses greatly.

Julian's comment about the family atmosphere of KU basketball is nothing new. We've all heard it before - it's part of what makes Kansas basketball great. Julian's example of what it means to be a part of that family is admirable, though, because on that night, the proudest and seemingly happiest Jayhawk I spoke to was Julian. And for the second time in the four years I've known him, he wowed me in a way that had nothing to do with basketball.

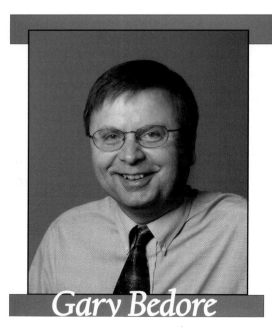

*Gary Bedore is regarded as one of the most knowledgeable sources in the country on Kansas athletics. He began working at the Lawrence Journal-World in 1983 and was promoted to the Kansas beat prior to Roy Williams' first season in 1988. A Las Vegas aficionado and an avid Chicago White Sox fan, Bedore was named Sportswriter of the Year in Kansas in 2008.*

I've been asked this question countless times by KU basketball fans who, more often than not, seem puzzled by my sincere, yet somewhat unsatisfying (to them), answer: "Who's your favorite Jayhawk of all time?"

"Ryan Robertson," I say without hesitation, drawing blank stares from folks expecting the names such as Danny Manning, Paul Pierce, Kirk Hinrich, Brandon Rush, Nick Collison, Drew Gooden, Scot Pollard, Jacque Vaughn and/or Wayne Simien - players I've covered the past two decades - to roll off my tongue.

Why Robertson, KU's eighth leading assist man of all time?

Because Robertson - who is tied for second with Collison in most games played as a Jayhawk (142, five fewer than Manning) - was the most polite, colorful, quotable, accessible Jayhawk I've ever been around. A guy who never even once hinted he'd rather be somewhere else than talking to the media - heck, he worked in KU's Media Relations Department his senior year - will forever lead my all-time favorite player list.

As far as the best player I've ever seen up close and personal in a Jayhawk uniform? That'd be Manning, the best big-man passer to play the college game. Manning has one KU record that will never be broken: most points in a career (2,951). Collison is second, but way, way back at 2,097.

The four other players on my personal all-KU first team (ability regardless of position) would be: Paul Pierce (just call him Mr. Smooth), Collison and Raef LaFrentz (one Iowan shot righty, one lefty, both were money) as well as the pride and joy of the state of Kansas, Wayne Simien.

Simien played for both Self and Roy Williams. My favorite player ability-wise of anybody coached solely by Self would be Mario Chalmers. His ability to steal the basketball from unsuspecting foes is unparalled. Of course, he hit the biggest shot in KU history, the most baskets I've ever witnessed -- the three that sent the title game against Memphis into overtime.

As far as if anybody on the current team is in a class of Robertson as far as interviews go ... I'd say Sasha Kaun is about the friendliest guy you could ever meet. He never used the fact that English is his second language as a crutch and always was pleasant in an interview setting. Kaun may not steal headlines, but he's a darn good guy to talk to. I can honestly say that about most of the guys on the championship team.

*Al Wallace*

*Since joining the Fox 4 sports staff in 1985, Al Wallace has blossomed into one of the most successful and recognizable names on the Kansas City sports scene. In 1998, he was voted one of the "Most Influential African-Americans" in the area. Wallace loves covering the Chiefs and thinks the Royals are fun, too. But he's long said there is no assignment better than following the Jayhawks during the NCAA Tournament.*

We were covering the team in Michigan during the second weekend of the tournament, and one issue that came up was the fact that KU was going to play so late. The Sweet 16 game against Villanova didn't start until 9:45 Detroit time.

Someone asked Darnell Jackson: "What's your biggest concern about tipping off at nearly 10 p.m.?" Darnell said, "My biggest concern is that I have to hang out in the hotel all day, because Darrell Arthur is my roommate on the road, and he has some really bad gas. I'm going to have to sit in the room and deal with that all day."

Not the most pleasant story, I know. But it speaks to how candid those guys were. Any reporter would love to cover a team like that, where the players are always up front and honest. I can't remember a Kansas team that was as friendly and accessible as this group.

The main reason for that is Bill Self. He allows you just enough access before you cross the line, and because he does that you're less likely to cross the line. It's that way with everyone. Print, TV, radio.

I remember the Thursday before KU played North Carolina in the Final Four. Self and the team got back to the hotel from practice and there were some reporters there that hadn't been in town the night before when the team arrived from Lawrence. A lot of us had footage and interviews from that and had been using it, but the folks from Channel 9 and Danny Clinkscale from WHB radio had nothing. Nothing.

Anyway, Self gets off the bus and Clinkscale says, "Hey coach, do you have a minute?" Self said, "No, if I talk to you I have to talk to everyone." Self walked into the hotel and everyone was disappointed. Not even 30 seconds passed before he came back out. I guess he thought, "What's two minutes out of my day?" He gave

us two minutes and everyone was happy. This guy was nice enough and smart enough to know that, if he gave us two minutes, we'd all go away after that and wouldn't hound his team.

I definitely respected Roy Williams and liked covering his teams. But it's different under Self. If we would've tried to get close to one of Roy's players while they were cutting down the nets, he'd have said, "Get the hell away." He didn't want anyone interfering with their chorus line bow. He didn't want anyone near them.

Self doesn't mind you being part of the celebration. I think he realizes that that's what people in those small towns in western Kansas - people who didn't get to go to the game - want to see. Roy would make a point to get us out of there. Self would never do that. He makes it enjoyable to cover the team.

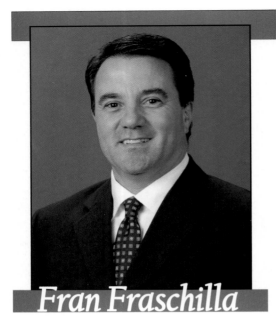

Fran Fraschilla

*Fran Fraschilla, who recently completed his third season as a color analyst for ESPN, has worked more Jayhawks games than any national announcer the last few years. He is the former head coach at Manhattan College, St. John's and New Mexico. Fraschilla resides in Dallas.*

Usually, I broadcast games with Ron Franklin. There aren't many places - if any - that we like better than Allen Fieldhouse. Lawrence has become a home away from home for us. You can't go into the Starbucks on Massachusetts Street or Jefferson's or Borders without someone saying, "Hey, what do you think of the Jayhawks tonight?" You almost become part of the fabric of the program.

For me, as a New Yorker, I went 25 years or so in college basketball without ever seeing a game in Allen Fieldhouse. Now I could probably get around the place blindfolded.

The fans are so close to the action that, right up until tipoff - when they really block access behind us - we're constantly getting bumped around. I feel like I'm on the New York subway in rush hour. People are trying to get to their seats and they're bumping into the back of your chair and saying excuse me. It's very cozy. It doesn't bother me at all. It's just funny how it's so cozy that the fans could come up behind you and scratch your back.

I've got people I always see that have season tickets that are constantly critiquing my ties and shirts. It's funny. I'm constantly getting wardrobe tips from people. You definitely can't wear a tie that has the school colors of anyone else in the Big 12. They'll say, "Is that a purple tie? You can't wear a purple tie in here!"

One of my favorite things to do is to get to Allen Fieldhouse early and go back where dinner is served. Whether it's talking to Max Falkenstien or any number of NBA scouts that come through there ... it's a great place to catch up on all things college basketball. The TV is on in the background and the Big Monday game may be on. You may see Kevin Pritchard or Mel Daniels scouting an NBA game. You talk about who's playing well and where you're going next. Larry Keating and Lew Perkins are always around to shoot the bull. It's just great camaraderie back there.

I've said on many occasions that Allen Fieldhouse is like the St. Patrick's Cathedral of college basketball. There's a certain reverence that you have when you walk into the place. Not just because of all the great players - going back to Wilt - that played in that building. But because Allen Fieldhouse represents Phog Allen and the man who invented basketball. I'm talking about Dr. Naismith.

There are other places with great basketball tradition - places like Kentucky and North Carolina. But there's nowhere that traces its roots back to the man who invented the game except for Kansas. For someone that studies the history of the game like I do, it's something you can't help but enjoy whenever you're in Lawrence.

It doesn't matter if it's the University of New Orleans in December or Missouri in late February, there are going to be 16,300 in the building every night. Some nights are crazier than others, but it always has that special feel. Every time Kansas steps on the court it's a big-game atmosphere. That's why what they did this season is so impressive.

Bill told me once that people don't realize the amount of pressure these kids are under. A loss at Kansas is like a five-game losing streak somewhere else. Every night they step on the floor they're going to face the other team's best shot. It's hard to be near perfect every night.

*Mark Ewing*

*WIBW-TV Sports Director Mark Ewing is a native Kansan who played high school basketball for Hall of Fame Coach Jay Frazier in McPherson. After two years at Cloud County, Mark lettered for Ted Owens at KU from 1981 to 1983. He played alongside Dave Magley and Tony Guy, as well as future Final Four players Greg Dreiling, Ron Kellogg and Calvin Thompson. His 24-year broadcasting career has taken him from Oberlin-McCook to Joplin, Green Bay and Wichita. He and his wife, Carrie, reside in Topeka. San Antonio marked his fifth Final Four assignment as an on-site anchor covering the Jayhawks.*

### "BILL SELF'S HOMETOWN"

Kansas was San Antonio bound, and so were we. Before starting the 13-hour drive from WIBW-TV in Topeka , I had already made arrangements to stop in Edmond, Oklahoma, to do a feature on Bill Self's hometown.

It was mid-morning when sports talk radio hosts began spreading the rumor that Sean Sutton was about to be forced out as head coach at Oklahoma State. The scenario was more than familiar. The coach of the Final Four-bound Jayhawks was about to be courted by his alma mater.

By the time we arrived in Oklahoma City, the story was blowing up. The Cowboys were prepared to offer Bill Self the financial deal of a lifetime. Sutton had yet to officially resign when we rolled into the parking lot at Edmond Memorial High School, but folks were already debating the probability of the return of one of the state's favorite sons.

Mike de la Garza is the school's athletic director. He was also Bill Self's basketball coach back in the day. He turned out to be the perfect person to paint a portrait of how things were when Self was a Bulldog. It turns out that Self is more than just a hometown hero. He's a legend – partly because Self made a key pass that helped deliver a state title. According to de la Garza, when Self was a senior, he swished six game-winning shots. "And I'm talking about '3...2....1... Self shoots and scores.' Six times he did that!" de la Garza said.

Later, de la Garza said that the charismatic personality for which Self is known began displaying itself early on. "He was the only sophomore to date senior girls," the coach said. "I probably shouldn't say that on TV, but you wanted something different, so there it is."

Edmond is a bedroom community of Oklahoma City. It's obvious that the school takes great pride in its athletic accomplishments, as well as one Bill Self. During the final minute of the Kansas-Davidson game, de la Garza said the entire town was holding its breath, and that everyone let out a collective sigh of relief when the Jayhawks won.

The bonus interview came when Bill Self's sister, Shelly, agreed to meet us. She's an elementary school teacher in Edmond. After a little nudging, she consented to an interview about growing up with Bill. Eventually, I had to ask her the question that was on everyone's mind: "Would an offer from Oklahoma State be too difficult to turn down?"

Shelly laughed. "Who knows," she said. "Bill might not do very well this weekend, and they might want him to leave." Later she said, "I think Bill knows what he has, and I really believe he'll stay at Kansas as long as they'll have him."

It was a prophetic statement.

As long as Self is in Lawrence, there will always be Jayhawk fans in Edmond, Oklahoma.

### REUNION

As Bill Self stepped to the podium, he looked out into a sea of men who had written the course of history he was presently directing.

It was the 110-year Anniversary of Kansas Basketball banquet. Clearly, the head coach of the Jayhawks was looking for just the right phrase to capture the moment.

From my seat in the audience, I was very aware that I was the only former letterman who was presently a member of the media. In my business, I was observing what's known as an "exclusive."

Self, who is blessed with the gift of gab, paused in his delivery and then went off-script with a statement that I will always remember. To paraphrase, Self said the best thing about Kansas is that the best coach has already been here (Phog), and we've already had the best player (Wilt), so we can never match that. Then he looked at all of us and said, "I've always thought it takes a lot of guts to play at Kansas because of what all of you have accomplished."

And there it was. Bill Self had put it perfectly.

In that room was the living history of Kansas basketball. Athletes who had played under Phog Allen, Dick Harp, Ted Owens, Larry Brown, Roy Williams and Bill Self exchanged hand shakes, hugs, updates and lots of smiles.

At the center of attention were the players from the 1988 national championship team. They were celebrating the 20th anniversary of their title. Danny Manning, who still looks like he could lace it up and play right now, was in a conversation with Russell, Mario and Brandon while some older guys named Archie, Chris and Scooter listened nearby.

As for me, I capitalized on the opportunity at hand and pulled out a copy of

# Kansas Jayhawks: **A Year to Remember**

The *Kansas CityStar* that I had stored away since April 5, 1988. I took advantage of the rare occasion to get as many autographs as I could. The headline on the front page read, "You did it, Jayhawks." Just above it, the coach of that team carefully wrote, "Best Wishes, Larry Brown."

When I gazed at it afterward, I couldn't help but wonder if another miracle would soon be at hand.

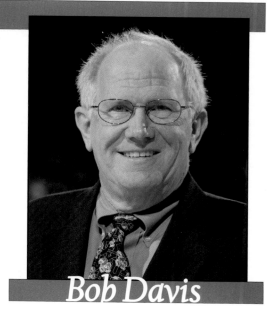

*Bob Davis*

*Bob Davis has been Kansas' play-by-play voice for the last 24 years. He also hosts Bill Self's weekly call-in show, HawkTalk, while serving as a play-by-play announcer for the Kansas City Royals' TV Network. During basketball season, Davis is joined on press row by color commentator Chris Piper, a starter on Kansas' 1988 national championship squad.*

I was a little nervous before the national championship game about my voice. It had been one of those weekends with games, talk shows, radio programs ... I had done a lot of talking and I was concerned that my voice might not finish the game. Plus, I had to fly back to Kansas City the next day for Opening Day with the Royals, so that was an issue, too.

That was the fourth time I've been in a championship game with KU. Seven Final Fours - but only four championship games. I didn't really have anything prepared in case they won. No speech written out or anything like that. Some broadcasters do that but I never have. When we won in 1988 Max (Falkenstien) linked that team with the 1952 team that won it all. He talked about how they were joining guys like Lovellette and Lienhard as national champions. So for this one I tried to expand it and link this team with both the '52 team and the '88 team. One of those guys (Chris Piper) was sitting next to me and another (Danny Manning) was sitting next to Bill Self.

A week earlier I was kind of feeling like the team must have felt before the Davidson game. I knew how big that game was for the kids and for Bill, and I also had a pretty good feeling of how good Davidson was. I mean, I watched that Wisconsin game and they just took the Big 10 champions apart. I was pretty impressed with that team - Curry and the other guys, too. You could see that was a losable game because they beat Georgetown. They were really good. They were very legit and that was a huge game. Everybody saw the tape of Bill crumbling to the floor in relief. I think all of us felt that way.

Even if we hadn't won the championship, I would've looked back on 07-08 as a fun year. Most of the players were veterans who had been around for awhile, so they were all really friendly. There were really good road trips this year, too. Places like Atlanta and Los Angeles. I still remember getting up at 4 a.m. to leave the Orange Bowl so I could meet the team for their game at Boston College.

I'm really going to miss some of these guys. They all had such great stories. Jeremy Case sticking it out for four years, Darnell persevering through his off-court problems and Russell bouncing back from a rough freshman season. It was quite a group.

If you're a broadcaster for a school and you say you don't want them to win or lose, you're lying. Of course, you want them to win, but there's a line between partiality and objectivity. You can be for your team, but I don't refer to the Jayhawks as "us" or "we." Still, you have to be tuned in to your audience, although even that's changing with the advent of satellite radio, where people can hear you all over the country.

*Harold Bechard has covered college and high school sports in Kansas for 32 years as a sports editor and sports writer. He worked at The Salina Journal from 1976-2002 and The Hutchinson News since 2002. A native of Grinnell, Kan. who lives in Salina, Bechard is a 1977 graduate of Marymount College of Kansas and has been a beat writer for the University of Kansas and Kansas State University since 1982.*

*Harold Bechard*

It's difficult to fathom any Kansas basketball team being all but overshawdowed in their own backyard.

But here it was, three months prior to winning the school's third national championship, and the Jayhawks were playing second fiddle to – OK, everyone steady themselves – the KU football team.

Yes, the football team.

You know, football – the sport that usually provides KU fans with a couple of thrills in September before reality sets in and "Late Night" rolls around in mid-October.

In this remarkable season, Mark Mangino's football program stole the thunder from KU basketball and didn't give it back until coming home from Miami with its school-record 12th win of the season and a victory over Virginia Tech in the Orange Bowl.

Kansas basketball, however, wasn't exactly shirking its duties while the football team was having all its fun. With all the hoopla surrounding KU's gridders, the basketball team seemed to relish its time under the proverbial radar. The Jayhawks entered the New Year with a 13-0 record and won their 14th straight game two days after the football team's win in the Orange Bowl.

And by the time March rolled around, no one was talking football any more on the KU campus. As bright as the spotlight had been in January, Mangino's bunch toiled through spring drills in near obscurity as the state of Kansas and city of Lawrence were held in the iron fist of March Madness.

That madness eventually consumed Lawrence, not once, but twice during a historic three-night stretch when Massachusetts Street put Bourbon Street to shame. Seriously, during the weekend of the Final Four, Lawrence felt like Mardi Gras, New Year's Eve and the Fourth of July all rolled into one.

Just how do you define a basketball season that ends with a national champio... hip?

Do you just go straight to the source - Mario's Miracle, the 20-footer just to the right of the key that was heard across the country, from Key West to Kennebunkport, from Seattle to San Diego?

Well, that's a good start.

It was such a stunning, memorable moment. Let's face it. That shot will be discussed (in Kansas) and cussed (in Tennessee) for as long as there is such a thing as an NCAA Tournament and all the buzzer-beaters that go with it.

It was a moment that will define Chalmers not just for the rest of his basketball career, but for the rest of his life.

Perhaps Mario should thank a few of his football buddies on Mt. Oread.

Maybe, just maybe, Kansas football had a little something to do with the Jayhawks' 2008 NCAA basketball championship.

After all, no self-respecting University of Kansas basketball player wants to take a backseat to those gridiron boys.

*Marty Wall*

*For the last three years, Marty Wall has co-hosted the "Neal and Marty" show each weekday on 610 Sports in Kansas City. Wall graduated from Kansas in 1986 with a degree in journalism and went on to earn a master's degree in education in 1993.*

The story about the Final Four that I told everyone when I got back happened after the final horn sounded in Kansas' win over Memphis. I walked over toward the Kansas section and looked into the stands, and what I saw says as much about Kansas basketball as anything I can ever remember.

In that section you had Greg Dreiling and Greg Ostertag, who was wearing a big cowboy hat. Ostertag was motioning and gesturing boldly as the two of them laughed and shared stories. And I thought, "You know, at most schools these guys wouldn't even know each other." Dreiling was a senior in 1986 and Ostertag's last season was in 1995. But on that night, it didn't matter.

Behind them I saw Walt Wesley talking with Bud Stallworth. Scot Pollard was just in front of them. The most striking sight was across the aisle, where I saw Larry Brown and Ted Owens. Remember now, Ted Owens was fired to make way for Larry Brown. But on that night they were talking like old friends. The only person sitting between them was Larry Brown's wife. Roy Williams was there cheering, too. And R.C. Buford was crying – crying!

Another moment I witnessed happened after the celebration had pretty much ended. Most of the team had left the court, but then a player ran out to get Julian Wright to take him back to the locker room. Julian said, "No, no, no. This night belongs to you guys. Don't worry about me." But the player said, "No – get back here. You're a part of this, too."

A few minutes later, I was in the tunnel. There was hardly any media around, and Bill Self was making his way toward the interview room. He passed Chris Piper, stuck out his hand and said, "Pipe … 20 years … man, can you believe it?"

That's what I'll never forget – standing there amongst 40 years worth of Jayhawks. We classify them by era or as NBA players. Or we associate them with a certain coach. But what they really are is a family. I know this sounds sappy, but they're Jayhawks. It was a really powerful thing to witness.

**Kevin Haskin**

*Kevin Haskin is a sports columnist for the Topeka Capital-Journal. A graduate of Kansas State University, Haskin covered the Wildcats for 10 years and the Jayhawks for four before moving into his current position in the summer of 2007. He loves spending time with his grown children. He also enjoys water sports and tolerates golf.*

Even as a sportswriter, it's hard not to cheer -- keeping it to yourself, of course -- for Bill Self. Unlike many head coaches in this era who share a clandestine paranoia when dealing with sportswriters, Self is often glad to receive phone calls and doesn't mind engaging in a little casual conversation.

In short, he gets it.

His trust of the media helps stem any harsh criticism, though he probably begged to differ after his first-round defeats at KU, as well as the string of defeats in the Elite Eight that kept him from reaching the Final Four for so many years. His fortunes changed with the national championship the Jayhawks captured in 2008, though I doubt the title will change Self personally.

I'll never forget calling him about something in the summer of 2006. It was shortly after I began divorce proceedings, and when I told him the news, he expressed genuine concern. A simple five-minute phone call for a story turned into a 45-minute discussion about my family, the potential effects of the divorce and his well-wishes. For several months after alerting him to my situation, he always asked how I was getting along.

Major-college coaches don't need to do this. I'd never expect them to. But the fact that Self did makes him special. I know there will be times when I must be critical of both him and his program, but nonetheless, I value my relationship with Bill Self, both the coach and the man.

*Not many sportswriters know the Jayhawks as well as Rick Plumlee, who has covered Kansas athletics for The Wichita Eagle since 1979. A Wichita State graduate, Plumlee has been honored numerous times by the Associated Press Sports Editors, who deemed his 2003 account of Kansas' loss to Syracuse as the best game story in the nation that year.*

Not all of the games Kansas players played this season were on the court. In keeping with a time-honored tradition, many of them play a game off the court with reporters. It's called "interview avoidance."

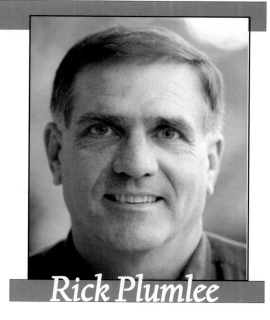

*Rick Plumlee*

Wayne Simien used to be very good at it, often taking a back entry to the practice court to avoid the arranged interviews before workouts. And then there are those who stand still for the interviews but roll their eyes - or give answers so quiet that you aren't sure if they actually said something or if they were just breathing a little harder.

All of that is understandable. KU players are in high demand for interviews throughout any season. But the demand for interviews goes off the charts during a national championship run. No stone - or grain of sand - is left unturned by the media. It can be very draining for everybody, and certainly for the players.

Russell Robinson was a stand-up guy throughout the process. So was Sasha Kaun. But few are in such high demand as the starting point guard. Robinson was there every time. After good games, after bad games, before practices, after practices. He met the throng of reporters and cameras without blinking. No rolling of the eyes, no heavy sigh as if to say, "OK, I'll do this, but I'm doing you a big favor."

What you saw of Robinson on the court - steady, cool and calm - is what he was off the court this past season. The kid from New York, New York, took the time to explain every detail he was asked about. And he almost always did it with a smile. You could always count on Robinson giving a straight answer. Direct and to the point. No dancing around.

Even when he was asked about his days as a pouty freshman - when he chose to stay on the bench rather than enter a blowout victory at Baylor - Robinson calmly pointed toward his immaturity at the time. No doubt Robinson still has more basketball days ahead. But wherever his life takes him, it's a fair assumption that he will do it with the class he showed during a national championship season.

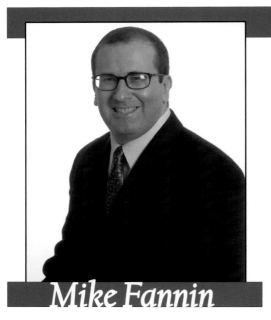

Mike Fannin

*During the past few years, no editor leading a sports department has enjoyed a string of success quite like The Kansas City Star's Mike Fannin. In 2008, The Star was the only big-circulation newspaper in the country to capture the prestigious Triple Crown at the Associated Press Sports Editors Convention. The award is given to publications that are deemed to have one of the Top 10 daily, Sunday and special sections in America. Fannin is a Longhorn fan who attended the University of Texas.*

There's always a special energy in the sports department the night of a championship game or the Final Four. Thanks to Kansas, we'd been in this situation a few times before.

The Jayhawk graduates at The Star were understandably nervous. Copy editors like Dave McQueen and Mark Zeligman and our assistant managing editor, Holly Lawton. During Saturday's North Carolina game, their superstitions were on full display. After the Jayhawks' furious start, we quickly designed a front page that was geared around the Hawks winning. Because of the tight production deadlines, you have to stay ahead of the game whenever possible.

The headline blared "TARRED AND FEATHERED!" But, literally, as we were applying the finishing touches on the layout, North Carolina began to rally. A 28-point lead shrank to single digits – and then it got all the way down to four.

The room was hushed and, for the first time all night, the Kansas State and Missouri fans had reason to hope. A new headline – "DADGUMMIT!" - was crafted in case the Tar Heels won. As we scrambled for fresh photos, we tried to understand what had happened, how Kansas could've blown a 28-point lead.

Then suddenly, the momentum changed again. This time it was Kansas fighting back. We had all but decided that we'd end up with Plan B, but now Kansas was resisting the script. Somehow our front page seemed to be causing bad karma. After losing so many big games since 1988, the Beakers just couldn't afford the presumptuousness of a "KU WINS!" headline until it actually happened.

"Don't change it!" the Jayhawkers pleaded as the minutes ticked down. I gave in. We would simply wait for the verdict. When KU won, we went back to the Roy slammer: "TARRED AND FEATHERED!"

Monday night was similar, with our front page design changing each time the game took a wild swing. Later, Saturday's unpublished "DADGUMMIT!" page was discussed reverentially, mystically. Someone suggested we sell the page online and tell its story. Crazy KU fans, I thought. This is what happens when you only win a championship every 20 years or so.

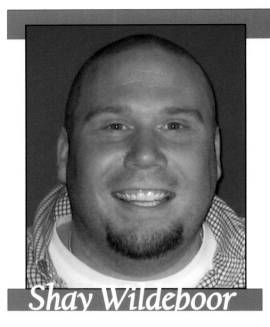

Shay Wildeboor

*Shay Wildeboor is the senior editor of JayhawkSlant.com and has been a recruiting analyst for Rivals.com since 2001. He lives in Olathe with his wife, Anne; son, Kemper; and black lab, Hercules.*

Bill Self's first graduating class at the University of Kansas will long be remembered for delivering a National Championship to Allen Fieldhouse for the first time in 20 years – something so many previous classes failed to do.

However, as Russell, Darnell and Sasha climbed the championship ladder to retrieve a piece of the net shortly after defeating Memphis, I found myself reflecting back on how each of the aforementioned seniors actually arrived in Lawrence.

While Russell, Darnell and Sasha came to Kansas for some of the same reasons, there is absolutely no question that each came from different walks of life. One arrived in Lawrence via New York, one via Oklahoma and one via Florida (from Russia).

Just as Russell, Darnell and Sasha came from different locations, they also arrived at Kansas with different stories to tell.

### HERE'S TO YOU, MR. ROBINSON

Russell's journey to Lawrence actually began on September 27, 2003. During that time, the former five-star guard and No. 27 ranked player in the class of 2004 spent a weekend on campus for an official visit.

Having already visited Connecticut and Georgia Tech, Russell was beginning to wind down his recruitment visits. However, I had no idea what was coming at that particular time. As I sat in my office the Monday following his visit, the phone began to ring. As I looked at the caller ID on the phone, I immediately knew it was Russell.

As Russell and I talked, he informed me that he'd decided to give a commitment to Bill Self and Kansas. Instead of taking one or two more official visits, the elite guard from New York had decided to shut things down.

As we continued to talk, it became clear that Russell ultimately decided to commit to Kansas for a variety of reasons. The opportunity to compete for a national championship was a big factor. As was the opportunity to play for a program filled with tradition and prestige.

As we continued talking, Russell told me about something that took place during his visit that had a profound effect on his decision. Shortly after Kansas had defeated Missouri on the football field, fans immediately rushed the field and tore down the goalposts.

As it turned out, Russell lost his host and found himself alone in the madness, so he helped carry the goalposts to Potter Lake. According to Russell, what took place that Saturday afternoon helped lead him to his decision.

### MEANT TO BE

Darnell Jackson became the first member of Bill Self's recruiting class back on July 12, 2003. There is no question that the former four-star prospect and No. 54 ranked prospect in the class of 2004, has a completely different story to tell.

For as long as Darnell can remember, he wanted nothing more than to be a member of the University of Kansas basketball program. As the spring and summer AAU Circuit slowly came to an end, and as Darnell was close to the start of his senior year, he felt the need to make a decision about his future.

The thing I remember most about that conversation was the emotion coming from Darnell and his mother. Most players aren't fans of the school they play for, but that certainly wasn't the case for Darnell.

While he didn't start playing basketball until late in his career, Darnell was always a big-time Kansas fan. He was, without question, born to play basketball in Lawrence.

When Darnell and I spoke the night of his commitment, he talked about how important bringing a national championship to Lawrence would be during his career. On the final night of the college basketball season, and during his final game, Darnell helped the Jayhawks do just that.

### DUKE OR KANSAS?

Sasha Kaun's decision to attend the University of Kansas didn't come as easy as the decisions of his future teammates. Kaun, No. 34-ranked player in the class of 2004, picked Kansas over Duke, but the decision-making process was far from easy.

Sasha arrived at the Florida Air Academy via Russia with no knowledge of college basketball. When he began to emerge as an elite college basketball prospect, he was forced to research each school and find out as much about each coaching staff as humanly possible.

Sasha's recruitment was difficult to cover. It wasn't the language barrier that made things tough. Instead, Sasha's schedule at Florida Air Academy was very strict and strenuous, and it was often hard for him to get to the phone.

The recruiting process was certainly new to Sasha, which meant he would need help along the way. He received that help from Aubin Goporo, the head coach at Florida Air Academy.

Sasha, along with Coach Goporo, knew this decision wasn't just about basketball, but academics, as well. I distinctly remember the conversation Sasha and I had after he'd committed to Kansas.

He talked about how much work he put in and how diligent he was about researching each school. The decision making process wasn't just about basketball. In fact, the decision to attend Kansas was probably based more on education than anything else.

### CAN'T HELP BUT BE HAPPY

As I watched Russell, Darnell and Sasha celebrate after winning the national title, I realized just how far each had come. Not only as individuals, but as teammates.

I couldn't be any happier for those three guys. The 2004 recruiting class was the first class I covered during my time with Rivals.com and JayhawkSlant.com. My career with the company was just getting started when they signed their letters of intent.

They certainly made my new job seem easy at times. There were occasions when I reached out to Russell, Darnell and Sasha - but there were also times when they reached out to me, too.

As each got closer to making a decision, the conversations between myself and each player became more frequent. I would generally call - or they would contact me - after an official visit or after an in-home visit.

Nothing about this class was complicated. It didn't matter if I was talking to Russell or his father, Russell, Sr.; Darnell or his mother, Shawn; or Sasha or his coach, Aubin Goporo. They were all more than willing to spend time with me on the phone.

For that reason, this senior class will always have a special place in my heart.

*Erin Bajackson*

*Erin Bajackson has been an anchor/reporter for Metro Sports/KCTV5 since June of 2004. She also worked two years at KAUZ-TV in Wichita Falls, Texas. During that time, Erin has covered everything from football to swimming, basketball to golf, volleyball to soccer, track to tennis and wrestling to log rolling (no lie). However, Kansas' national championship has been the most exciting event she's reported on thus far. She also works as a play-by-play announcer for various sports.*

I covered the Jayhawks throughout the NCAA Tournament and, for me, one of the most memorable moments came after they advanced to the Final Four by beating Davidson. Once the players left the court with pieces of the net in their hands, the media had to wait about 10 minutes before entering the locker room. However, when we got inside, the guys had no problem sharing with us the special moment they had just experienced with their head coach. It involved an ice bucket poured all over Self's back and a few minutes of free-flowing tears.

The players spoke openly of how they wept when they saw the watery eyes of their coach who, admittedly, had thought about that moment nearly every day since entering the profession. They got a little emotional again talking about how special it was for them to be part of Bill Self's first Final Four. They took a lot of pride in the fact that Self will never forget his first team to get him there - no matter how many more may come afterward.

It wasn't just how the players felt about their coach that made that night such a joy. It was also how they felt about each other. Russell Robinson told me how, as soon as the game was over, he ran up to backup guard Jeremy Case. He hugged him and told him he loved him. He said that they wanted to win that game for all of the walk-ons and reserves that made them better each and every day in practice but never received a whole lot of playing time in return. He said that those are the true heroes on the team, because practice at Allen Fieldhouse was often harder than the challenges they faced on game day. Case told the same story of their embrace at mid-court, adding that neither one could keep the smile off of their face. I appreciated both of them being so candid. I realized that neither of them was obligated to be so open with the girl holding the microphone.

The other moment that stands out also involves Kansas' victory over Davidson – and, more particularly, Sasha Kaun. For years I'd had heard stories about how Kaun needed to be more physical. I listened to people complain about his lack of consistency and I watched him get yelled at by his coaches on the bench. That's why I couldn't help but be happy for Kaun during his 13-point performance against Davidson. It was yet another outstanding effort by a player who clearly saved his best for last.

Self gave Kaun credit for his monster-like performance in the postgame interview, but the real reward came when the Jayhawks returned to Allen Fieldhouse. Thousands packed the gym to congratulate their San Antonio-bound team. As he concluded his address to the fans and prepared to hand the microphone to Kaun, Self passed along a compliment that I'm sure the big Russian will never forget.

"Did the big man play great today, or what?" said Self, raising Kaun's hand as if he were a boxer who'd just won a fight.

Instant hysteria broke out as Kaun smiled and attempted to make a speech. The problem was that the fans couldn't hear him. They were too busy chanting his name: "Sa-sha Kaun! Sa-sha Kaun!"

All Kaun could do was wait for the crowd's cheer to die down a little bit before talking. Still, it was a moment that you could tell moved him. And for all of us in the media who had witnessed him break out of his shell over the course of a few weeks? We couldn't help but be fans, too – just for a little while.

*Jay Bilas*

*It's almost impossible to turn on ESPN during basketball season and not see Jay Bilas. Whether it's on the set of College GameDay, ESPNEWS or SportsCenter, Bilas is included in almost any story or discussion related to college hoops. A Duke graduate, Bilas was a member of Mike Krzyzewski's first No. 1-ranked recruiting class in 1982. He scored 1,062 points in his college career before playing professionally in Italy and Spain. Bilas joined ESPN in 1995.*

It was obvious from the beginning of the season that Kansas was going to be one of the four best teams in the country – especially if Brandon Rush was able to come back from his knee injury and be the star-caliber player that everyone knew he could be.

When I went to Lawrence in November to do the Arizona game, Bill said, "I'm only going to play Brandon for 15 minutes. That's it. We're going to have a clock on it." Well, the game went into overtime, and Brandon ended up playing 36 minutes because he was playing so well and looked so structurally sound.

After the game I said, "Is that Oklahoma State math? How do you get 36 out of 15?" Bill said it just happened that way. He didn't want to do that, but Brandon was playing so well, and if he didn't play him, Kansas would've gotten beat.

During the NCAA Tournament, there was never a time during the Jayhawks' championship run when I didn't think they were the best team on the floor. With the teams they were playing ... they had so many mid-majors in their path. There's a feeling players get sometimes when they're playing not to lose. You know you're better than the other team, but instead of just going out and going for it and playing loose, you play tight. That's what happened against Davidson.

Kansas played very well defensively in that game. They were the only team to hold Davidson under 70 points, and they did an excellent job on Curry. But offensively, they just weren't the same team.

I think I said this a thousand times, but I thought Kansas was going to play great against North Carolina because the cuffs were off. With the monkey off Bill's back, and not having to worry about how they would be portrayed, they could play with freedom again. I thought that's what happened in the Final Four. They played loose and free – and really hard. With all of those images of Bucknell and Bradley ... it couldn't have been easy to let those things go and not think about them. But they did it.

To me, what stood out in the championship game was the way the players reacted to everything. They were so positive. Even when they were down, you could sense that they still had a run in them because they never seemed to lose that energy.

They still could have lost, because Memphis had that game. Obviously, the steal by Sherron Collins and his ensuing three-pointer was probably the biggest play of the game other than the shot by Chalmers. They had so many guys that played so well all season. It was really hard to pick an MVP from that team.

*Brady McCollough recently completed his first year as the Jayhawks beat writer for The Kansas City Star. The previous two seasons he covered high schools. McCollough penned some excellent features during KU's national title run and was also one of the top game story writers on the beat. A Michigan graduate, McCollough resides in Lawrence. Fortunately, his car was at the airport – and not parked near his Mass Street loft – when KU defeated Memphis.*

I watched in total disbelief on the night of April 7, 2008, as the Kansas Jayhawks celebrated their national championship on the Alamodome floor. Looking over at a colleague, I remember shaking my head and saying something like, "I can't believe these guys just won it all."

That was no slight against this collection of Kansas players and coaches. It was more about me being blown away by the fact that I had covered a national championship season during my first year on the KU beat. I wondered if I should just go ahead and retire right there on press row in San Antonio.

For a beat writer, it doesn't get any better. Sure, sports writers get the reputation of being cynics who are actually more concerned with what type of food is being served at the media buffet or whether or not there is media parking available at the arena. But really, we're fans at heart. We watch sports to see greatness, and during the past year on this beat, I got so close that I could smell it.

Covering the beat, I experienced many small moments that, taken together, gave me the feeling that these Jayhawks were capable of something special. Here's a glimpse into a year covering a national champion.

### June 7, 2007 – Cole Aldrich's dorm room

I first met Aldrich, the 6-foot-11 freshman center, outside Jayhawker Towers on move-in day. We went up to his dorm room. He rapped on the door of his new digs, hoping that roommate Tyrel Reed was home, and opened it with a twist of a key.

"Where you at?" Aldrich yelled.

Sure enough, there was Reed, ready with a handshake. Reed would soon learn what I had learned minutes earlier: Before shaking hands with Aldrich, you should go ahead and start grinding your teeth, because it's going to hurt.

Walt Aldrich, Cole's father, gave Reed some advice about life with Cole.

"When he gets mad," Walt said, "all you gotta do is give him food!"

Cole talked that day about the excitement of finally getting to play in front of the KU fans. But at "Late Night at the Phog" four months later, Aldrich was more nervous than he had ever been playing basketball. Even though he came in glowing with the confidence of a McDonald's All-American, Aldrich needed all of his first year on campus to get himself ready for big-time college basketball.

You got the feeling that his maturation peaked when the Jayhawks played North Carolina and Aldrich matched up with Tyler Hansbrough. On that night, "Psycho-T" met "Tenacious-C." Aldrich exploded onto the national radar with eight points and seven rebounds in KU's 84-66 victory, a performance 10 months in the making.

### October 31, 2007 – Allen Fieldhouse

Brandon Rush really shouldn't have been sitting with me, doing an interview about his relationship with Kansas coach Bill Self. He should have been in the NBA, but a twist of fate – an awkward landing in a pickup basketball game that tore his right ACL – changed everything.

Truly, the narrative of the Jayhawks' season began on Thursday, May 24, 2007, when Rush went down. Self was saddened for Rush, but deep down, he knew that KU just got a lot better.

Self and Rush needed each other this season. Self needed Rush to be more aggressive, putting aside his passive personality, and Rush needed Self to make sure that he would be in a position to get drafted high in the 2008 NBA Draft.

Their relationship had been complicated, but it had always worked for some reason. Rush had never been coached before, and he said something that day in October that stuck with me, that told me Rush really cared for Self.

"He helped turn my whole reputation around, saying I'm a good kid, saying that I'm doing good in school, saying all these great things about me," Rush said. "It has changed the way everybody thinks of me."

In turn, Rush wanted to do something for his coach.

"I want to get him to the Final Four, since he's never been," Rush said.

### January 10, 2008 – Allen Fieldhouse

Watching Mario Chalmers play this season, I knew that something had to be driving him. He was suddenly an explosive dunker – we all learned that when he posterized a Georgia Tech player in December – and his three-point percentage was way up from his sophomore season.

Chalmers is a supremely confident guy, so I figured that his being cut from the 2007 USA Basketball Pan American Games team was a motivating factor. Turns out, my suspicion was right. In fact, teammate Darnell Jackson told me that Chalmers had cut out a list of names from a newspaper when the final team was announced.

Wayne Ellington, North Carolina

238

Derrick Low, Washington State
Eric Maynor, Virginia Commonwealth
Drew Neitzel, Michigan State
Scottie Reynolds, Villanova

Chalmers was on a mission to prove everybody that he should have been on that team.

"It affected me a lot personally," Chalmers said. "That's the first team I've ever been cut from. It was a tough experience for me."

Chalmers certainly made his point when he was named the Most Outstanding Player at the Final Four. And he got to take out Ellington and Reynolds along the way.

### February 6, 2008 – Russell Robinson's apartment

Robinson decided to live by himself during his senior year, away from the chaos of Jayhawker Towers. He and Jeremy Case were the only Jayhawks who chose to live alone.

"I do spend a lot of time by myself," Robinson told me. "It's fun. Just to chill and relax and not have the stress of having to entertain anybody."

Self would say that Robinson's ability to separate himself from his teammates made him a better leader. Guys listened when Robinson spoke because of his independent nature.

One thing struck me over and over again during my time in Robinson's apartment. The guy was focused. From the color-coordinated bathroom towels to the Chinese blinds on the windows, Robinson found comfort in the details.

Robinson guided me over to the corner of his apartment, where he had a book shelf filled with memorabilia from his KU career. The corner looked like a shrine to Russell – a poster of himself hung from the wall.

"People ask me, 'Oh my God, you're too into yourself. Why do you have your picture up?'" Robinson said. "But this is why I do those things: When I'm down, I constantly see my accomplishments and all the things I've done. It reminds me of all those good times. That's how I deal with my stress and get over things."

When KU lost to Kansas State on Jan. 30, Robinson visited that corner and looked at his three Big 12 regular-season championship rings.

"Hey," he acknowledged, "if we have another game like that, we're not going to win a fourth one."

Robinson, of course, ended up with a fourth ring. And another one for good measure.

### February 20, 2008 – Oklahoma City, Okla.

The names were written on a white sheet of paper, and Shawn Jackson wouldn't let them go. She was giving me a tour of Darnell Jackson's Oklahoma City. Not the places. The people.

Darnell and Shawn went back and forth about who to include on this list, but they finally came to an agreement. It was so typical Darnell, deciding that his story should be told through the voices of others.

"Don't give your credit away, Darnell," Shawn has often told her son.

With Darnell, it is never about him. That's why he wanted me to meet Cory Colbert, Mary Deaton, Kenya Kraft and Don Davis.

Colbert was his mentor and coach who taught him to play basketball and saved him from the city streets. Deaton and Kraft were high-school teachers who took an interest in Jackson. Davis was a friend and Kansas graduate who helped Jackson get over the loss of his father – Jackson's dad was killed when he was 13 – and ended up getting Jackson in trouble with the NCAA during his sophomore year.

Shawn referred to all of the names on the list as her village.

"Everybody that came through my life," Darnell said, "I took a little bit from each person and put it all together, and I guess it came out as me."

Jackson became KU's emotional leader largely because of those people. They showered him with unconditional love, teaching him how to open himself up to others.

"If you're lucky enough to have him as a friend," Kraft told me, "he'll be your friend forever."

## NCAA Tournament

The bigger the game, the better Kansas played. That was no coincidence for Darrell Arthur and Sasha Kaun. Both guys, for very different reasons, were just figuring out how important it was to win in March.

Arthur is an "AAU baby," raised by non-stop ball from the time he was a sixth-grader. In one year, Arthur could play as many as 300 games.

"If you lose," Arthur told me, "you know you're going to be playing again."

But as I talked with Arthur before the UNLV game, he understood the stakes were higher now.

"These are the biggest games of my life," he said.

Arthur would score 20 points and grab 10 rebounds in the biggest game of his life on a Monday night in April.

Kaun realized that these games matter more, too – just in time. The big Russian scored 13 points to push KU over Davidson in the Elite Eight. Afterward, he said he wouldn't have cared so much about winning a year ago. He had to taste bitter defeat against UCLA in 2007 before he could understand.

"Last year, knowing how great it felt before the Elite Eight and then losing that game and how bad it felt afterward," Kaun explained. "I felt this was going to be a special year for us, and it meant so much more to me."

It was obvious all along that Robinson, Jackson, Chalmers and Sherron Collins would have given anything to win the title. But seeing how much quiet, laid-back types like Rush, Arthur and Kaun wanted to taste tournament glory told me everything I needed to know about KU's chances to finish on top in San Antonio.

KANSAS
00

*profiles:*
A YEAR TO
REMEMBER

# Jayhawks Bond Through Tragedy

Yahoo! Sports: March 21, 2008

OMAHA, Neb. – What would you do if your uncle was beaten to death with a hammer?

Would you lie in bed all afternoon, despondent and depressed? Or would you wipe away your tears and go to history class like Kansas' Darnell Jackson?

What if someone called with news that your baby son was dead? Would you drop out of school and move back home? Or would you leave after the funeral like Sherron Collins and drive eight hours to lift weights and play pickup basketball?

What if you were Rodrick Stewart, whose adopted brother was shot and killed while waiting at a traffic light? Or Sasha Kaun, whose father was likely murdered in Russia? Would basketball really seem all that important?

"We're probably the No. 1 team in the country when it comes to dealing with death and tragedy," Stewart said. "Any time one of us starts feeling down, we know we can step into this locker room and find strength."

Their roster is stocked with McDonald's All-Americans and future NBA draft picks. They've won four straight Big 12 titles and 46 of their last 50 games. Still, as successful as they've been on the court, the most impressive thing about the Kansas Jayhawks is how they've persevered off of it.

"I heard a quote the other day that said, 'Ten percent of life is what happens to you and 90 percent is how you deal with it,' " guard Russell Robinson said. "We've played the hands we were dealt as best as we could."

Dead parents. Murdered friends and relatives. Gang-infested neighborhoods. Absentee fathers. Almost every key member of Kansas' team has achieved college stardom after overcoming obstacles that would've forced a weaker person to wilt.

The more you hear their stories, the tougher it is not to root for the Jayhawks in the NCAA tournament, where they will face UNLV in a second-round game Saturday at the Qwest Center. Relating to these players is easy because, in many ways, they're just like us. Athlete or not, everyone faces adversity at some point. Each of us will deal with hurt, anger and grief. But while some are forced to do it alone, the Jayhawks persevered together. It's a team full of players that, in tough situations, have made all the right choices for all the right reasons.

Now, more than ever, it's paying dividends on the court.

"Everything that's happened has brought us closer together," forward Darnell Jackson said. "We've got a tight circle, a tight family. You see some teams out there arguing with each other on the court. We don't do that. When we're out there you can see how much we enjoy playing together."

No Kansas player has experienced more off-court trauma than Jackson, a

senior who's averaging a career-high 11.6 points.

In the eighth grade Jackson's absentee father, James Howard, was shot and killed by Oklahoma City police after he attacked a jogger. As a high school senior, Jackson arrived at the scene moments after a friend's murder. A few years ago his close friend, Glen Davis, died after being shot in the head by gang members.

Jackson's uncle was murdered, too, and his grandfather died in 2006. Just last month his cousin was killed in a shooting. The worst tragedy, though, occurred in the summer of 2005, when a car carrying Jackson's mother, Shawn, and grandmother, Yvonne, was struck by a drunk driver in Las Vegas. Yvonne Jackson died a week later from the injuries she sustained in the collision.

"I don't know of anyone," coach Bill Self said, "that's had to deal with more at such a young age than Darnell."

At times, the tragedies seemed to be taking their toll on Jackson. Last January he drove home to Midwest City, Okla., with no plans to return to Kansas. Self caught a flight to meet Jackson and convinced him to return.

This season Jackson broke down crying as he left the court at halftime of a game, but a hug from teammate Mario Chalmers assured him that he was in the right place.

"There are a lot of people out there that think we get the red-carpet treatment because we play basketball," Jackson said. "I wish those people could trade places with us so they could see how hard it is to be a college athlete and a student at the same time.

"We go through so much. You're away from home and so much stuff is happening, but you can't do anything about it. You can't go back home. You have to stay."

Collins may have felt like giving up after his son, Sherron Jr., died a few days after his birth in the summer of 2006. But then he remembered the rigorous trek he'd made to get to Kansas in the first place.

Much of Collins' childhood was spent in the Lathrop Homes housing project in Chicago, where fights, prostitution and drug deals were commonplace in the courtyard. Collins' father had gang ties and was in jail for drug-related incidents for most of his childhood.

As a teenager Sherron's best friend, Cedrick, was shot in the head and killed seconds after leaving Sherron's home. Earlier this month, Crane High School – Collins' alma mater – made national news when gang members shot and killed a student and hospitalized another by beating him with a golf club in broad daylight near the front steps of the campus.

Because he had basketball, Collins managed to stay clear of such riffraff and earn his diploma. When he experiences tough times at Kansas, he knows his teammates are there to help him cope.

"Sometimes we all need somebody," Collins said. "I think overall we've got a good core of guys that really cares about each other. We're like brothers on this team. When someone is down we try our best to pick them up."

That kind of gesture was certainly needed when Stewart's adopted brother, Allen, was shot as he sat alone in his car at a traffic light last month in Seattle. The murder happened the same week that Jackson's cousin was shot and killed.

"We had two murders this week within the immediate family," Self said at the time. "I've never coached that before. I don't know the coaching manual on that."

There are other stories, too.

Kaun's father, Oleg, was found dead in a parking garage when Kaun was 13. The cause of his passing remains a mystery, although Kaun's family believes it was related to Oleg's job as a computer programmer for one of Russia's biggest banks.

Brandon Rush grew up without guidance from a father figure and Russell Robinson was reared in the hardscrabble streets of Brooklyn.

Even the ancillary members of Kansas' program have encountered tragic times in recent weeks. Mary Hudy, the mother of Jayhawks strength coach Andrea Hudy, lost her battle with cancer the morning before the team's regular-season finale against Texas A&M.

Before they took the court that day, the players sent Hudy a text message offering their condolences.

"She wrote back and told us to go win another ring," Collins said.

A few hours later Kansas returned to the locker room as Big 12 champions for the fourth consecutive year. Now they're five victories away from accomplishing something even more special.

Kansas (32-3) has not won a national championship since 1988.

"This would be something positive we could hang our hats on," Robinson said. "After all the negative things we've been through, we've got an opportunity now to do something great."

In some ways Robinson is missing the point.

The Jayhawks already have.

# The Great Escape

KU freshman guard
Sherron Collins discovers
that life is a lot different in
Lawrence after growing up
on the mean streets
of Chicago.

Kansas City Star: March 21, 2008

*Sherron Collins*

CHICAGO | Some say Sherron Collins' neighborhood is getting safer, but a few weeks ago, on North Leavitt Street, a girl was stabbed in the temple with a scalpel.

Happened just down the sidewalk from the Chicago Boys and Girls Club, where tonight members of the Kings and Deuces linger on the porch, smoking cigarettes while rehashing the gang fight that erupted a short time ago in the gymnasium.

"You missed it by 10 minutes," says program coordinator Nick Sanchez, still somewhat out of breath from breaking up the fracas. "This one was pretty bad."

A block away, on the corner of Damen and Diversey, a middle-aged man paces back and forth, almost to a cadence, never taking more than three steps before reversing his course. He's babbling to himself and flailing his arms in unpredictable directions, a sign that he may be on crack.

The man holds out his hand as two women approach near the intersection. He asks them for money, but they pretend not to see him as they wave and peer through the window of each passing car.

Treena and Charisma wear white mini-skirts and black leather boots that extend above their knees. They won't give their last names, but they admit to being prostitutes. Treena, 19, interlocks arms with her friend. They always work together.

"Around here," she says, "you never go anywhere alone."

Nearly 600 miles away, at Buffalo Wild Wings in Lawrence, Collins is plowing through a basket of mini corn dogs as he watches a college basketball game. On Saturday he'll be the one playing on national television when Kansas takes on Texas for the Big 12 title.

Collins, a freshman, is averaging nearly 10 points a game for the third-ranked Jayhawks. Still, as impressive as he's been on the court, the amazing thing about Collins is that he's even here.

Here, instead of in jail like his father, a gangbanger who spent most of Sherron's childhood in prison for selling drugs.

Here, instead of a coffin like his best friend, Cedrick, who was hit in the head with a bullet during a drive-by shooting just 50 feet from Sherron's front porch.

Here, instead of holed up at his mom's place back in Chicago, depressed and defeated over the death of his infant son last summer. Born four months early on June 3, Sherron Jr. lived just 10 days before an infection overtook his lungs.

"Sherron's only 19, but some of the stuff he's been through -- some of the stuff he's seen -- most people will never experience stuff like that in their whole life," said Walt Harris, Collins' uncle. "He had every opportunity to let his situation get the best of him.

"But he saw there was a different path."

• • •

Thirty seconds after the door slammed at Apartment 2868, Sherron Collins heard gun shots. And, eventually, screams.

Cedrick Collins (no relation to Sherron) had been hit with a stray bullet moments after walking out of Sherron's living room at the Lathrop Homes housing complex on the near northwest side of Chicago. By the time Sherron made it outside, his best friend of 10 years was basically dead.

"His hat was lying a few feet away and his head was in a big puddle of blood," Sherron said. "He moved a little bit, but whenever I tried to get him to talk, he couldn't say anything."

A few days later, at a local hospital, Cedrick was taken off of life support. He was 16.

"Sometimes I see interviews on TV or hear people talking about how tough they had it growing up," Collins said. "I never say anything out loud but, in the back of my head, I'm thinking, 'You have no clue.' "

The book on Sherron Marlon Collins was established early.

Within a year of his birth in March 1987, Sherron had learned to dribble a basketball in front of his walker. By the time he was 9, he was embarrassing grown men in pick-up games at neighborhood picnics.

Sherron's mother, Stacey Harris, worked two jobs as a certified nursing assistant and rarely came home before midnight. Then there was Dad, who couldn't offer much support from his jail cell.

Like his son, Steven Collins was once a standout on the Chicago high school basketball scene, playing at St. James against the likes of Windy City legend Tim Hardaway.

Steven, though, dropped out of school his junior year. He eventually joined a gang and began selling drugs, a trade he practiced even after fathering Sherron and his older brother, Steve.

"We were living in the projects, but we had all the nice clothes and all the latest video games," said Steve Collins, now 21 and a student at West Valley College in San Jose, Calif. "But he was never there for us. He was never that male figure we needed because he was in and out of prison.

"People in the neighborhood called him the Gym Shoe Daddy, because buying Sherron and me gym shoes was the only way he knew to show us love."

Even with their father incarcerated and their mother busy with two jobs, Sherron and his brother felt safe in their surroundings during their elementary school years. Each day after school they went straight to the Boys and Girls Club, where you couldn't touch a basketball until you'd completed your homework.

Steve said the Boys and Girls Club is paying his college tuition, and Sherron shudders when he thinks of what he may have become had his mother not

walked him through those doors more than a decade ago.

"In a lot of ways," Sherron said, "you could say that club saved our lives."

Still, while he felt safe inside the walls of the Boys and Girls Club, nothing could protect Sherron from what he saw outside.

By the time Sherron reached junior high school, the feeling of safety that existed in the projects had all but vanished. From the Kings to the Deuces to the Stones, gangs of every race were growing right along with the crime rate. It was impossible to ignore.

One morning Sherron could open his door and see men slicing a tattoo off the chest of a rival gang member. Other times things got even more violent.

"I still remember that maroon Suburban," Steve said. "A bunch of guys would jump out and everyone would yell, 'Get down!' We'd start hearing shots. I'd look up and people were running past Sherron and me, shooting.

"They didn't even look at us because we were so young. They just kept chasing people through the neighborhood with those guns." It all became too much for Stacey Harris. Disheartened by the murder of Cedrick Collins, she moved her family into a Madison Avenue apartment on Chicago's west side.

That neighborhood wasn't any better, and the situation only got worse.

Stacey said she experienced the scare of her life shortly after settling into her new home. Around midnight Sherron's friend, Bobby Fisher, stormed through her door and told her someone was trying to rob her son.

When Stacey ran outside she found Sherron's blue Los Angeles Dodgers cap lying in the street.

"I thought someone shot him," Stacey said. "I thought he was dead."

And Sherron easily could've been had he not fled when a man hopped out of the driver's seat of a car and brandished a gun. Sherron said the man slipped on the icy road, which gave him a head start on a chase through the neighborhood. Eventually Sherron flagged down a stranger, who gave him a ride back to his apartment.

After that Sherron began spending more and more time at Uncle Walt's house. As for his mother and that place on Madison Avenue?

"I picked up and moved back in with my mother in the suburbs," Stacey said. "I'd seen all I needed to see."

• • •

Lunch trays and aluminum chairs flew through the Crane High School cafeteria during a 200-person, gang-related melee.

Even if he wanted to, Collins couldn't have gotten involved.

"I knew all of the security guards," Collins said. "One of them grabbed me and told me to go home. Everyone there made sure I stayed out of trouble."

People have always looked out for Sherron Collins. Not just administrators, relatives and mentors, but gang members and drug dealers, too.

In elementary school he was known simply as "the kid who could play basketball." So impressive

was Collins on the court that some of the neighborhood's most-feared hoodlums would show up at the Boys and Girls Club to watch his sixth-grade games.

It was the same way in high school, where Collins was popular with everyone from the student body president to the kid who'd try to fight you if you looked at him the wrong way in the hall.

That's the thing about Collins: The people that laud him for steering clear of mischief also realize he probably couldn't have joined a gang or gotten involved in the drug game if he had tried. And it was all because of basketball.

"If you're a ballplayer in Chicago, you're off limits to that kind of stuff," said Anthony Longstreet, Collins' high school coach. "It's an unwritten rule: Gangs don't draft ballplayers. Those guys are left alone."

Collins put it more simply. "They didn't mess with me," he said. "They respected me and what I was trying to do."

Before he ever played a game at Crane, word of Collins' prowess on the basketball court had spread throughout the city. Stacey Harris said coaches used to "flood" the nursing home where she worked, trying to persuade her to enroll Sherron in their high school.

"Until then I didn't know seventh-graders got recruited," Stacey said.

Eventually Collins picked Crane off of a list that included Westinghouse and Simeon. Longstreet had worked with NBA All-Star standout Kevin Garnett back in the mid-90s, and the year before Collins enrolled he'd sent Will Bynum, one of the country's top guards, to Arizona.

"The first time I saw him play I was like, 'Oh my God!'" said Longstreet, who made Collins a four-year starter. "He was Will Bynum all over again. The crossover, the strong body, the aggressiveness. It was like they were long-lost brothers."

Collins found a mentor in Longstreet, who handled his college recruitment. His time at Crane also saw him grow closer to his uncle, who he'd considered a father figure since childhood.

Collins began to appreciate his uncle more and more. He moved in with him as a junior and, for the first time in his life, had to abide by a strict set of rules. No phone calls past 10, only one house guest per night, curfew on the weekends.

It was the kind of guidance Collins never received from his father -- and it was almost taken away when Walt had a liver transplant in 2004. Harris lifts his shirt to expose a scar that runs from hip bone to sternum on each side.

"I called him at 4:30 in the morning as I was going into surgery," Harris said. "I said, Hopefully I make it out of this, but if I don't, don't let that stop you. Let it push you more and more. I want to be able to celebrate with you, but if I can't you push forward. You go on with your life.' "

Walt pauses.

I've tried to help that kid," he said, "but in a lot of ways he helped me."

• • •

Before he shoots each free throw, Sherron Collins glances at the tattoo on his right forearm. Below a pair of clasped, praying hands are these words: "Sherron

Jr. R.I.P."

His stint as a father lasted fewer than two weeks, but during that time, it would have been tough to find a dad as proud as Collins. He phoned Longstreet so the coach could hear the baby crying through the receiver. Callers who were sent to Collins' voicemail were treated to the song "Daddy" by Juelz Santana.

""I was so happy," Collins said, "to be a father."

It didn't last long. About 10 days after his birth, young Sherron's lungs stopped getting oxygen. The infection, doctors said, couldn't be reversed. Walt said he'll never forget what happened after Sherron arrived at Rush Medical Center.

"When Sherron got to the hospital, I told him it was time to say goodbye to his son," Walt said. "He just broke down. We went into the room, the doctor unhooked the tubes and then handed Sherron the little baby. He sat there holding him for about 30 minutes, until ..." The sentence was left unfinished.

Collins, who had moved his things to Kansas a few weeks earlier, returned to Lawrence depressed. Friends and family members from Chicago had a tough time reaching him on the phone, and his weight ballooned to 228 pounds.

Suddenly the 5-foot-10 bulldog who threw down the left-handed tomahawk slam at the McDonald's All-American game was one of the first ones winded during conditioning drills. His knees hurt. His back ached -- and his playing time diminished.

A busload of folks from the Boys and Girls Club came to watch KU take on DePaul in Chicago, but Collins played just 14 minutes. Afterward KU coach Bill Self delivered a message: Get down to 200 pounds, or you're not going to play.

For the next month Collins endured three cardio workouts a day. He also ate every meal in the presence of a KU staff member.

While the pounds -- 26 of them -- melted away, Collins' playing time began to increase. Midway through the Big 12 season, he'd become one of KU's best performers, and some would argue he's been the best.

His 23 points helped KU eke out an 80-77 victory over Missouri at Allen Fieldhouse, and he had 20 in the Jayhawks' win over K-State in Manhattan. Suddenly a Kansas offense that sometimes appeared stagnant had life thanks to Collins, who during one stretch had 14 assists and only two turnovers.

"Everyone here admires Sherron," Self said. "It's obvious that, at some point in his life, he came to a crossroads where he had to choose one kind of life or the other. That he is where is he now shows you that, deep down, he's a winner."

• • •

Back at Buffalo Wild Wings, Collins can't stop thinking about playing against Texas. The Longhorns have defeated Texas A&M, meaning a victory Saturday would give KU the outright Big 12 title.

Uncle Walt and Mom are flying in for the occasion, a treat considering she missed almost all of his high school games because of work.

Afterward Sherron hopes they can all gather for a nice dinner and then maybe meet up with roommate Brady Morningstar, a KU guard whose parents live in Lawrence.

"Sherron and I do everything together," Morningstar said. "He doesn't like to be alone."

The Morningstars have become Collins' second family, their house — complete with a pool table and big-screen TV — a second home.

"That family has been a godsend for Sherron," Longstreet said. "It's good for him to know that there are people like that in this world. People that care about him for who he is instead of who he can be."

Collins and Morningstar push away from the table, leaving their wing bones behind as they walk out the door onto Massachusetts Street. It's cold and rainy outside, but Collins doesn't seem to care, as he struts slowly to the car, sending text messages along the way. There's no threat of gunfire, no gang members on the street corner. Just a free night to see a movie or hang out at Wal-Mart, where Sherron and Brady sometimes spend hours walking each aisle until their basket is full of things they probably don't need.

"Getting away from that stuff ... sometimes I feel like I'm on a vacation," Collins said. "I'm just glad there are people in my life that made me see a different way."

Sasha Kaun

# Sasha's Journey

Yahoo! Sports: March 7, 2008

LAWRENCE, Kan. – If only they'd given him more time to talk. Maybe then, Kansas forward Sasha Kaun would've told the rest of his story.

Perhaps he would've discussed that night 10 years ago, when his father was found dead – murdered, some believe – in the corner of a cold parking garage in Kaun's native Russia.

Kaun could've mentioned that emotional moment three years later when, at 16, he wrapped his arms around his mother at the airport, knowing that the hug would be the last they'd share for more than a year.

Or maybe Kaun could've explained how he blossomed into a top post player for one of the country's most storied programs just a few years after playing organized basketball for the first time.

"When you look at all the things that happened that led Sasha to this point ... it's an unbelievable story," KU coach Bill Self said.

Yet it's a story that can't be told in three minutes, which is the time Kaun was allotted for his Senior Day speech Monday at Allen Fieldhouse. Still, at least he got to say thanks.

Thanks to his coaches. Thanks to his teammates and fans. And thanks, most of all, to Olga, who waved to her son from Row 8 as he stood in the middle of the hardwood, clutching a microphone as a sellout crowd of 16,300 watched and listened.

"When I look at him running around the court during games," Olga said through an interpreter, "I see this grown-up boy – this man!

"I can't believe this is all real."

• • •

Shortly before midnight – as he raced through his neighborhood to comfort his mother – 13-year-old Sasha Kaun could see the lights from the ambulance flickering against the dark sky.

Minutes earlier he'd answered the phone and heard Olga sobbing.

"It was terrible," he said. "She was in hysterics."

Kaun said his mother told him she'd become concerned when her husband,

Oleg, failed to come home from work, and that her search for him had ended at the family's single-car garage a few blocks away.

Olga entered and found Sasha's father on his knees and unconscious. His body faced a wall, his torso sloped forward and his right hand was behind his back.

"A strange, awkward position," Sasha said.

Paramedics attempted to resuscitate him knowing there was little hope. On Jan. 16, 1998 – in the biting, unforgiving cold of Tomsk, Russia – Oleg Kaun was dead.

There were no clues, no witnesses. Instead of opening an investigation, Sasha said Russian authorities cited "gas poisoning" as the cause of his father's death and moved on.

"We've never thought it was a suicide," said Sasha, now 23. "He was a happy person. He wouldn't have done that."

Instead Olga believes Oleg was killed, and that the murder was somehow related to his job as a computer programmer for one of the largest banks in Russia. Not only did he create the programs used by the bank and all of its branches, but it was also Oleg's responsibility to prevent hackers from getting into the system.

A few weeks before he died, Oleg told his wife that he was "having some problems" at work and that someone had broken into the program and was stealing money.

"Russia was very unstable during the 1990s – especially the banking system," Olga said. "My friends and I have come to the same conclusion: Someone just got rid of Oleg so he wouldn't cause any problems.

"Oleg was a very good person, very goal-oriented. Everyone loved him. He was handsome and he was respected as an expert."

Throughout his college career, Kaun has chosen not to speak publicly about the death of his father, who he described as "very private."

But earlier this week, as he reflected on the tragedy during an interview at Kansas' Burge Union, Kaun was open and matter-of-fact when discussing Oleg's passing and the way it shaped his future.

"I didn't cry much when it happened," Kaun said. "But after the funeral, at the reception, all these people came up to me and paid their respects. People started talking about the different things he'd done in life. That's when it really hit me. There were a lot of things I didn't know."

One man told Sasha about the actions his father took to benefit the community. Another mentioned Oleg's impeccable reputation as a computer programmer, adding that he was regarded as one of the best in Russia.

"I was sad that I'd never get the chance to find those things out on my own," Sasha said.

Kaun reaches into his backpack and pulls out his billfold. Inside is a black-and-white picture of Oleg taken from an old passport. He's wearing a sport coat and has mangy, black hair. Once or twice a week, Kaun looks at the photo says hello to his father through prayer.

Just like Oleg, Sasha has plans to become a computer programmer when his basketball career is finished. Despite the Jayhawks' rigorous schedule, Kaun has managed to earn Academic All-Big 12 honors three times and will graduate in May. Kaun puts away his dad's picture and smiles.

"I definitely think I'm making him proud," he said.

• • •

As painful as Oleg's death was emotionally, it also caused a change in lifestyle for Sasha and Olga, who was left alone to raise her only son.

"All of a sudden," Sasha said, "it was just the two of us."

Olga, though, was confident they would persevere because of a comment Sasha made moments after he arrived outside the garage on that dreadful January night.

"On that cold winter evening, his first words to me were 'Mom, don't worry. From now on I'm going to help you with everything," Olga said. "That was the end of his childhood. He became very serious, very grown up."

On nights when he used to hang out in the streets playing soccer, Kaun now found himself shopping for groceries. He'd clean the apartment between homework assignments and often cooked dinner for his mother, who had to work extra hours to pay the tuition fees of Sasha's private school.

The routine worked well until high school, when Sasha fell into the trap that threatens so many children in single-parent homes. With so much freedom, Sasha said he became lazy and blew off homework assignments. His grades begin to slip right along with his work ethic. Luckily, the problems didn't last long.

The summer before his sophomore year, Sasha received a call from a friend who'd just graduated from a high school called the Florida Air Academy.

Located in Melbourne, Fla., the boarding school had long been lauded for its efforts in attracting foreign students. Kaun's friend said the school wanted to add more Russians to its student body and suggested he enroll.

"I looked at the situation and realized I could be doing a lot better in school," Kaun said. "Going to the states was like a wake-up call. It was like, 'Hey, you have this chance. Take it.'"

The only problem was that the situation would pull Kaun away from the mother with whom he'd experienced so much. But Olga Kaun knew an American education had more value than one obtained in Russia, where diplomas can be purchased off the street.

So she borrowed about $2,000 from her parents for a plane ticket and a visa. Just like that – without knowing a word of English – Sasha was on a plane bound for Florida.

Years later, Kaun couldn't be more appreciative of Olga's decision. It's one thing for a parent to send a child to a new high school on the other side of town or even a college in a different state.

But for a mother to allow a 16-year-old son to enroll at a school in another country shows how eager she is for him to succeed. "It wasn't all that tough for me," Kaun said. "I liked challenges and experiencing new things. But it was difficult for my mother. I kept telling her that, if I didn't like it after a year, I'd come home."

But that never happened.

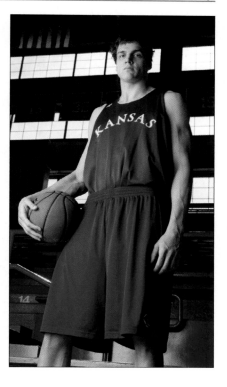

Kaun went 18 months before returning to Russia. Instead he and Olga talked twice a week on the Internet. In the meantime he was earning good grades in school – he aced Calculus as a sophomore – while continuing to learn more and more about computers.

"He was chasing his dream – just like his daddy," said Aubin Goporo, a faculty member at Florida Air Academy. "The first time I met him I asked him what he wanted to be and he said, 'A computer engineer.' I asked him what else he may want to do and he said, 'I don't know, maybe own my own business.'"

Goporo pauses and chuckles. There was another reason he'd called Sasha into his office that day.

"Did you ever think about making a living playing basketball?" Goporo asked Kaun.

No, Sasha said. Never.

• • •

From the day he arrived on campus, everyone at Florida Air Academy knew Sasha Kaun. At 6-foot-10, he was easily the tallest student at the school – and the ironic thing was that he had never played organized basketball.

Kaun's inexperience was glaring during his first few weeks on the court. He said he felt "lost" when the team tried to run plays, and the fact that he spoke little English made it impossible for him to understand Goporo, who is also the school's coach.

Physically, Kaun, then 175 pounds, didn't have the strength to match up against anyone in the paint. One day in the weight room, he said he attempted to squat 135 pounds but fell over as soon he lifted the bar from the rack. Kansas assistant Joe Dooley remembers watching one of Kaun's practices during his sophomore season.

"Anyone who says they saw him as a sophomore and knew he was going to be a good player is lying," said Dooley, an assistant with New Mexico at the time. "But with big kids you can never tell. You never know how they're going to develop."

Still, even the ones who improve rarely do so as rapidly as Kaun, who began logging extra hours in the weight room and gym. Kaun might have had an advantage when it came to size but, even today, he credits hard work – and not natural ability – as the main reason for his success.

"He's one of the most disciplined kids I've ever coached," said Goporo, who counts Florida's Walter Hodge among his proteges. "He doesn't say much, but he pays attention to everything that goes on around him. You won't find many players smarter than Sasha."

After just two years of organized basketball, Kaun began excelling on the summer AAU circuit. A standout performance at the Boo Williams Invitational catapulted him near the top of college want-lists across the country. In the end, Kaun named Kansas, Duke and Michigan State as the finalists for his services.

Not that the Blue Devils and Spartans ever stood much of a chance.

Goporo, who had become Kaun's mentor, had long been infatuated with KU coach Bill Self when Self was coaching at Illinois. Goporo traveled to Chicago to listen to Self speak at clinics. He had an Illini backpack and subscribed to the school's newsletter. When Self came to Florida to visit Kaun he noticed Goporo had a picture of him on his screensaver.

"I tried to hide it but it was too late," said Goporo, laughing. "College basketball has become such a business. It's hard to find someone who's going to put his career aside and take care of you as a human being. But I knew that's what Sasha would have with Coach Self."

Kaun averaged 8.2 points while starting all but four games as a sophomore. His scoring average dipped to 5.9 a year ago, when nagging injuries stymied his progress.

Still, Kaun, at 250 pounds, has developed a reputation as one of the Big 12's strongest players in the paint. Rarely does he get out-muscled, and right now he's on pace to achieve season-highs in both points and blocks despite losing his starting job to Darnell Jackson.

Self said Kaun is having his best season ever for the 27-3 Jayhawks, who can clinch their fourth straight Big 12 title with a win Saturday against Texas A&M.

"This is the healthiest he's been," Self said. "He was prepared to come in and have a good year. He hasn't had lower body problems like he's had in the past. There were two summers in a row where he couldn't work out because of health reasons.

"In my mind he's a starter. Since he hasn't been starting he's playing at a higher level and Darnell has been playing at a higher level. So in the long run the move has helped our entire team."• • •

Back at Allen Fieldhouse, Kaun is standing at center court, still clutching that microphone. He begins to address his mother and then cuts a joke.

"She probably won't understand half of what I say," Kaun said, "because she doesn't speak much English."

Olga doesn't mind. She and Sasha have spent plenty of time together the past few months. Because she wanted to be present for all the big events during her son's final semester of college – Senior Day, the NCAA tournament and graduation – Olga has been living in Lawrence since December.

Each and every night she sleeps on the couch in Sasha's living

room. He also doesn't mind that she cleans his dishes, does his laundry and occasionally cooks pelemeni, a Russian ravioli.

"I am proud that my son did not fail," Olga said. "I'm proud that he showed manhood and patience and is getting an education here – just like his dad. I think the tragedy that occurred in our family helped form my son's character and helped him fight against everything to reach great accomplishments."

Kaun will graduate May 18 with a degree in computer science. Beyond that, he's not sure what's next.

An NBA scout said last week that Kaun – because of his size, strength and intellect – might be selected in the second round of this summer's NBA Draft. If that doesn't happen, he could almost certainly earn solid money playing basketball overseas.

Kaun isn't thinking that far ahead. On Tuesday, he couldn't stop talking about the Big 12 title race, the NCAA tournament and Kansas' chances of winning the national championship.

But most of all he kept bringing up the emotions of Senior Night, the ovation he received and the sense of love he and his mother felt inside Allen Fieldhouse.

Lawrence may be thousands of miles from Russia. Still, now more than ever, Sasha Kaun couldn't feel more at home.

# In No Rush

Star freshman grows up, chooses to stay in college after discovering the meaning of team at Kansas

Kansas City Star: March 19, 2006

*Brandon Rush*

LAWRENCE - He was taught to stand up straight, to keep his feet still and establish eye contact. But as Brandon Rush stands before 22 of his peers, the rules of public speaking are becoming difficult to follow.

The assignment in Communications 130 is this: Talk about yourself. Tell your classmates where you're from. Tell them about your family, about your interests, about your ambitions.

That should be simple for Rush, the Kansas star and Freshman All-American who some argue has more potential than his legendary older brothers.

Surely the class would love to hear about the month last summer when Rush kicked it with the Lakers in Kareem's four-story beach pad near Los Angeles. Or about the time JaRon shattered a backboard during a high school basketball game.

So many fascinating stories to hold their attention. Yet Rush never tells them.

Instead he leans against a wooden lectern and stares down at his notecards, rarely lifting his head as he mumbles and stutters his way through his speech.

"My hands were shaking, my palms were sweating," Rush said later. "I could feel myself getting hot underneath my sweater. I hate talking in front of groups like that. I get nervous."

So do a lot of normal college kids, which is what Rush is feeling more and more like each time he strolls through the Kansas campus.

The strange thing? He likes it. Brandon Rush actually likes college - so much, in fact, that he announced after Friday's NCAA Tournament loss to Bradley that he'll be returning for his sophomore year rather than entering the NBA draft.

"College," Rush said, "is a lot different, a lot more fun, than what I thought it would be."

• • •

A few weeks before he signed with Kansas last summer, Rush told The Star that his time with the Jayhawks would probably be limited to one season, that Lawrence would be no more than a restroom stop on his way toward becoming a top pick in the upcoming draft.

But then something strange happened.

As the season wore on, Rush began caring about his teammates more than his statistics. He went more than two months without making a day trip to his native Kansas City because he was too busy enjoying the social scene near campus.

Rush is still soft-spoken and, at times, introverted. But at least now he smiles and waves at the strangers who call his name or honk their horns on campus.

In Lawrence, he's finally found a place where he can be Brandon Rush - not JaRon and Kareem's little brother.

"When you step back and look at it, the whole thing was kind of like a trade," KU guard Jeff Hawkins said. "Kansas needed Brandon, but even more than that, I think Brandon needed Kansas."

Before you can truly appreciate how far Rush has come, you must first know where he's been.

Rush's story starts here, in the home of Jeannette Jacobs, the grandmother with an NCAA Tournament bracket on her kitchen table and pictures of Brandon, JaRon and Kareem strewn across her living-room walls.

On most days, Rush's mother, Glenda, was still at work when school let out in the afternoon. So Rush retreated to the basement of his grandmother's home near 59th and Prospect in Kansas City.

There he would spend hours playing video games with his younger cousin. Rush's father was not a part of his life - and, truthfully, neither were his brothers.

Brandon is six years younger than JaRon and five years younger than Kareem. Some say JaRon, a former UCLA star, was the best high school basketball player in Kansas City's history. But it's Kareem who went on to earn NBA millions with the Los Angeles Lakers and the Charlotte Bobcats, his current team.

While Brandon rotated between his mother's and grandmother's house, JaRon and Kareem spent their summers traveling on the AAU circuit. All those backyard pickup games you'd expect between brothers? They rarely occurred.

"We never were the type to sit around at a family dinner and talk about things," JaRon said. "We just kind of came and went on our own."

Kareem regrets he didn't spend more time with Brandon.

"That bond that most brothers have wasn't as strong as it should've been," he said.

Glenda Rush said JaRon and Kareem teased her youngest son for being a "Big Baby" and a "Mama's Boy." So shy and insecure was Rush that when accepting an

award for JaRon at age 12, he couldn't utter a single word into the microphone.

"He walked up to the microphone and got all ready to say something," Jacobs said. "But then he couldn't get any words to come out. So he stood there until people started clapping and then went back to his seat."

Eventually, Rush began playing AAU basketball. At 6 feet 2, he was dunking - and wearing a size-12 shoe - by the time he reached eighth grade. With long arms and strong coordination, it was obvious Rush had what it took to become something special.

Thing is, that's not what he wanted.

"When he was younger, like 14 or so, he told me he didn't even like basketball," said UMKC guard Tim Blackwell, one of Rush's closest friends. "It's tough being a Rush brother in Kansas City. Even then, people were watching every move he made.

"People would be like, `Hey, there's little Rush.' Brandon would just turn away and pretend like he didn't hear them."

• • •

Brandon Rush can't read. At least that's what fans in opposing arenas like to chant.

He's also arrogant, self-centered, uncoachable and just an all-round bad kid, according to a flock of people whom, strangely, he's never met.

"I met this girl (at Kansas)," Rush said. "She told me that before I got here, everyone was saying that I was dumb. She said she heard I was stuck on myself and that I was a real lazy player with a bad work ethic.

"Most people out there ... they don't know me. That's why I can't figure out why someone would say stuff like that."

Perhaps it's because of the reputation Rush earned during his high school days in Kansas City. By the time Rush was 16 he had spent time at three different high schools. Because of poor grades, however, he didn't play his first prep game until the second semester of his sophomore year at Westport, where he led the school to its first state tournament berth in 25 years. By the following winter, Rush had been declared ineligible again.

Rush admits now that he was a follower at Westport and not a leader. He said he was running with a bad crowd. He said he associated with people who experimented with drugs and others who didn't give a flip about school.

"I got tired of getting called up to school to hear about his problems," said Jacobs, the grandmother. "He wasn't fighting or getting into any major trouble, but he was disrupting class and telling jokes - just being lazy. Brandon just didn't like school."

Even away from the classroom, Rush didn't seem motivated.

"I'd go over there, and he wouldn't want to get off the couch," Blackwell said. "All he wanted to do was watch TV and play video games all day."

He may not have been excelling in the classroom, but it's not as if Rush didn't have the wherewithal to realize he was headed down a disastrous path.

Eventually he decided to leave Kansas City for Durham, N.C., and Mount Zion prep school, the alma mater of a bundle of Division I standouts as well as NBA superstar Tracy McGrady.

At Mount Zion, Rush said, life was more about basketball than books. But this wasn't team basketball. With each player talented enough to attend a top-notch college, Rush said it was every player for himself.

"We were all trying to get our own little shine on," he said.

Heck, Rush may have been one of the worst when it came to selfish play. By this point his brother, Kareem, was playing for the Los Angeles Lakers.

Rush had seen the four-story house in Marina Del Ray, the one with the plasma TVs in every room, the one with the whirlpool and the pool table and the beautiful women who came by for parties.

If Rush needed to run an errand on his visit to Los Angeles, he was free to drive Kareem's Cadillac Escalade - if, of course, it was in the garage. If not he could always take the Hummer, the BMW or the SL 500.

"Those NBA players ... they're living the life," Rush said. "Cars, jewelry, nice houses and furniture. They've got the freedom to buy anything they want. You see that stuff, and it makes you want it. It makes you want it bad."

No surprise, then, that Rush snickered a few years ago when Shawn Taggart asked Rush where he wanted to go to college.

"College? I ain't messin' with college," Rush told his Mount Zion roommate. "I'm going straight to the league."

• • •

Watching what happened to JaRon and Kareem during high school helped create the skeptical and guarded nature Brandon carries with him today. The story is well-known in Kansas City: After leading Pembroke Hill to three state championships from 1997 to 1999, the older Rushes were named in a scandal involving their AAU coach, Myron Piggie.

In 2000, Piggie pleaded guilty to paying $35,000 to JaRon, Kareem and three other players on his summer team. Piggie was sentenced to 37 months in federal prison while JaRon and Kareem each received suspensions from their college teams.

"It was horrible," Jacobs said. "It was embarrassing. Myron got us into a mess and we didn't even know we were doing anything wrong. I don't ever want to see something like that happen again.

"Brandon was old enough to realize what went on. He knows right from wrong when it comes to that kind of stuff."

Rush's leeriness of outsiders became an issue during his days at Mount Zion. Although he declined to provide any names, Rush said someone he thought was a friend began trying to help him financially and even offered to give him a car.

"He kept trying to get into my business," Rush said. "Wherever I went, he wanted to know everything: Where I was going and who I was talking to. I had to cut him off and quit taking his calls.

"Sometimes I feel like a piece of meat. I don't know what people are after. That's why I don't trust anyone. People try to get close to me, but I never know what for. So I just end up isolating myself."

Even today, the only adult Rush seems to fully trust - outside of his family members - is John Walker, who coached all the Rush brothers on the AAU circuit.

Rush leaned heavily on Walker a year ago when he decided to make himself eligible for the NBA draft. Along with performing well at the pre-draft camp in Chicago, Rush impressed the scouts and coaches of the four teams with which he worked out.

In the end, though, it was unclear whether Rush would be a first-round selection and, thus, receive a guaranteed three-year contract. After a workout with the Houston Rockets, Rush found a fax machine at Hobby Airport and sent notice to the NBA that he was withdrawing from the draft.

"It was actually a little scary," Rush said. "It was late June, and I had no idea what I was going to do."

Kansas had already signed a top-10 recruiting class in Julian Wright, Mario Chalmers and Micah Downs when it joined Indiana, Illinois and Oklahoma in the recruiting war for Rush. Adding a surefire NBA draft pick to the mix would make KU's haul the best in the country.

The only problem was that Rush's family wasn't keen on the idea. JaRon had had a negative experience while being recruited by former KU coach Roy Williams, and Kareem had starred at archrival Missouri.

Rush, though, couldn't help it. Hours after returning to Kansas City from his official visit, he caught a ride back to Lawrence and spent the weekend hanging out with Chalmers, whom he has known since eighth grade.

Even though he waited until he was deemed eligible before making an announcement, Rush said he told Chalmers that weekend that Kansas would be his home. Not that he expected to stay very long.

"It's no secret," Rush told The Star on Aug. 8. "Most of the coaches I talk to ... I don't even have to tell them. Instead they tell me. They're like, `Don't worry, we know you're only going to be here a year or two.' They're cool with it."

From an individual standpoint, Rush's first year at Kansas couldn't have been much more of a success. He started every game, averaged a team-high 13.5 points and became the only freshman in Big 12 history to earn first-team all-conference honors.

Still, ask those close to Rush, and they'll tell you his time at Kansas has been more about what happened off the court than on it.

Before this season Rush didn't know what "we" meant. It wasn't his fault. He had never been around team-oriented basketball. He knew what it was like to achieve success as an individual, but not as a group.

"Watch him out there," said UMKC's Quinton Day, another close friend from

Kansas City. "I've never seen him show this kind of emotion. Once you realize how fun it is to win, your feelings start to come into play.

"He used to dunk on someone and run down the court without even smiling. Now he's high-fiving his teammates and hugging them. He cares."When Kansas won the Big 12 tournament title last week, Rush was the only KU freshman not to be picked to the all-tournament team. A year ago that would've bugged him.

But when he climbed the ladder toward the iron rim in Dallas, he carried with him a sign that read "Big 12 Champs" and propped up against the backboard. Afterward he snipped away a piece of the net and gave it to his grandmother.

"I want her to frame it for me," Rush said.

• • •

The locker room doors swing open, and a throng of media surround the Jayhawks after their final game of the season. Back in the corner sits Rush, who offers up a reason to smile during a moment that's filled with angst.

"I'll be back next year," he said after KU's loss to Bradley. "I can't go out like this. I can't do that to my team."

Let's not kid ourselves. Rush isn't Shane Battier. There are things he doesn't like about college.

He's said publicly that he's not a fan of going to class - even though he earned a 3.6 grade-point average last semester. He doesn't enjoy the tutoring sessions each night and, sure, there are times when practice is a little more strenuous than he would like.

Still, Rush has found something here in Lawrence, something much more than a place to play basketball until he decides to turn pro.

Ever since he became a good basketball player, it's always been about the final destination for Rush. But now he's stopping to enjoy the journey.

College isn't a nuisance. It's a chance to sweat bullets in speech class and to exchange text messages with the dozens of girls who call his cell phone and to have pillow fights with teammates in the dorm.

Rush will grow up soon enough. Right now, for the first time in his life, he's discovering how neat it is to be a kid.

"I never could've imagined," Rush said, "that I'd have this much fun."

# Jackson Perseveres

## Kansas forward, who has fought through family tragedy, grabs 11 rebounds as Jayhawks tie for first place

Kansas City Star: Feb. 15, 2007

*Darnell Jackson*

BOULDER, Colo. | His uncle was beaten to death with a hammer.

His cousin and close friend were killed by gang members outside an Oklahoma City nightclub, and his grandmother died after her car was hit by a drunken driver in Las Vegas.

When Kansas forward Darnell Jackson walked into Bill Self's office on a dreary day over Christmas break, he didn't need a coach.

He needed a friend.

"I just started crying," Jackson said. "I cried and cried until he came over and hugged me. Coach just said: 'Darnell, God is doing this to you for a reason. He's making you a stronger person.' "

Listen to him talk. Watch him on the court and pay attention to his smile.

It's obvious the Darnell Jackson who grabbed 11 rebounds in KU's 75-46 victory Wednesday at Colorado is a different player from the one who for two years yo-yoed between decent and dreadful.

Finally -- after more than two seasons -- Jackson is having fun. Finally, he's able to relish his achievements on the court rather than grieve over the tragedies that have occurred off of it.

"He's got more juice than he's had in a long time," said Self, whose team is tied with Texas A&M for first place in the Big 12 standings. "From a personal standpoint he feels better than he has in a while. He's maturing."

In his last three games, Jackson has averaged nine points and nine rebounds. The 11 boards he grabbed Wednesday came in just 17 minutes.

As the season inches toward its climax, it's clear Jackson -- once a seldom-used reserve -- could play an integral role for a Kansas squad that has legitimate Big 12 and national title hopes.

There were times, though, when Jackson questioned whether he'd ever get to this point.

The trouble began when Jackson's grandmother Evon was killed in 2005 in Las Vegas. Also in the vehicle that afternoon was Jackson's mother, Shawn, who sustained serious injuries to her legs. She spent more than a month in the hospital before being released.

A few months later, Jackson's childhood friend was shot in the head along with his cousin, Glen Davis. The two were leaving an Oklahoma City nightclub when bullets began spraying from a passing car.

"Back at home everyone thinks it's cool to be in a gang," Jackson said. "In Oklahoma City you don't fight. You shoot. It's sad."

As if that heartache wasn't enough, Jackson learned in November that he was suspended for the first nine games of the 2005-06 season for receiving impermissible gifts from KU booster Don Davis.

Jackson said he'd been friends with Davis since his high school days and therefore didn't think he was doing anything wrong by accepting small amounts of cash and occasional rides from Oklahoma City to Lawrence. Still, that didn't stop the NCAA from leveling its punishment.

"Ever since I've been here stuff has been falling in my lap," said Jackson, who's also dealing with the recent death of his grandfather. "It was eating me up on the inside because I was holding it all in. When I was out there, coach Self knew I wasn't playing good. He knew something was wrong, so he'd take me out."

Jackson averaged two points as a freshman and only 6.3 as a sophomore. Because he had trouble sustaining any sort of focus, Jackson was rarely in the lineup when the game was on the line.

Even worse was that Jackson often felt as if he didn't have anywhere to turn. But that finally changed during this last Christmas.

During a trip back to Oklahoma City, Jackson was out on the town when a stranger approached his group, brandished a gun and opened fire.

"Just imagine walking down (Massachusetts Street) on a Friday night in Lawrence," Jackson said. "It was just like that. This guy just came up and shot one of my friends in the leg. It's just been one thing after another. I felt like everything was going downhill."

Only this time, instead of bottling up his feelings, Jackson went to Self.

He said the meeting steered him toward the path he's on today.

"It helped me a lot," Jackson said. "I don't have male figures or role models in my life, so I look at all the coaches as role models. I grew up without a dad.

"Sometimes that's hard for me. I look out there and see Mario Chalmers shooting around with his dad (Ronnie) there, and I wish I had that. But things happen for a reason.

"I'm a more positive person now. I feel like I'm getting stronger as I go."

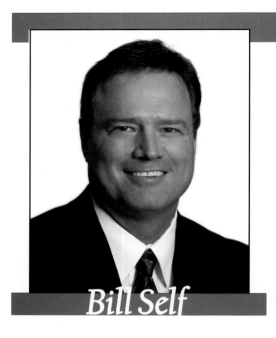

*Bill Self*

# Top Billing

### After a tough start, Bill Self has truly made the KU basketball program his own

Kansas City Star: Nov. 9, 2004

LAWRENCE - The coach of America's No. 1 basketball team cuts the ignition and turns off the Springsteen that booms in his black Lincoln Navigator. The speech begins in 20 minutes, and he's still not sure what to say.

"Any suggestions?" asks Kansas' Bill Self, now snaking through the banquet hall of the Lawrence Holidome. "Hopefully I'll think of something."

If only he had the time.

Fresh off a workout on his treadmill, Self scores a Diet Pepsi from the bar and begins rattling the ice in the plastic cup. Heads turn. People whisper. A group of Jayhawk boosters that has Kansas legend Danny Manning pinned against a wall is now pointing toward Self, who seems oblivious to the attention as he spots Lew Perkins.

"Haaay there, Mistuur Puurkins," howls Self, sounding like Gomer Pyle as he slaps five with KU's athletic director. "Whut's goin' on, bud?"

Self saunters toward the food area. Just look at him. The buffet is stocked with mashed potatoes, steamed veggies and chicken as tender as a mother's love. But Self doesn't eat. Instead he makes his way up and down the chow line, shaking the hand of each and every person in attendance for tonight's roast of former Kansas coach Ted Owens.

"You from Oklahoma?" he asks one woman. "What high school did you go to?"

Self turns to his wife, Cindy.

"I don't think I'm gonna eat, babe," he says. "I gotta watch this girlish figure."

People chuckle. This is vintage Self. Even more than his success on the court, this is why Kansas fans love him, flock to him, praise him.

Self's as at ease around his boss as you are your favorite drinking buddy. He erases the tension of star-struck fans within seconds, conversing with them as if they're his barber - as if they're his friend.

"It's amazing," a man in the line says to his wife. "He's as normal as he can be."

• • •

Here's the thing about Bill Self: He's not normal.

His personality, the situation he's stepped into at Kansas, the fact that his Jayhawks are No. 1 in the opening The Associated Press poll for the first time since 1956-57 - everything about Self and his tenure at KU is about as ordinary as Marilyn Manson.

"I hear that all the time, about how normal he is," Kansas assistant Tim Jankovich said. "I'm telling you, this guy is anything but normal. How many people do you know who could handle the pressure he's under, yet make the job seem so easy and stress-free? And how many people do you know that are so genuine and kind - people that talk to strangers each day not because they have to, but because they want to?

"Bill has a unique gift, and when I say unique, I mean one in a million. It's something we should all be envious of."

To an outsider, Self's first 19 months at Kansas couldn't have unfolded any more beautifully. After reaching the Elite Eight of the NCAA Tournament last season, the Jayhawks will enter the 2004-05 campaign boasting four seniors who have appeared in two Final Fours.

No team in the country is as battle-tested as KU - and few feature such depth. So talented is Self's first recruiting class that all five newcomers are expected to log significant minutes as true freshmen.

Everyone in the college basketball world is buzzing about the Jayhawks. If ever a Kansas team seemed destined for a national title, this would be the one.

"Our fans who bought (season) tickets were wise," Self said. "This could be a really fun year."

And at the center of it all will be Self, the former Illinois coach who was hired by Kansas during one of the most tumultuous times in the program's history. Jayhawk fans were still smarting from the sudden departure of Roy Williams when Self stepped off a plane at Lawrence Municipal Airport back in April 2003.

Eager as he was to begin his job at one of the country's most tradition-rich programs, Self realized his first year would be a difficult one.

He knew there would be comparisons to Williams, who was beloved by KU's three most-talented returnees: Wayne Simien, Keith Langford and Aaron Miles. How could he make those players - Roy's players - his own? And how, Self thought, could he put his own imprint on a team that had just played for a national championship, a team that had already experienced so much success?

"I came into a situation that didn't need to be fixed, a situation that wasn't broken," Self said. "And that was the biggest challenge of them all. I had to put my stamp on things, because I can't be something that I'm not. I can't coach what I don't believe in."

Self's confidants say he's the best in the business at masking aggravation, that his "every-day-is-a-good-day" mantra is baffling in its ever-presence. But as he reclines in his leather office chair, Self admits now just how frustrating things became.

"I went through phases when I didn't have much fun," he said. "There were times when I had buyer's remorse, just like you do when you buy a house or a car."

Self pauses.

"I wondered if I made the right decision."

• • •

Christmas was just three days away but, as Self sunk into a chair at the Reno, Nev., airport last December, he was hardly in the mood to sip eggnog and sing "Jingle Bells."

He looked at his assistant coaches.

"Fellas," he said, "the honeymoon is officially over."

Indeed, this was hardly how Self had envisioned his first year at Kansas. The Jayhawks were at the end of a road trip that included an awfully played victory over Cal-Santa Barbara and a 14-point loss to Nevada. Self could hear it now: "Roy never would have lost to Nevada!"

A few weeks earlier guard Michael Lee told reporters that the Jayhawks were in a "tug-of-war" with Self. And it eventually came to light that players were making frequent, in-season calls to Williams, who had moved on to North Carolina.

It wasn't that Kansas' players didn't like Self. They did. The problem was that the Jayhawks weren't buying into Self's system. Mainly because of the loss of guard Kirk Hinrich, a team that was used to playing at an up-tempo pace found itself adjusting to Self's high-low offense. When the Jayhawks struggled to execute, they couldn't help thinking, "The old way worked - why change it?"

"Not only is it difficult to teach 12 or 13 brand-new guys a new system," Jankovich said, "but some of them were resistant to change. It wasn't a defiance or any plotted, planned behavior. It was just a lack of enthusiasm toward what was asked of them.

"It's very easy to feel when a team hasn't completely bought in. You could tell that everyone didn't have both feet in the circle."

Looking back on it now, Self said he may have been too "soft" on his players during his first month on the job. He said he was sensitive to the Jayhawks' emotions after the coaching change, and that he wanted to give them time to enjoy their run to the 2003 title game, an accomplishment that had fallen by the wayside in the midst of Williams' departure.

"They saw me as being pretty laid back initially," Self said. "Then when I felt like guys were feeling better about themselves, I probably became more of a jerk in their eyes. I couldn't shove things down their throats. I had to be respectful of what they accomplished, but they had to understand that there was a new guy

in town."Even during the most trying times - which included a 20-point loss to Oklahoma State and a 19-point embarrassment at Nebraska - players said they respected Self from day one. Just as the Jayhawks were faced with obstacles, Lee said everyone realized Self had hurdles to conquer, too.

"Coming into a program like this, I'm sure he felt that pressure of, `I've got to win games here,'" Lee said. "Last year he was so intense. He'd jump on us about everything. But things are different now. We're still going to do things his way, but he's willing to make adjustments because he respects us - just like we respect him."

That's because, by the end of last season, the Jayhawks finally began to flourish by playing Self's style of basketball. The Jayhawks ended up finishing tied for second in the Big 12 regular season. During the NCAA Tournament, Self said his team was playing about as well as it possibly could have.

At the end of a long year, the future of Kansas basketball couldn't have appeared in better shape.

• • •

On a Friday evening last April, Bill Self turned off the lights in his office around 6 and prepared to head home. He was just two weeks removed from hernia surgery, and it hurt just to walk.

Still, just as Self was about to leave, he noticed a man in raggedy clothes standing with his young son in the foyer of KU's basketball headquarters.

"What can I do for you folks?" said Self, smiling.

The little boy's face lit up as his dad began to speak.

"I know the deadline was earlier today, but I just got off work," said the man, his fingers caked with auto grease. "Is there any way I can still sign him up for your basketball camp?"

Self: "Oh, I'm sure we can work something out. What grade are ya in, buddy? Seventh? My daughter's in seventh grade. Let me show y'all around the office."

Think that kid didn't have a tale for his friends at school?

There are hundreds of Self stories like that, stories that make you realize that Self's demeanor - just like his time at KU thus far - is anything but ordinary.

Perhaps you've talked baseball with him - Self loves Barry Bonds - after an impromptu encounter at Biggs, Pat's Blue Ribbon or any of the other barbecue joints he frequents in Lawrence.

"Bill eats barbecue eight days a week," Jankovich said.

Maybe he's waved at you while driving down 23rd Street as Journey, Styx or Springsteen plays on his car radio. Or you could be a reporter who has called Self's cell phone (he freely gives out his number, want it?) at all hours of the night.

"My mother and father always told me to treat everyone the same and that you're never any better or any worse than anyone else," Self said. "Sometimes people are friendly only to those that can help them. But to me it doesn't matter what role you're going to play in my life. I just enjoy people."

Yes, as he prepares for his second season with the Jayhawks, Lawrence has fallen in love with Bill Self. And his players have, too. That's why this season has the potential to be so special.

Simien will contend for national player of the year honors and Miles will shatter the Kansas assist record. But there's an x-factor there, a cohesion and harmony that permeates throughout the basketball offices and in the locker room. This isn't Roy's program anymore. Not even close. "That's a credit to coach Self," KU guard Stephen Vinson said. "One of the biggest differences between the two coaching staffs is that, with coach Self, you can go into his office and he'll make you laugh. He's just an approachable, down to earth guy."

• • •

The Jayhawks are preparing for practice as Self shoots the breeze with a few writers near the baseline. Jankovich and Manning are on the court, swishing three-pointers with ease. Someone asks Self to name the top shooter on his staff.

"I don't know," he said. "Tim's pretty darn good. And then there's Danny and Joe (Dooley). We've probably got the best shooting staff in America."

Self begins to walk away, but then turns back toward the writers.

"Don't forget," he whispers, "that I'm pretty freakin' good, too."

Perkins, the boss man, cracks up when he hears the story - just like he did when Self shot Perkins a barb about his controversial ticket policy during his speech at the Ted Owens banquet.

"Lew wanted me to tell everyone that the money you paid to be here tonight doesn't count toward the points system," Self said.

Perkins hee-hawed at that one.

"I'll get him back, but don't you just love it?" Perkins said. "Everyone knows he's a great guy, but that doesn't mean he doesn't have a cocky side. You have to in this job. He couldn't be any better to work with. There are low-maintenance coaches, and then there's Bill Self."

As long as Self is on the bench, Perkins said he likes KU's chances no matter who the Jayhawks are playing.

"Bill's legacy is still ahead of him," Perkins said. "The best days of Kansas basketball are right around the corner."

# Miss Match

Yahoo! Sports: April 2, 2008

*Roy Williams*

CHAPEL HILL, N.C. – Outside the door and down the steps, they're waiting for him with cameras.

Roy Williams' press conference begins in 2 minutes, but as he paces about his digs at the Smith Center, the North Carolina basketball coach hardly seems hurried as he points toward the wall and begins to count.

"That's Drew Gooden and I at the Wooden Award ceremony," says Williams, motioning toward a photo. "There's Nick Collison ... Jeff Boschee ... Paul Pierce ... Allen Fieldhouse on Senior Day."

Each shelf is stacked with stories, each wall mounted with memories from Williams' 15-year tenure as Kansas' head coach.

A final tally reveals that 34 pieces of Jayhawks memorabilia adorn Williams' second-floor office. There's even a picture of North Carolina and NBA legend Michael Jordan – wearing a Kansas shirt. Jordan requested it after working one of Williams' camps more than a decade ago.

"He was on his way to speak at a Boys and Girls Club," Williams says. "And he told me he wanted to let everyone to know where he stood."

Williams reaches for his desk and fiddles with a Kirk Hinrich bobblehead. His eyes sparkle and his voice booms with energy. Each time he talks about his former team - his former school – he says he can't help but smile.

If only folks in Lawrence could do the same.

Three days before North Carolina takes the court in the Final Four, the coach who tells his players to "enjoy the ride" is having trouble heeding his own advice. That's because the Tar Heels are matched against Kansas – the one school Williams prayed he'd never have to play.

"He's dreading this for a number of reasons," Williams' son, Scott, said. "He's thrilled to be in the Final Four, and he won't lose his focus when he's on the court. But from a personal standpoint I know this is bothering him a great deal."

As if trying to defeat his former school isn't burdensome enough, Williams

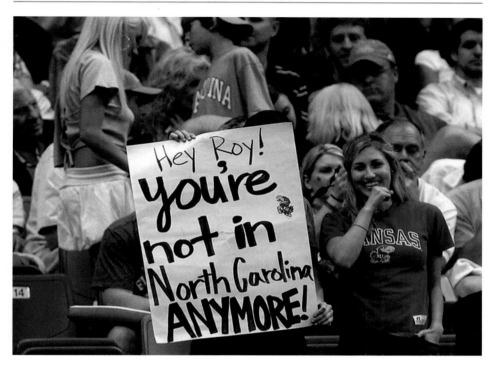

is aware that a large group of Jayhawks fans are still livid with him for leaving Kansas for North Carolina – his alma mater – in 2003.

Williams guided Kansas to four Final Fours during his time in Lawrence, yet the crowd goes bananas when a losing North Carolina score is announced at Allen Fieldhouse. He won more games than any coach in the 1990s, but "Benedict Williams" shirts are still seen frequently throughout town.

Kansas claimed conference championships in nine of Williams' final 13 seasons, but in the Jayhawks' pregame highlight video, his image is shown only for a few seconds.

And even then, almost on cue, fans hiss.

"I know he hears those stories, and I know it hurts him," said Boschee, who played for Williams from 1998-2002. "He's a sensitive guy. He doesn't care what people think about his coaching. But I think he listens to comments about what type of person he is. He takes great pride in his character.

"It really is ridiculous. The people who boo him are childish. They need to get over it."

Some have, but even Williams' staunchest supporters know the focus of Saturday's national semifinal won't be Kansas vs. North Carolina. It'll be Kansas vs. Roy. That, more than anything, has Williams on edge as he prepares for the most emotional game of his career.

"We can sit here for two hours and talk about all the negative things," Williams said. "But the negative things should only take about one percent of our time. This should be about a great Kansas team playing a great North Carolina team. That other stuff should command about one percent of our attention.

"The fact that it's not isn't very pleasant."

• • •

Tuesday night, in the middle of all his game prep, media responsibilities and film sessions, Roy Williams found time for a quiet dinner at his home with family friend Ted Seagroves.

The crab legs and Caesar salad were delicious. But when he looked across the table at his buddy, Ted sensed something wasn't right.

"It was obvious," he said, "that Roy was hurting."

Earlier in the day, Williams read an Associated Press article about the family-owned barbershop where he used to get his haircut in Lawrence. Williams' picture was once displayed prominently in the front of the store. Now it hangs near the commode in the restroom – or as it's been re-named, The Roy Room.

"We figured if Roy had stuck around, they would have named a building after him," owner John Amyx said. "So we decided to name a room after him. That seemed to be the best place to see his picture, too."

Seagroves said Tuesday wasn't the first time his friend had been disappointed by a derogatory article.

"He still reads the paper and hears those comments," Seagroves said. "You can see the hurt in him when he talks about it now. I don't think he expected such strong resentment from the fans and folks there. He loves Kansas. There's a part of him that would still love to be there."

As much as those situations upset Williams, some Jayhawk faithful say they have plenty of reasons to be angry, too.

Many of them refer to Williams as a traitor and a turncoat and say he "betrayed" them when he left Kansas for North Carolina.

"People view the situation like a messy divorce or an ugly breakup," said Scott Buxton, one of Williams' closest friends in Lawrence. "It's a shame they have to be so mean-spirited about it."

For most Kansas fans, the biggest problem with Williams' departure wasn't so much that he left, but that he did so three years after vowing to finish his career as a Jayhawk.

Williams flirted with the North Carolina job when the Tar Heels tried to woo him in 2000. Then, with nearly 15,000 Kansans watching on the Memorial Stadium JumboTron, he gave his famous "I'm stayin'" speech. The future of the Jayhawks' program seemed set.

Things changed, though, over the next few years.

The Jayhawks enjoyed tremendous success on the court – reaching the Final Four in 2002 and 2003 – but away from it Williams was often miserable. The athletic director who hired him, Bob Frederick, had been forced out in the spring of 2001 and replaced with Al Bohl.

Williams' relationship with Bohl was strained from the get-go, and the

administrative goings-on caused him so much discontent that, when the Tar Heels offered him the job again in 2003, he accepted even though Kansas had tried to appease Williams by firing Bohl less than a week earlier.

Even today, there is a faction of Kansas fans who believe Williams-to-North Carolina II was scripted, and that he and the Tar Heels administration had worked out the deal months before he officially accepted it following KU's loss to Syracuse in the national title game.

"That's so far from the truth that I wouldn't even do it the dignity of discussing it with someone," Williams said. "Other than a serious thing happening to someone in my family, there is no way a situation could bother me any worse."

Indeed, so torn was Williams that, during the week when he was attempting to make his decision, he'd wake up in the middle of the night, dart toward to the toilet and throw up.

The weekend after the Final Four, Williams still hadn't reached a decision. He flew to Los Angeles to attend the Wooden Award ceremony with Collison and stayed at the home of close friend and Kansas booster Dana Anderson.

Anderson said he and Williams discussed his situation in his living room a few hours before he drove him to the airport.

"He had tears in his eyes the whole time," Anderson said.

Williams told Anderson that his mentor, former North Carolina coach Dean Smith, had told him that he was the only coach who could get the Tar Heels' program turned around and that it was time to come home.

Smith, ironically, is a Kansas alum, and Anderson reminded Williams that the Jayhawks once tried to lure Smith back to his alma mater after it hired Ted Owens.

"Dean turned us down," Anderson said. "He told us, 'No, I've built something special at North Carolina and I have to stay.' Then they built the Dean Dome. I told Coach Williams that there will never be a Williams Dome at North Carolina. Apparently I wasn't a very good salesman."

There were other factors.

Williams' sister was not in good health, and he wanted to develop a better relationship with his father, with whom he'd never been close. His wife Wanda's family was in North Carolina, too, and his daughter, Kimberly, attended school there.

Anderson talked about those things with Williams on the drive to the airport that morning. Once they dropped the coach off, Anderson turned to his wife.

"We've lost him," he told her.

The following day Williams announced he was leaving Kansas for North Carolina. By Easter Sunday the Jayhawks had hired Illinois coach Bill Self, who led Kansas to two Elite Eight appearances prior to this year's 35-3 record and Final Four berth.

Still, five years later, there are still plenty of people who snarl at the mention of Williams' name. Not long ago a Kansas writer published an article about Williams on Dec. 25. When the writer went to church that morning he was approached by an angry fan.

"Thanks for ruining my Christmas!" the man snapped.

Joe Holladay hears those stories and shakes his head.

"Most of the people that are griping have changed jobs at least once in their life, I would think," said Holladay, Williams' top assistant at both Kansas and North Carolina. "Who hasn't changed jobs? Who hasn't moved?

"He changed jobs because he wanted to come home. His dad was sick. His wife's family lives here. His kids live and work here. He wanted to go back to where he grew up. A lot of people want to do that.

"It's been five years. You've got a great coach at Kansas. You've got a great program. It's like, get a life, you know? Get over it. Move on."

• • •

Sunday evening, less than an hour after the Jayhawks catapulted into the Final Four with a victory over Davidson, Williams called close friend and Kansas basketball secretary Joanie Stephens.

"Make sure you tell Bill (Self) that I said 'congratulations,'" Williams said.

Despite the animosity that has hovered in Lawrence since his departure, Williams continues to be a huge Kansas fan. He allows the children who attend his North Carolina basketball camp to wear Jayhawks jerseys, and he said his passion for the school will prevent him from ever trying to schedule a game against his old team.

A few years ago Williams said he had trouble watching Kansas on television because former players such as Wayne Simien, Keith Langford, Aaron Miles and Michael Lee were still on the team.

"It was exhilarating to watch them win," Williams said, "and gut-wrenching to see them during the few times they'd struggle."

These days, though, Williams said he couldn't get any more enjoyment over watching players such as Sherron Collins, Russell Robinson and Darnell Jackson.

"The greatest thing – and please emphasize this – the greatest thing is that Bill is doing such a good job," Williams said. "His teams are winning, they're great kids. The program is moving on. That part I love.

"Those are the things I wish could dominate our feelings and our conversations this week instead of stories about someone hanging my picture over a commode."

Williams leans forward in his chair and takes a sip of his Coca-Cola.

"I don't want to come across as crass," he said, "but if someone can't come to closure with everything by now, it's almost an insult to Bill and his team. And it's an insult to me, because my gosh, it wasn't like I was there two days and left. I was there 15 years."

For all of his detractors, Williams also has scores of supporters – the main ones being his former players.

Hinrich, Collison and Billy Thomas have visited Williams in Chapel Hill. Simien, Rex Walters and Greg Gurley were among those who traveled to Springfield, Mass., for his Hall of Fame induction ceremony last fall.

Sunday night, when it became apparent that Kansas would take on North Carolina in the Final Four, Williams fielded phone calls from ex-Jayhawks such as Ryan Robertson and Moulaye Niang.

"The way people have reacted to him leaving says a lot about what kind of coach he is," said Collison, now a forward with the Seattle SuperSonics. "If he hadn't done such a good job people wouldn't care that he's gone.

"Rationally, it might not make much sense. But sometimes, when people really love something like they love Kansas basketball, they don't think rationally."

Back in Lawrence, Williams still counts Buxton, Frederick and Lawrence golf pro Randy Towner among his closest friends. Self has repeatedly praised the job Williams did with Kansas' program over the past few days.

Hall of Fame coach Larry Brown, who coached Kansas to its last national title in 1988, also expressed his admiration for Williams on Tuesday.

"Roy shouldn't have to feel bad about anything," Brown said. "He should be proud of what he did there and happy that Bill Self is carrying it on.

"If there is anyone out there that's angry, it's because he did such a special job there (and now he's gone). If people would think about it a little while – if they thought about all the positive things he did for that program and how Bill is carrying it on – they'd realize it's a win-win for everyone. If I talked to Roy, I'd tell him that."

Brown said he believes that time will eventually heal the wounds that still seem to fester among

certain Kansas fans. The process, albeit slowly, may already be under way. *The Kansas City Star* on Tuesday conducted an online poll asking readers to vote on how they would respond if they saw Williams on the famous Riverwalk in San Antonio, the site of this year's Final Four.

Twelve percent of readers said they'd push Williams into the water. Sixty-eight percent said they'd shake his hand and thank him for his time at Kansas.

"Print that out for me, would you?" Holladay said. "I want to make sure I show that to him. It will make him feel good."

Williams isn't excited about either event.

"There are two things I'm not looking forward to," he said. "I've got to answer questions about me and Kansas all weekend. And I've got to be able to stand up and listen if someone wants to yell something at me."

Williams is asked how he'll react, if he'll grit his teeth and shrug it off.

"I don't know," he said. "Probably. We'll have to see."

• • •

He knows the timing isn't right, and that it may not be for the next few years. Still, Anderson – Kansas' biggest donor – said he's "made it known" that sooner rather than later, the Jayhawks need to honor Roy Williams during halftime of a game at Allen Fieldhouse.

The mention of such a gesture seemed to cause a basketball-sized lump to swell in Williams' throat Tuesday.

Asked if he hoped it would happen one day, Williams said: "I do – almost to the extent where I'd hope that it wouldn't be that big of a deal. It'd be nothing more than a coach coming back to watch one of his two favorite teams play."

In the meantime, Williams has plenty of other things to keep him busy. There's a team to coach, a game to play and, ugh, more questions to answer.

"Kansas wants so desperately to beat North Carolina so it can proceed toward a national championship," Buxton said. "But there's this other level of intensity, where it wants so badly to beat Roy, to show him he made a mistake or 'We're just as well off without you.' "There's a lot of that undertone to the conversations that are going on in Lawrence. I'm sure he'll be glad once this one's behind him."

Especially if the Tar Heels win. That would put North Carolina one step closer to its second national championship in the last four seasons.

Then again, Williams also realizes that Kansas is an elite team, too, and that the possibility exists that his squad could lose.

If that happens Williams isn't sure what he'll do. Buxton said Williams told him he'd like to remain in San Antonio to cheer on Kansas against either UCLA or Memphis. But he's not sure he'd be welcomed in the Jayhawks' section of the stands.

It's a decision Williams will make when – or rather, if – the situation presents itself. Right now only one thing is certain.

"I talked to Pops Sunday night," Scott Williams said. "Some people may not believe this, but he literally said, 'Worst-case scenario, I know I'll have someone to pull for Monday night.'"

Darrell Arthur

# Bear of a Decision
## Picking KU over Baylor a struggle for Arthur

The Kansas City Star: January 24, 2007

WACO, Texas - They arrived just before noon, in their television trucks. One by one, reporters marched through the parking lot of the Dallas YMCA, anxious to hear the state's top high school basketball player announce his college intentions and then channel the news to the rest of the world.

No one ever got through the front door.

"Press Conference Canceled," a sign read. "Come back tomorrow at 12:30."

A few miles away, Darrell Arthur paced throughout the kitchen of his Oak Cliff home. It was May 8 -- nearly six months after signing day -- and he still didn't know where he wanted to go to school.

That morning he was set on Baylor. A few hours later, it was Kansas.

"It surprised me," said KU guard Russell Robinson, who was following the situation back in Lawrence. "If it's between Baylor and Kansas, you'd think someone would (pick) Kansas automatically. To me, the choice seemed easy."

For Arthur, it was anything but.

Arthur ended up signing with the Jayhawks the following day, but the decision was as painful as the boos he's expecting to hear when he returns to Waco tonight for Kansas' game against Baylor at the Ferrell Center.

This is the school his grandmother, Ruby, begged him to attend because of its religious background and proximity to Dallas. This is where he and Bears sophomore Kevin Rogers, his friend and teammate at South Oak Cliff High School, talked about ruling the court together once again.

This is the place that coach Scott Drew persuaded Arthur to call home.

Almost.

"We recruited him for three years," Drew said. "Losing him was a knockout. There was no standing eight on that one. We were down for 10."

• • •

There were times during Arthur's senior year at South Oak Cliff that he dreaded going to school. Whether he was walking to class or talking with a reporter after practice, Arthur was always peppered with the same question: Know where you're going to college yet?

"I tried to zone them out," Arthur said. "People were getting upset that I wouldn't pick a school, but I just didn't know."

Arthur certainly had plenty of options. Much of his senior year was spent trekking across the country for visits to some of the most well-known programs in America.

Indiana one week, North Carolina the next. Arthur visited Kansas during "Late Night in the Phog" and LSU just weeks after the Tigers' Final Four appearance. During a Texas game, a group of students wore crowns and held signs that read: "King Arthur's Court."

Arthur, though, was a no-show in Austin. Happened a few times at Kansas, too.

"One week you'd feel comfortable you were going to get him, and the next you felt like you were out of it," said Shay Wildeboor, a recruiting analyst for Rivals.com. "With Arthur, no one ever knew. It was a complete circus."

And Baylor was the bearded lady.

While the other schools on Arthur's list boasted national titles, league championships and first-round NBA draft picks, the Bears hadn't even been to the NCAA Tournament since 1988.

Never had they experienced a winning Big 12 season, and attendance had been down ever since forward Patrick Dennehy was shot and killed by teammate Carlton Dotson in 2003. An investigation that occurred after the murder revealed numerous instances of wrongdoing by former coach Dave Bliss, which almost led to the death penalty for Baylor.

Still, the Bears' lackluster history didn't do anything to turn off Arthur, who made frequent visits to Baylor's campus.

"They're doing a good job of coming back from that little mishap that happened a few years ago," Arthur said. "I looked at Baylor as a program that's on the rise. Plus, it's close to home. I'm real close with my family."

Arthur's mother, Sandra, said Drew and his staff made an impression on her son.

"They outrecruited everyone that was interested in him," Sandra said. "He was going to Baylor. If he would've gone through with that first press conference, that's where he'd be right now."

But Arthur never showed up at the YMCA that afternoon. Instead, he went home.

"He was almost in tears," Sandra said. "He wanted me to make the decision for him, but I wouldn't do that. I didn't know what to say to him, so I just told him to pray."

• • •

While Arthur mulled over his decision on the evening of May 8, KU coach Bill Self was a nervous wreck in Lawrence. The two hadn't talked in weeks, leading

Self to believe that KU was out of the running for Arthur's services.

While Arthur's choice - KU or Baylor - may have seemed elementary to outsiders, Self was hardly shocked to find himself in a recruiting war with Drew, who signed a McDonald's All-American (Tweety Carter) last year and may have another one (LaceDarius Dunn) coming in next season.

"Baylor is a player in the recruiting game," Self said. "The other schools in our league are aware of that now. They're getting guys from the Big 12 region and from Louisiana that are serious difference-makers.

"That's a compliment to their staff, considering what happened there four years ago."

Still, in the end, Baylor's up-and-coming program wasn't good enough to beat out tradition-rich Kansas.

Arthur awoke on the morning of May 9 and told his mother he had a dream in which he was wearing a KU uniform and running down a court. At that point he'd all but decided to become a Jayhawk, but he called Self anyway to allow him the chance to make one last pitch.

"He just told me how great it was here and how good we were going to be," Arthur said.

Later that day, shortly before his 12:30 news conference, Arthur sent Self a text message. "I'm coming 2 Kansas," it read.

• • •

As Self and his staff began their celebration, Drew could hardly stomach the news in Waco. With guards such as Carter, Curtis Jerrells, Aaron Bruce and Henry Dugat, the Bears' backcourt is regarded as one of the best in the conference.

But there's a serious dropoff in talent down low. Without Arthur, Baylor is an NIT team at best. With him, they would've contended for an NCAA Tournament berth this season, and Drew knew it.

"He's a franchise type of player," Drew said. "It wasn't just a want, it was a need. Adding a guy the caliber of Darrell would've speeded up the rebuilding process. We'd recruited him since we got here three years ago. It's a lot tougher

to lose a guy like that than one you just started recruiting."

Not just for Drew, but for Arthur, too.

"I really think that was a bittersweet day for Darrell," Sandra said. "He was excited about going to Kansas, but he also knew he'd left a lot of people feeling brokenhearted. The whole thing was just really, really tough on him."

• • •

A few weeks ago, Sandra Arthur packed her bags and headed for Lawrence. Not to watch a game, but to look after her son.

Darrell, Sandra said, was experiencing a bout of homesickness. He'd returned to Dallas over the Christmas break and reunited with a few of his friends and relatives. When the time came to return to Kansas, Arthur wasn't ready to go.

"I moved into his apartment with him for a few days," Sandra said. "I cooked for him -- even laid right there in the bed with him sometimes to talk. A lot of kids his age probably go through that. I know he likes it at Kansas. He and his teammates get along real well, and the coaches are great."

So, too, is Arthur, who, if not for Texas' Kevin Durant, probably would be the leading candidate for Big 12 Freshman of the Year.

Arthur leads the league with 1.95 blocks per game, and he ranks second on KU's squad in scoring (11.6) despite averaging just 21 minutes.

The 6-foot-9 Arthur tallied 19 points in the Jayhawks' victory over defending national champion Florida on Nov. 25. And he and fellow freshman Sherron Collins accounted for 17 of Kansas' final 19 points in last week's 80-77 Border War win over Missouri.

So good is Arthur that one Web site, NBA draft.net, is predicting that he'll be the No. 16 pick in this summer's draft. Arthur, though, hasn't even hinted about the possibility of leaving school early.

"(Arthur) has a long way to go before you can start talking about him as one of the top players in the country," Self said. "But I think it's obvious that he's capable of some pretty special things."

Arthur hopes to use those abilities to the fullest when Kansas travels to Baylor for tonight's game.

He said he expects Bears fans to boo him, and he knows any exchange with Drew could be awkward.

Still, in the end, Arthur said he made the right decision. His coaches and teammates couldn't be any happier.

"His presence is felt," Robinson said. "He's brought toughness to this team, and a little personality as well.

"It's going to be kind of tough for him (at Baylor), because the fans there probably aren't too happy. But he's tough-minded. He's going to be ready to play. As always."

# A Bronx Tale

## Kansas is a world away from the one Robinson is used to

The Kansas City Star: December 18, 2004

*Russell Robinson*

LAWRENCE - One by one, they swing open the glass doors of Allen Fieldhouse.

Practice ended 45 minutes ago, and now the Kansas Jayhawks jog toward the parking lot, trying to escape the chill that's left a frosty film on their windshields. No one thinks to offer the freshman guard a ride.

Russell Robinson doesn't mind, though. As he steps out into the 29-degree air, he doesn't even zip up his coat. Whether it's a fall hike through the apricot leaves and campus hills or tonight's peaceful stroll to his apartment, Robinson has come to cherish walks like this. They remind him of where he's been - and make him appreciate where he is.

No honking horns, no neon lights, no winos arguing in front of a liquor store. Just silence.

Robinson, a Bronx native, pulls his hood over his head.

"It's nice," he says, "to be able to walk somewhere without having to look over your shoulder."

• • •

Some days, Robinson can't decide if the silence is good or bad.

In just six college games, he has established himself as one of the top freshmen basketball players in America. He's averaging 7.3 points - and playing some maddening defense - as the first guard off the bench for No. 2 Kansas.

Dads are buying replicas of Robinson's No. 3 jersey as Christmas presents for their sons. Strangers stop him in Wal-Mart and ask for autographs. Coach Bill Self marvels at the 18-year-old's comfort level in running KU's offense.

"Russell is the only freshman that's not overwhelmed right now," Self says.

Ask Robinson about his first six months of college, and he will tell you some challenges simply aren't tough enough. After all, this isn't New York. This isn't home.

"I'm having to grow up," says Robinson, reclining in a leather chair at Allen

## 290

Fieldhouse. "I've started to realize that maybe my way - the way I've grown up - isn't the only way."

Robinson's parents, Theresa and Russell Sr., separated when he was in the third grade. When Army duty called for his father to move from New York to Killeen, Texas, Robinson went with him. They stayed 15 months before relocating to Fayetteville, N.C.

Robinson had trouble relating to classmates from well-to-do suburbs and felt isolated, often spending his recess time alone. He missed the brash streets of the big city, the pickup basketball games in the parks, and the subways that whisked him from borough to borough to see his buddies. By junior high, he was back with his mom in the Bronx.

"I'm a city kid," Robinson says. "And I thought New York was one of the best cities in the world."

And yet, when Robinson walked out the doors of Rice High School each afternoon, he saw gang members lingering in the parking lot. When he rolled home, he sometimes passed childhood friends who had become dropouts and peddled drugs on a street corner in his neighborhood. When he visited his father's apartment on Mosholu Avenue, he often passed an adult bookstore or stepped over homeless people sleeping near the front stoop.

Robinson became immune to it all. He was an "A" and "B" student in high school whose passions were drawing, making collages of his newspaper clippings and spending quiet nights with his girlfriend.

New York and all its temptations were the ultimate challenge, and staring them down made Robinson feel as big and bad as the city.

"I don't want to make it sound like a danger zone," said Demetrius Hicks, Robinson's former teammate and a current senior at Rice High School. "But there are plenty of obstacles around here that make you grow up - fast. You either go one way or the other."

Robinson went the other.

• • •

Blood speckles dotted the hardwood under Robinson's feet. It was the summer before his senior year, and a pickup game against some roughnecks from Jersey had turned nasty at a local gym.

Fighting for position in the paint meant a forearm to the chin. Layups were met with a shove in the back. A simple jump shot was reason enough to trash-talk.

"It wasn't basketball; it was a boxing match," Russell Robinson Sr. says. "And Russell caught one of the best shots of the day."

After examining his son on the sideline, the elder Robinson insisted they rush him to a hospital for stitches. Robinson's bottom lip was split wide open, the aftermath of a vicious elbow to the face.

"He wouldn't do it. He wouldn't go - not until after the game was finished," Robinson Sr. says. "He went right back out there and kept playing, basically drinking his own blood."

Robinson saved his battles for New York's basketball courts, where street-ball legends attract fans and filmmakers on famous blacktops such as Rucker Park and West Fourth.

"Where I'm from, a foul ain't a foul unless you see blood," Robinson says.

For Robinson, summer afternoons meant catching the subway with friends and moving from park to park - or as he calls it, "traveling." Winners played until they were defeated. Lose one time, Robinson says, and you might as well call it a day, considering how many players were waiting for a game.

"Sometimes my community traveled with as many as 15 people," Robinson says. "The games were five-on-five. But it was always good to have a lot of your boys there to watch your back ... you know, in case something happened."

From Manhattan to Harlem to Brooklyn to Queens, Robinson developed a reputation as one of the best ballers in the area, even though he was often going up against men 10 and 20 years older. Hicks remembers a game when his and Robinson's team matched up with a group of players who were "on the wrong path in life."

The more Robinson beat them to the basket or made a steal, the angrier they became.

"They kept getting in Russell's face and threatening to beat him up," Hicks says. "I got a little worried, you know, thinking we should leave. But Russell wouldn't do it. He just kept on schoolin' 'em. When it was over, they had no choice but to hug him and pay him respect."

That toughness paid dividends for Robinson at tradition-rich Rice High, alma mater of NBA players such as Felipe Lopez and Kenny Satterfield. Robinson led his team to the state title as a sophomore.

Fueled by his summer-league success with the AAU Gauchos, Robinson entered his junior year as one of the nation's top recruits. But one particular recruiter stood out.

Norm Roberts, a former Kansas assistant under Self, was raised in Queens and related to Robinson so well that "he could finish my sentences," Robinson says.

Roberts knew it would be difficult persuading Robinson to move halfway across the country. In the 106-year history of the program, only five players from

New York had worn a KU uniform. Still, each time he watched Robinson play, Roberts knew he couldn't give up.

"When the game got tougher, he got better," says Roberts, now head coach at St. John's. "When he needed to get a stop defensively, he could do it. When he needed to make a big shot, he could do it. He's one of those kids who's always smiling. He's soft-spoken in a lot of ways. But it's amazing how he transforms when he gets on the court as far as personality."

After touring campuses at Kentucky, Connecticut and Georgia Tech, Robinson agreed to visit Kansas the weekend of the KU football team's upset victory over Missouri in September 2003. He was among the thousands of fans who rushed the field after the game and joined the mob as it carried the goal posts to Potter Lake.

"That day I felt what everyone else was feeling - I felt the KU spirit," Robinson says. "I knew right then that this was where I wanted to be."

Robinson announced his commitment the following week. The Jayhawks had a new style of player.

"New York kids bring a different kind of toughness," Roberts says. "There's nothing tougher than playing in a Rucker Park tournament. You've got your whole community watching. There's nowhere to hide. You've got to be tough all the way through.

"Russell grew up with all of that. Kansas needed a player like him."

And Robinson needed a place like Kansas.

• • •

The phone stopped ringing in September.

Theresa Robinson had grown used to getting calls from her son during his first month in Lawrence. Eventually, though, hearing Mom's voice became too painful for Robinson. He missed her, missed his girlfriend and his boys back in the Bronx. He missed the whole lifestyle.

Robinson couldn't walk out of his apartment and buy a hot dog from a street vendor or eat chicken fried rice at his favorite Chinese

restaurant down the block. He didn't have a car, and there were no subways to sweep him away for an afternoon of shopping.

When he attended KU summer school in June, it all seemed like one big road trip. Once he moved for good, the enormity of the change set in.

"I started to think, `This is what I'm going to be dealing with. This is my life for the next four years,' " Robinson says. "I started getting homesick, and calling back to New York just made it worse."

Robinson pauses, looking down as he twiddles his thumbs.

"Everything here was just so different."

It wasn't just the atmosphere. It was the people. Everyone was friendly as could be, but Robinson couldn't relate. Like the grade-school kid who sat alone at recess, Robinson was once again socializing with the upper crust, and he stood out as much as his accent. "I came here thinking the New York way of life was the only way - the right way," Robinson says. "Now I'm realizing that's not exactly the case."

Robinson has had no choice but to adjust. In the last two months, he's spent more and more time talking with classmates from different backgrounds and cultures. He's letting his guard down a bit, opening his mind to new ideas and his heart to new people.

"I haven't met one arrogant person in Lawrence - not one," Robinson says. "Seeing how other people do things has helped me grow as a person. Everybody thinks their way is the right way. Now I see that there are a lot of right ways."

Things are taking shape for Robinson when it comes to basketball, too. He's averaging 14.7 minutes a game as the first player off the bench and is one of the Jayhawks' top defenders, the label he embraces the most.

"For me defense is a pride thing," says Robinson, who ranks second on the team in steals. "I just think, `Hey, I'm not going to let this guy go by me. I'm not going to let him outplay me.' It should hurt when someone scores on you."

Self marvels at Robinson's composure. He said the trend for most freshmen is to follow a good play with two bad ones, or a strong game with a lousy game. Robinson has been steady - just as he was on the unforgiving asphalt of New York.

"That's the reason I don't get rattled," he says. "I've been playing in pressure situations like this my whole life."

• • •

Back in the Bronx, Robinson's father has ordered the Full Court Package through his cable provider. A postal worker, he's yet to see his son play for Kansas in person. But, even a thousand miles away, he can see that things are going well in Lawrence.

"You can tell Russell is happy - shoot, he plays happy," Robinson Sr. says. "It's good to see him smiling again. The people there have embraced him. He feels welcome at Kansas."

Hicks, the high school friend, senses it, too. He says Robinson told him a few weeks ago that he can envision himself making his home in Lawrence once his basketball career is finished.

"I know there are about 47,000 people out there," Hicks says. "But the way Russell talks, it's like one, small community where everyone knows each other and gives each other love. I think he's appreciating that more and more each day."

A few months ago, Robinson learned to drive. He's got his license now and, before long, his father will buy him his first car. Robinson is hoping for an SUV; Dad says he'll suggest something smaller and a bit more modest.

Either way, Robinson is looking forward to those afternoons when he's alone, when he can cruise through Lawrence with no particular destination in sight.

"I'll just drive around," he says, "where everything is open and free."

*Mario Chalmers*

# Mr. Big Shot

Yahoo! Sports: April 8, 2008

SAN ANTONIO – The greatest shot in the history of Kansas basketball can be traced to, of all places, Alaska.

Mario Chalmers used to hide behind the couch until his mother, Almarie, sang the national anthem. Then he'd waddle around the corner and onto the "court" he'd constructed on the living room floor of his family's Anchorage home.

"Three ... two ... one," Almarie would count as four-year-old Mario heaved shot after shot at the miniature Nerf rim. "Three ... two ... one."

Chalmers' father, Ronnie, chuckles as he tells the story.

"He won a lot of national championships in that living room," Ronnie said.

Perhaps that's why Chalmers felt so at ease at the Alamodome on Monday. Seventeen years after those impromptu games in his den, Chalmers again found himself with the ball in his hands and the clock winding down. Only this time there were 43,257 fans watching – and the national championship really was on the line.

No matter.

With one swift flick of the wrist, Chalmers helped Kansas accomplish what only two other teams in its storied history have achieved. His heavily guarded three-pointer with two seconds remaining against Memphis forced overtime – where the Jayhawks escaped with a 75-68 victory and their first national championship since 1988.

Chalmers' heroic shot was the cherry on top of a ferocious Kansas rally that saw the Jayhawks come back from a 60-51 deficit with 2:12 left in regulation.

"It's a great feeling," Chalmers said. "I'll get older and look back on this day, and I'll always be able to watch that last shot. It's something I'll never forget."

Neither will Kansas coach Bill Self, who needed just five years to attain at Kansas what predecessor Roy Williams couldn't in 15: a championship trophy. Self hoisted it high as he and the Jayhawks stood atop a platform at center court Monday.

Danny Manning, Clyde Lovellette, Wilt Chamberlain, Paul Pierce, Raef

LaFrentz, Kirk Hinrich, Nick Collison and Drew Gooden. As many successful players and seasons as the program has had, never has a Kansas squad won as many games as Self's 37-3 Jayhawks.

"I told them tonight that they'll be remembered as the best team ever in the history of the program," Self said. "That, to me, it's very humbling to know that, of all the great players and teams, this one will go down as the best ever."

Indeed, as hard as he may try, Self may never be able to assemble a squad with the same mix of talent and experience as the 2007-08 Jayhawks.

Three of Kansas' top seven players were McDonald's All-Americans, and six of them likely will be selected in the NBA draft either this season or next.

Included on that list is Chalmers, whose stock surely rose after being selected as the Final Four's Most Outstanding Player. Along with his game-altering three-pointer, Chalmers made four steals Monday while dishing out three assists.

One of them came early in the overtime period, when Chalmers elevated for what appeared to be an open jumper from the free-throw line. But at the last second Chalmers lobbed a pass to Darrell Arthur, who finished the play with a dunk that gave Kansas a 67-63 lead and a momentum it never would relinquish.

"Before he was ever formed in his mother's womb, God had a plan for Mario's life," Almarie Chalmers said. "He's lived his whole life for a moment like this."

As if he hadn't already done enough, Chalmers wrapped a bow around Kansas' victory by swishing a pair of free throws that extended Kansas' cushion to 73-68 with 45.1 seconds left.

Chalmers made all six of his foul shots Monday.

"We call him Mr. Clutch," teammate Brandon Rush said.

Years from now, perhaps at a reunion or in the streets of Lawrence, Kan., fans still may be using that name when they refer to Chalmers. To many it seemed so fitting that one of the most memorable national title games in history ended in such dramatic fashion.

But to Chalmers, it was something he'd come to expect.

As confetti danced through the air around them, Chalmers embraced his father – a Kansas assistant – on the Alamodome Court.

"I told you something like this would happen someday," Chalmers said as he hugged Ronnie. "I told you."

# *Acknowledgments*

Most sportswriters enter the profession because they love covering games. For me, it happened because I decided to drop theater. Plans were underway at Hillcrest High School in Dallas for a big production of "You're a Good Man, Charlie Brown," and it looked as if I were going to play Linus, which meant I would have to sing. Linus also carried a blanket, and that would've cramped my style.

Anyway, the academic counselor placed me in Journalism-I, and few weeks later I went home and told my parents I wanted to be a sportswriter. For that, I'd like to thank Mr. Tate.

Dow Tate will always be a Mr. to me. He was my teacher in the ninth grade, and he's still my teacher today. When I covered my first high school football game for The Dallas Morning News – as a 15-year-old – Mr. Tate was sitting right beside me in the press box, showing me how to keep stats. When I wrote stories for my college newspaper, it was Mr. Tate who listened late at night as I dictated my articles over the phone, stopping me every paragraph or so to make suggestions. Even now – whether I'm struggling to find the words for a profile on Sasha Kaun or rushing to meet a postgame deadline at Allen Fieldhouse – Mr. Tate is always a call away, willing to give advice.

For all I know, I would've ended up selling door-stoppers or working in a toll booth if I hadn't walked into Mr. Tate's journalism class that day in the fall of 1988. Instead, I wound up with one of the best jobs in America – and also a best friend.

There are scores of other journalists who count Dow Tate as their mentor, and one of them is Laura Nelson. At the time this book was produced, Laura was 18 years old and one of Mr. Tate's students at Shawnee Mission East, where he now teaches. Along with drafting the striking cover, Laura designed each and every page of this book during the three-week stretch before her high school graduation. Even more importantly, Laura was a sounding board and calming force when the stress of this project began to wear on yours truly. For that, I will be forever grateful.

Three other people have influenced my career to lengths they'll never fathom. Mike Fannin gave me my first job covering preps at The Kansas City Star in 1998 and promoted me to the Kansas beat a few years later. Jason Whitlock, my friend and former colleague at The Star, helped me become a more versatile journalist and has shaped many of my beliefs and philosophies about the profession. Mark Konradi of The Dallas Morning News gave me the first newspaper job I ever had in the summer of 1994, when he worked for People Newspapers.

Others to thank: Kansas' administrative staff — namely athletic director Lew Perkins — for supporting this project. Dave Morgan and Gerry Ahern, my editors at Yahoo! Sports, for being so encouraging and patient.

Freelance photographer Steve Puppe, for supplying the majority of the photos. Topeka-Capital Journal photographer Ann Williamson, for also providing pictures along with Russell Robinson. John Holihan, for conducting four of the interviews in this book.

Stephen Nichols and Sam Logan, for transcribing countless hours of tape. Bernadette Myers and Paige Cornwell, for helping with pagination.

Thanks also to the folks who proofread hundreds of pages of copy: Christie Cater Nelson, Sam Mellinger, Derek Samson, Michael Pulsinelli, Jason, Lara and Marsha Farley and Mike and Susan Fitzgerald. Brandon Ivie, Melissa Jezek, Ricky Sanders, Bekah Randolph and the folks at Ivie & Associates, Inc. in Dallas couldn't have been more pleasant and professional throughout the printing process.

Needless to say, Kansas coach Bill Self had a tremendously hectic schedule the month after his team won the national title. Still, he found time to answer every phone call and return every text message relating to this project.

The same can be said for Self's players, many of whom welcomed me into their homes for the interviews found in this book.

The final three people I want to thank are the three people I love the most. My parents, Martha King and the late J.C. King, for letting me find my own place in the world instead of trying to nudge me down a certain path.

And Jennifer, my beautiful wife, who after five years had finally heard enough about how much I wanted to publish a book about the Jayhawks.

"Quit being a talker," she told me. "People get tired of talkers. Be a doer."

Thanks, Jen. I love you.